पुरातत्त्व

पुरातत्त्व

PURĀTATTVA

Bulletin of the Indian Archaeological Society

No. 1 1967-68

Editors
A.K. Narain
M. Seshadri
S.B. Rao

Assistant Editors
P.C. Pant
P. Singh

D.K. Printworld (P) Ltd.
New Delhi

Cataloging in Publication Data — DK
[Courtesy : D.K. Agencies (P) Ltd. <docinfo@dkagencies.com>]

Purātattva : bulletin of the Indian Archaeological Society, no. 1, 1967-68 / editors, A.K. Narain, M. Seshadri, S.B. Rao ; assistant editors, P.C. Pant, P. Singh.

p. cm.

Includes bibliographical references.

ISBN 8124602778

1. Archaeology — India — Periodicals. 2. India — Antiquities — Periodicals. 3. India — Civilization — Periodicals. I. Narain, A.K. II. Seshadri, M. III. Rao, S.B. IV. Indian Archaeological Society.

First Reprinted in 2005
ISBN 81-246-0277-8
Price for volume 1 (1967-68): Rs. 600 US $ 30

Reprint authorised by
Indian Archaeological Society
New Delhi - 110 016

The Editors are not responsible for the opinions expressed by the Contributors.

Purātattva is published annually.

Manuscripts (whether in the form of articles or notes or book reviews) offered for publication should be sent to the Editor, Purātattva, Indian Archaeological Society, B-17, Qutab Institutional Area, New Delhi - 110 016.

Published and printed by:
D.K. Printworld (P) Ltd.
'Srikunj,' F-52, Bali Nagar
New Delhi – 110015
Phone : (011) 2545 3975, 2546 6019 Fax : (011) 2546 5926
E-mail : dkprintworld@vsnl.net
www. dkprintworld.com

DEDICATED TO

LATE PROFESSOR B. SUBBARAO

AN EMINENT ARCHAEOLOGIST

&

A DISTINGUISHED SCHOLAR

CONTENTS

Reviews

Editor's Note

After independence, Archaeology in India got the long awaited momentum and this resulted in the enormous expansion of archaeological activities. Whether they were within the process of natural growth or they brought about a chaos in Indian Archaeology, it cannot be denied that the new enthusiasm led to some of the remarkable discoveries and rewarding fieldwork. It gave new dimensions to Archaeology and greatly expanded its scope.

In view of the accumulated mass of data and the immense scope of work lying ahead, the necessity of such a coordinating body, which can also give a sense of organisation and proper direction needs hardly to be emphasised. It should further serve as a suitable forum for academic discussions and thus provide opportunities to the archaeologists of the various parts of this vast country to exchange views on the diverse problems. With these primary objectives in mind, the Indian Archaeological Society has been formed, somewhat on the lines of similar institutions in other countries.

That an association like the Indian Archaeological Society should have a bulletin of its own, which can inform the world periodically about the recent trends and discoveries and the work done in India is an obvious imperative; hence this bulletin, *Purātattva*, to be published bi-annually. It will primarily include first hand reports of archaeological field work, including exploration and excavation, and their interpretation, but, at the same time, it will be fairly comprehensive in its scope. Articles dealing with scientific analyses of the past relics are particularly welcome.

In the recent years natural sciences have contributed a great deal to the study of the chronology, technology and environment of the past, especially in the countries abroad. We feel that there is a significant scope for such studies in this country. The Society and its organ '*Purātattva*' will strive in this direction and try to bring about a worthwhile collaboration between the archaeologists in the field and natural scientists working in the laboratory.

The late Prof. B. Subbarao, the noted archaeologist of India, was among those who gave birth to the idea of the formation of the Indian Archaeological Society. It is most unfortunate that he is not alive to see it materialised. We dedicate this very first number of *Purātattva* to his cherished memory.

Obviously the present number has been printed in a very short time. Hence some omissions are quite likely. For these we crave the indulgence of the readers.

Archaeology and the Rāmāyaṇa Or Dating the Rāmāyaṇa*

by H. D. SANKALIA

The *Rāmāyaṇa* has been our most popular epic. How old is it in its present form ? And how old is the story of Rāma ?

Tradition and legend invariably assert that the *Rāmāyaṇa* is at least 5000 years old, and that Rāma lived much before Kṛishṇa, the hero of the *Mahābhārata*.

No doubt, scholars, Indian and Western, orthodox and critically-oriented, have tried to date the *Rāmāyaṇa* as it has come down to us, as well as the kernel of the story, viz., the Ikshvāku dynasty and the King Janaka of Mithilā, families in which Rāma and Sītā were respectively born, and the kidnapping of Sītā by Rāvaṇa.

Leaving out the very high dates, some Indian scholars seriously believe that Rāma lived between 2850 B.C. and 1950 B.C. Pargitar, a famous English scholar after his critical collation of all the Purāṇas placed Rāma in 1400 B.C. Other German and English scholars thought that the kernel of the story might go to 800 B.C., that is a few centuries before the Buddha.

It was, however, agreed almost unanimously that the *Rāmāyaṇa* in its present form was quite late, composed between 400 B.C.-200 A.D., though scholars like Radhakrishnan thought that its philosophical views might belong to the 6th century B.C. Nevertheless, there are scholars who would accept the society described in the *Rāmāyaṇa* as belonging to the Vālmīki age—a view which appears to be very uncritical.

On both these points viz., the kernel of the story—and the stages of the composition of the *Rāmāyaṇa*, archaeology can now throw much more positive light. For, in the last 20 years, several excavations have been carried out in different parts of India which give factual evidence regarding the layout of the cities, nature of houses, palaces, religious buildings, dress and ornaments, cloth, food and drink, and methods of disposal of the dead, against which the *Rāmāyaṇa* data can be checked.

The *Rāmāyaṇa* refers to very few cities. In the Bālakāṇda Viśvāmitra tells Rāma about the origin of the cities of Kauśāmbi, Vaiśāli, Mithilā, Girivraja, Ayodhyā and others. All these are situated in the present U. P. and Bihar. Excavations since 1947 have enabled us to say that all these cities were founded before 6th century B.C. and, according to a few C-14 dates their earliest existence might be placed around 1000 B.C. This has an immense bearing upon the antiquity of the Rāma story. For the first time we can confidently say that the kernel of the story, if true, could not have been earlier than 1000 B. C., because prior to that there was no organized city life in the Gangetic Valley.

But the same cannot be said about the foundation of Takshaśilā (Taxila) and Pushkalāvatī (Chārsada), near modern Rawalpindi and Peshawar respectively. According to the Uttarakāṇḍa these cities were founded by the sons of Bharata, viz. Takshaka and Pushkala respectively,

*This is a preliminary summary of a series of lectures to be delivered at the Maharaja Sayajirao University of Baroda. The published lectures will be documented.

after defeating the Gāndharvas. Excavations by Sir John Marshall at Taxila, and Mortimer Wheeler at Chārsada have shown that these cities were founded about the 6th century B.C. and hence Wheeler said :

" Briefly, then, if these later impacts be omitted, the story of Pushkalāvatī is essentially the story of Taxila. In affirming that the two cities were founded at the same time, the *Rāmayāṇa* has more semblance of historical authority than is commonly accredited in detail to the Indian epics ".

But a little consideration of the description of the two cities in the *Rāmāyaṇa* definitely indicates that the epic had in view ***not*** the simultaneous foundation of the *earliest* cities at these places, but the simultaneous foundation of the Indo-Greek cities at Sirkap near Taxila and Shaikhan near Chārsada respectively. These are laid out in a chess-board pattern with arterial roads, and answer closely the description of Takshaśilā and Pushkalāvatī of the *Rāmāyaṇa*, whereas the earlier city at Bhir Mound, Taxila is characterized by narrow irregular lanes and houses. The Indo-Greek city at Shaikhan was excavated by Dani in 1965. C-14 dates accurately place its foundation to 132 B.C. Archaeology thus confirms the traditional and scholarly view that the Uttarakāṇḍa of the *Rāmāyaṇa* was added later. However, the description of cities like Ayodhyā, and Laṅkā with seven and eight storey buildings, are certainly imaginary, because even at Mohenjo-daro, the tallest building could not have been more than two storeys in height. One could however concede these cities had ramparts and moats (though how Laṅkā which was on a hill could have both these is inconceivable !!). For excavations have exposed remains of ramparts at Rajgir (Rājagṛih, Bihar), at Śiśupālagarh (Orissa), and moats at Taxila, Chārsada and Ujjain.

Thus some of the cities in the *Rāmāyaṇa* can claim hoary antiquity, but not the life led by the people. This would appear to reflect the great prosperity that India experienced because of favourable foreign trade, particularly with Rome and other Western countries. As a result Roman gold, wine and women literally invaded India. The *Rāmāyaṇa* not only speaks of golden ornaments and vessels, but doors and walls covered with gold sheets. Wine flowed freely and abundantly. One would normally associate it with the Rākshasas who were known for their un-Aryan life. But it is not so. It was common in every walk of life, and enjoyed at Ayodhyā, Kishkiṅdhā (the Vānara capital) as well as at Laṅkā. And also in the āshrama of Bharadvāja which was located in a forest !! Here two kinds of wine—Maireya and Saura—were offered to the army of Bharata. This may appear strange and extremely incongruous, but the Roman amphora often with a black resinous residue still sticking to its inner wall has been found not only on the coastal towns—Dwarka, Kolhapur, Pondicherry—but at such inland towns as Junnar and Nevasa, and had also reached the Buddhist monastery at Devnimori, District Sabarkanthe in North Gujarat and Nagarjunakonda in Andhra. The effect of this widespread use of Roman wine is reflected in the posture of amorous couples in the caves of Western India, in the sculptures on the stupa at Amaravati, Nagarjunakonda and Mathura. It is this Bacchanalian life which the interpolators must have witnessed and which they have depicted while describing the harem of Rāvaṇa, for instance in the Sundarakāṇḍa.

Roman wine had become a fashion, just as it has today, in high society, in which both men and women—including Rāma and Sītā—occasionally drank. Archaeology would date this precisely to a period between 1st century, B.C. and 4th-5th century A.D. The name for this Western wine, I think, should be *Vāruṇī*, a term for wine, I am told which appears only in the epics. For Varuṇa is the lord of the sea and the guardian deity of the West.

Another important criterion for dating the *Rāmāyaṇa* is iron. It occurs under the name, *Ayasa*, *Kālāyasa* or *Kārshṇāyasa*, *Loha* and is translated as wrought iron, and steel. While the last three certainly refer to iron, even the first—*ayasa*—here stands for iron. For in the Ayodhyakāṇḍa [1] it is said that the mother of Rāma must surely have had a heart of iron (*āsyasa hṛidayam nūnaṁ*), for it does not break on seeing him go to a forest. Copper is soft, and hence no one would compare a stony heart with it. Not only defensive and offensive weapons such as armours, swords, and arrowhead were made of iron, but even bolts for doors, and chests are said to be made of this metal. The most noteworthy is no doubt the chest, several feet long with 8 wheels, in which King Janaka had kept the famous bow. Rāma alone could wield this and thus win Sītā.

For assuming the existence of such an 8-wheeled iron or steel chest, one has to postulate the existence of advanced iron technology. This technology India had acquired only after the 5th century B. C. reaching its zenith with the manufacturing of the Iron Pillar at Delhi, which after 1500 years has not yet rusted.

The late dating of iron has been amply confirmed by numerous excavations during the last 20 years. Only at one site, Atranjikhera, District Etāh, U. P. has iron occurred in a context which C-14 method would date it to 1000 B.C. But everywhere else it has been proved to be not so early, not before 7th century B.C. And we must remember, nowhere in the world iron was used before 1500 B.C. Thus on this one ground alone the very high dating of the *Rāmāyaṇa*, and even the kernel of the story cannot be accepted. It cannot be before 1000 B.C., though the probability is that it was considerably late when iron technology was well known, and iron had replaced copper in every day use.

Among smaller items, the most curious is the mention of Lakṣmī seated on a lotus and bathed by two elephants, one on either side. This—Gajalakṣmī—Hanumān saw depicted on the Puṣpaka Vimāna (" aeroplane " of Rāvaṇa) at Laṅkā [2]. Just as Air India decorates its Boeings with typical Indian scenes, the artist might have done then. But when ? About the 2nd century B.C. For this is a familiar motif depicted in sculpture on the stupas at Bharhut and Sanchi. On these Buddhist monuments, this scene represents the nativity of the Buddha. Later it was adopted by the Hindus, with whom the goddess became Lakṣmī. This conversion itself as well as the name Lakṣmī suggests a date later than at Sanchi or Bharhut.

Such instances can be multiplied. Suffice it to say that archaeologically we might place the Ikshvāku dynasty and its hero Rāma to about 1000 B.C., but the *Rāmāyaṇa* in its present form—as the abundant use of gold, pearls, silk, wine, iron and camels, and the occurrence of Lakṣmī with elephants on the Puṣpaka Vimāna testifies—should be between the 3rd century B.C. and 4th century A.D. And certain portions which mention palaces or temples with 1000 pillars and temples with high *śikharas* still later, not before 700 A.D. Also late are references to Mars, Saturn and days etc. named after them. For until the 2nd century A.D., the Indian Calendar mentioned only the season, the *nakshtra* (constellation), the two halves (*paksha*) of the month and the *tithī*, but not the day. The last entered our life only after the Roman contact. These appear for the first time in the Gupta Period (c. 300 A. D.).

Now that the critical editions of the *Rāmāyaṇa* and the *Mahābhārata* are compiled, it is time we plan or undertake the preparations of these national epics based on higher criticism. When these are ready then only we shall know what were the *Ur* or original *Rāmāyaṇa* and the original *Mahābhārata*.

NOTES

[1] Cr. ed., 2.35.20.

[2] Cr. ed., 5.6.14.

Inter-relations between Archaeology and Plant Sciences

by VISHNU-MITTRE

Introduction

In the synthesis of knowledge, co-operation of diverse disciplines of science and humanities is very imperative chiefly with the object of enlarging the spheres of knowledge and providing solutions to the jumble of problems beyond the limits of an individual discipline. At the high level of the fuller exposition of knowledge, the various diverse disciplines are so inter-digitantly related to each other that without this realisation and without utilising the humble aid the diverse disciplines are worth, no progress in knowledge can be made. Archaeology, for instance, is directly related to history and evolution of man and obviously to anthropology and sociology. For dating of cultural horizons, physics comes to its aid and for the interpretation of former environment geology, pedology and climatology and even chemistry contribute their humble bit. Likewise there are numerous areas of common interest between archaeology and plant sciences (botany, agriculture and forestry),which can be profitably explored to provide solution and elucidation of knotty problems arising out of intensive studies in each of these disciplines.

The relation of man with plants dates from the antiquity of man although during a long span of his history he did not exercise direct and much influence on the destiny of the plant world. This indirect relation refers to the period of food gathering which covers the entire Palaeolithic and the Mesolithic. During this period he influenced vegetation through digging of roots apparently to provide food, and the discovery of fire. How far these humble influences of early man on Vegetation were able to create imbalance in the equilibrium of vegetation with the environment and thereby affected the course of its natural development may be of particular interest to students of plant sociology. Howsoever small his influence was, the early man's contact with the plant world can hardly be denied.

The direct influence of man on vegetation commenced late in the history of man and it dates from the New Stone Age—the Neolithic period. It comprised the domestication of plants and animals—the commencement of agriculture. Some scholars rightly attach great importance to this direct influence of man on vegetation and consequently distinguish the Old Stone Age from the New one on this basis. It is, therefore, of considerable mutual interest to know more and more of the plant economy of the New Stone Age through the botanical investigation of the plant remains unearthed from archaeological excavations. To an agriculturist the earlier methods of domestication and the kind of wild animals and plants domesticated are of considerable interest, for they not only provide factual information of the wild progenitors of our cultivated plants and domesticated animals but also serve as a touch-stone to prove the validity of the results of their present-day cytogenetical probing into the problem.

How far plant economy should be given the credit, it deserves, in the evolution of metallic cultures (Copper—Bronze and Iron Ages) cannot be said with certainty. But the diffusion of farming traits and cultivated plants in the post-Neolithic cultural evolution has been of considerable interest from both historical and botanical view points. The cultural diffusion must have been slow and at times rapid accompanied by peaceful and violent events resulting in the rise and fall of cultures, their amalgamation and progressive change into subsequent cultures thus eventually building up the personality of India. The role of plant economy has, therefore, not been small in the evolution of cultures.

Vegetation as we understand today is the expression of prevailing environment and in it are integrated the effects of geology,soil, climate and the biota. The reconstruction of former vegetation provides information of past environment which can, however, be built up from other sources also, but the response of plant communities even to slight or minor fluctuations in environment is a decided advantage over the other methods. The importance of environment in the evolution of human cultures can be assessed from the fact that most knotty problems in archaeology are often left to the environment to explain. Botany in this respect comes to the aid of archaeology in unfolding the past environment which was the chief driving force governing the evolution of human cultures.

Together with the animal remains, the plant remains have helped in building up the chronology. The radio-carbon assay is largely dependent upon organic remains. Combining the changes in past environment with the radiocarbon assay a dating time-scale can be built up for the past events in the history of man.

The importance of such a dating mechanism in archaeology is well realised and its importance is equally well understood in dating the shifts in plant populations, the advent and extinction of certain plant genera and the introduction and progressive development of agriculture and such other events as the shifts in climates, the uplifts of mountains, changes in river courses, the origin, extension and drying up of lakes and several other features of physiographical importance.

It becomes apparent from the above that there are some areas of considerable common interest between archaeology and plant sciences. A good deal has been done abroad in exploring these common areas thus widening the horizons and opening new vistas of knowledge for both archaeology and plant sciences. The application of the above information to India is not free from difficulties and pitfalls on account of vast differences in climate, vegetation and the local problems obtaining here but the guide-lines laid by researchers abroad can be successfully followed though with small and suitable modifications. Below are discussed some common areas of mutual interest between Indian archaeology and plant sciences, which need exploration through the co-operation of respective specialists. The discussion also includes a resumè of research work hitherto carried out in this regard.

The Dating mechanism

There are several ways in which botany helps directly or indirectly in dating archaeological periods. Dendrochronology or Tree-ring analysis is one of them. It is an interesting coincidence that this method of dating prehistoric sites is the work of prehistoric people and is known as early as 1811 when De Witt Clinton estimated by this method the age of trees growing upon earth works in New York [1] but it was suggested as a method by Charles Babbage in 1837 [2]. He is the earliest natural philosopher who visualised the ultimate connection of this method with the chronology of man.

The method has been successfully applied abroad in correlating with one another the growth rings of different trees—the inner rings of young trees with the outer rings of older trees and thus from the timber used by historic and prehistoric man in the construction of his houses, it has been possible to build up chronology. Conifer woods have been found to be better over the hard woods because of regular ring formation in them. In the temperate regions, however, the method of tree-ring analysis has been found to work well and has provided a calendar comprising continuous and discontinuous series going back to more than 3000 years, although a reliable calendar in relation to archaeology has been built up upto about 2000 years.

Similar kind of work has not been extended to tropics where the rings are not so regularly formed and the effects of temperature and humidity cause several irregularities and at the same time timber may not have been used by the Prehistoric man for construction purposes. Greater possibilities of dendrochronological research exist in the temperate regions of India such as the Himalayas where timber derived from pine, deodar [3] , spruce and fir is even today used for construction. The wood of oaks (*Quercus*) in the Himalaya has been more used as fuel rather than for construction, the possibility of finding beams of oaks in the Himalayas seem to be remote. Chowdhury [4], Chowdhury and Ghosh [5] and Chowdhury and Rao [6] have examined the possibilities of age determination of Indian woods through growth rings. In the tropical India the *Kalpa-vṛiksha* tree (*Adansonia digitata* L.) believed to be of African origin, is one of the long lived trees known. This may prove suitable for dendrochronology.

Apart from the chronological importance of tree ring analysis, the recognition of prehistoric timber provides information of the selective use of timber and the decline of such genera at the hands of prehistoric man. This information can go a long way in substantiating the trends in forest development inferred from pollen records. The increase in our knowledge of useful timber yielding plants may be economically exploited through their increased plantations.

The importance of plant material for C-14 determination needs no exaggeration. It has provided in Europe and elsewhere with an absolute chronology extended down from the Late Palaeolithic and has made it possible to date the events in human history much more precisely within the age range upto 70,000 years ago [7] . Some difficulties in the application of C-14 dates to archaeological periods have been pointed out by Tauber [8]. Samples of organic matter picked up from the same cultural horizon may sometimes give unidentical dates as for example samples of prehistoric cotton cloth from Paracas, Peru, showed a difference of 400-700 years [9]. Such instances are not uncommon. The difficulties and discrepancies of the kind mentioned by Tauber [10] can be overcome through improvements in methods and careful assessment before acceptance of C-14 date so that its application does not mislead.

Considerable overlap exists in Indian Neolithic and Chalcolithic as shown by radio-carbon assay and perhaps in the acceptance of C-14 dates we have not exercised the caution that ought to have been exercised. It is, therefore, very important to give due allowance to the nature and provenance of the organic matter (humus, peat, wood, charcoal) from the archaeological sites before accepting the date finally. Improved techniques have, however, tended to eliminate the wide differences in the radio-carbon assay of the same material by different labs. It is hoped that it will be possible to build up absolute chronology through radio-carbon dating of the Indian late Quaternary.

The precise dating of the commencement and decline of a particular cultural horizon is possible only where the plant matter in sections is examined inch by inch. It has become possible through pollen analysis which builds up climatically-controlled shifts in plant populations and which are designated as Pollen Zones. A standard pollen diagram built up from lake deposits and peat bogs and swamps gives a chronological sequence of pollen zones. Whearas the pollen of Cerealia points to a particular part of the diagram belonging to the commencement of the Neolithic (the post-Neolithic introduction of agriculture as at Nilgiris should, however, be determined from other sources), the correlation of pollen zones with archaeological periods is, however, determined through pollen spectra obtained from the soil sticking to implements or through pollen analysis of sediments in an archaeological excavation. If the sediments in archaeological provenanace fail to yield pollen as usually it happens in India [11], other indirect methods may be used in correlation of events from pollen diagrams from lakes and swamps with the cultural horizons. Table 1 shows a similar attempt towards the correlation of post-glacial events in the Kashmir Valley. The sediments are dated through the rate of deposition in relation to indirect adoption of a C-14 date from Burzahom the Neolithic site and information of plant economy from the pollen and written records. Other events have been carefully tied up with stratigraphy and shifts in pollen curves. The results are tentative but provide a skeletal picture of post-glacial chronology in the Kashmir Valley. Future work will, however, show how far the emergence of this tentative chronology is sound and dependable.

The dating of cultural periods and their correlation with shifts in plant populations are important to a botanist in the determination of the origin and progressive increase of biotic especially anthropogenous influence on vegeta-

TABLE 2

Occasional Cold Waves and reduction of Minimum Temperature*

	Date	Station	Average Minimum in Jan. upto 1950	Lowest minimum	Difference
1.	*Cold Wave in* 1905				
	31.1.1905	Jodhpur	9.2	—2.2	11.4
	1.2.1905	Jaipur	8.3	—2.2	11.5
	2.2.1905	Patna	10.7	2.2	8.5
	2.2.1905	Allahabad	8.6	1.1	7.5
	2.2.1905	Banaras	9.1	1.7	7.4
	2.2.1905	Jabalpur	9.0	0.0	9.0
	11.2.1905	Darjeeling	1.9	—5.0	6.9
2.	*Cold Wave in* 1935				
	15.1.1935	Bombay	19.3	11.7	7.6
	16.1.1935	Delhi	7.3	—0.6	7.9
	16.1.1935	Agra	7.0	—2.2	9.2
	16.1.1935	Rajkot	10.6	—0.6	11.2
	16.1.1935	Pachmarhi	8.7	—1.1	9.8
	17.1.1935	Poona	11.7	1.7	10.0
	18.1.1935	Bhopal	9.9	0.6	9.3
3.	*Cold Wave in* 1950				
	7.1.1959	Kodaikanal	8.1	2.8	5.3
	18.1.1950	Trivandrum	22.2	18.9	3.3
	10.2.1950	Mussoorie	2.6	—6.7	9.3
	11.2.1950	Ranchi	10.6	2.8	7.8
	12.2.1950	Gaya	9.6	3.9	5.7
	13.2.1950	Shillong	3.8	—2.8	6.6

*Date extracted from S. Basu, 'Weather and Climate' *The Gazeteer of India,* I, 1965, 67-116.

tion and for the study of the after-effects of disturbance in the equilibrium between the plant community and environment resulting in the decline and or extinction of some genera as oaks and alders in the Kashmir Valley [12] or *Celtis* in Kumaon [13] and their replacement by ecotypes or immigrants from near and distant regions. The progressive decline of the Shola forest in Nilgiris is also largely due to the cumulative effects of prehistoric people. How it was achieved and who did it and when and for what purpose are some of the interesting questions which can be answered through the coordination of archaeology and plant sciences.

Environmental Archaeology

Most discussions concerning the origin and evolution of a culture, may it be the Sohanian or the Madrasian culture, or the Mesolithic, the Neolithic or the Chalcolithic or the origin and decline of the Indus Valley Civilization, all eventually end up in the environment, about which, as regards India is concerned, is much less known.

Environment is a complex thing and broadly speaking it includes climate (temperature, precipitation and humidity), physiography, interaction of communities, etc. The last two factors may be strongly influenced by climate, although physiography may also be due to other causes such as earth movements. The nature and fluctuations in climate and their influence on physiography and culture can be built up from the nature of sediments as, for instance, the sequence of glacials and interglacials or pluvials and non-pluvials, loess and other special kinds of soils. The climatic fluctuations in the periglacial areas may be manifested in the river terraces, which may all be of glacial origin or some of them of interglacial origin. Attempts have been made to tie up the Quaternary climatic fluctuations in the north-west India with those in the central and southern India through nature of sediments (alternation of gravels and silts) and animal fossils [14]. The relation of Pluvial with Glaciation is still not determined and the determination of this may have far reaching significance on the above correlations.

The study of modern patterns of temperature and precipitation can provide useful clues to the reconstruction of past climates and the true nature of the pluvial and glacial periods. A large part of the country is swept by the Monsoons in summer season, abnormal fluctuation of which cause even torrential rains and floods in regions such as the NW arid zone. Floods are, therefore, correlatable in large part of India with the monsoons—a wet period—the pluvial. Temperatures are slightly lower during this wet period. Considerable increase in precipitation in summer (June, July) is able to reduce the maximum temperature by 3-4°, whereas a slight increase in winter is able to depress the maximum temperature by 3-5°. Considerable decrease in winter precipitation in Madras, Bangalore, Trivandrum and in eastern Himalaya depresses temperature by 2°. In regions of oceanic climate the decrease in temperature is normal. The recognition of a wet phase in tropical India from sediments and referred to the Pluvial period must have originated from a perpetual monsoon period.

Winter is mostly dry in the country and the lowering of temperature is largely due to the influx of Mediterranean climate although cold waves in India have also originated from south to north as in the years 1935 and 1950 (Table 2). It is also accompanied by precipitation which is the major source of snow formation in the mountains. During the occasional cold waves a drop of 3.3—11.5° in the minimum temperature is noted throughout the country [15]. Temperature below freezing point is noted in the plains of north India down to Rajkot and Pachmarhi. Thus the effect of refrigeration is felt throughout India comparatively less in the South. A perpetual continuation of the Mediterranean climate is equivalent to glacial climate. This reveals that a glacial climate was moist in the extreme west and dry in the rest of India whereas the pluvial climate was warm and wet. This analysis of modern climate suggests that the pluvial in India is correlatable with the Interglacial period more especially the climatic optimum and the Glacial with cool and moist (dry) climate.

The former alterations between the pluvial and non-pluvial climates during the Quaternary are reflected in the present day distribution of plants in India. During the pluvials (interglacial periods) the tropical element moved towards the north penetrating into the base of Himalayas. *Bauhinia*, *Acacia*, *Erthrina*, *Butea*, *Dalbergia*, *Milletia*, most leguminosae, *Bombax*, *Vatica*, *Nauclea*, Combretaceae, Verbenaceae, *Lagerstroemia*, *Grisleas*, *Jasminum* and *Bignonia* are the tropical members indifferent to cold which occur in NW Himalayas. The subtropical vegetational belt between the tropical and temperate belts is the cumulative result of these shifts. Members like *Osbeckia*, *Agrostemma*, *Plectranthus*, and members of Cyrtandraceae, Scitamineae, Araceae, Commelinaceae and orchids, were driven to the loftier mountains and some tropical genera as *Menispermum* and *Anandria* were driven to Siberia, where they still occur today. During the glacial or interpluvial periods several temperate plants including the arrivals from extra-Indian temperate regions such as Europe moved down into the south. Noteworthy among them are *Ranunuclus*, *Xanthium*, *Veronica*, *Anagalis*, *Polygonum*, *Juncus bufonius*, *Alisma plantago*, *Myriophyllum*, *Potamogeton*, *Vallisneria*, *Zannichelia*, *Stellaria plogionosa*, *Circead alpina*, *Sanicula europea*, *Brunella vulgaris*, *Geranium*, *Potentilla* etc. The typical Himalayan species of *Berberis*, *Hypericum*, *Rubus*, *Pedicularis*, *Artemisia* and *Rhododendron* in the south Indian hills may also be attributed to such climatic shifts especially the Glacial. Some species have, however, developed characters different from the corresponding Himalayan species.

The African, Mediterranean and European elements were driven into the country during glacial and periglacial climates and likewise the Japanese and Chinese elements. Through successive shifts in climates this alien flora moved inland step by step naturalising in course of time. The south Indian hill stations still serve as refugia (nunataks) for the immigrants from the cold climates and the Rajasthan desert is a refugium to the alien dry and arid species.

The knowledge of past climatic shifts can be more precisely built up through the application of pollen analysis to Quaternary sediments. This has recently helped in the determination of climatic shifts from the 1st Interglacial in the Kashmir Valley. And it is now possible on botanical evidence to separate the commencement of glacial epoch from the Pliocene [16]. The sediments of second interglacial have, however, been found barren and this in itself may have climatic bearing. It is hoped that the present lakes in the Kashmir Valley and elsewhere such as Kumaon, Nilgiris etc., may have preserved records of the entire Quaternary climatic fluctuation in pollen grains preserved in their sediments.

Post-glacial lake deposits have, however, given a record of climatic shifts from Kashmir Valley and Kumaon Hills [17]. The sequence is different from the one built up by De Terra and Hutchinson [18]. The dual effect of Man and Climate has, however, made it difficult to separate precisely their individual effects, but an important climatic shift towards the commencement of Neolithic has been found in the western Himalayas. Thereafter the shifts in plant populations are perhaps affected more by the human influence than climate suggesting very likely that no major climatic shift took place during the post Neolithic period. The progressive aridity in climate seems a plausible inference. This, however, may not be in accord with the inference of wet climate during the Indus Valley Civilization from wide drains and occurrence of Rhinoceros, and Elephant etc. and habitations in the Rajasthan desert corresponding to this time, although the lack of humus and the presence of aolian silts points to a drier climate when loessic deposits were formed in NW India. The discovery of habitation sites along the banks of rivers, amidst riparian plant communities, perhaps explains to some extent the anomalous situation.

The identification of charcoal and subfossil timber discovered from Harappa has led Chwodhury and Ghosh [19] to conclude that about 4000 years ago, there was scrubby forest with pockets of marshy land and tall grasses with rainfall probably limited to a few months in a year. A moist climate can be inferred from *Dalbergia latifolia* which occurs, occasionally to frequently, in the south Indian tropical moist deciduous forest in Mysore and Madras, but here *D. atifolia* is not associated with *Zizyphus* and *Ulmus*, the other two genera discovered at Harappa. *Zizyphus* does occur frequently in tropical moist deciduous forest at Mount Stuart, S. Coimbatore, but the other two genera are missing in this community. Their close occurrence at Harappa is only possible either through the transport of their woods from elsewhere by man or the shift of the southern plant communities to the NW and of Himalayan to the south but supporting evidence for the latter is yet to be discovered.

From the woods identified from Hastinapura, Chowdhury & Ghosh [20] conclude that they do not suggest any pronounced climatic change in the region within the last 3000 years. The evidence is based upon *Dalbergia sissoo* which is a riparian species whereas *Holarrhena antidyssentrica* occurs both in moist deciduous forest and dry deciduous rivarian forest. Both occur in subsidiary edaphic forest types. Likewise plant remains from the Chalcolithic site at Maski comprising *Chloroxylon swietinia* and *Acacia* [21] and frequent occurrence of *Acacia* and *Zizyphus* at other Chalcolithic sites such as Navdatoli-Maheshwar suggest warm and dry climate.

From a study of timbers from Sisupalgarh, Chowdhury & Ghosh [22] again arrive at the same conclusion that there has been no climatic change in the region since about 2000 years. The plant remains *Boswellia serrata*, *Acacia* and *Soymida febrifuga* suggest a *Boswellia* community which thrives in low rainfall (20-25″) on dry hills throughout peninsular India. *Casearia* sp. and *Holarrhena* are not misfits in this community.

Thus a large body of evidence from western, central and northern India suggests that Neolithic and post-Neolithic periods evolved in progressively dry climate. This was responsible for progressive expansion of the Rajasthan desert.

Besides extending help in Chronology, the growth rings in woods also provide evidence of former periods of drought, high precipitation etc.

Ancient Plant Economy

The distribution of cultivated plants and their wild ancestors have revealed that a large part of India leaving a strip in the north west belongs to the centre of origin for rice whereas the north western part belongs to the centre of origin for wheat (*Triticum sphaerococum*). India has also been the home of millets although considered to be a secondary centre of origin. Amongst the other useful plants *Dolichos Phaseolus*, *Cicer arictinum*, cotton are also attributed to India [23]. Several other cultivated plants have been introduced into India through diffusion of alien cultures into the country. The cultivated plants now used in the country can, therefore, provide background information of considerable significance to throw light on the evolution of the protohistoric cultures.

Researches hitherto carried out reveal [24] that *Dolichos biflorus* was an important legume amongst the Neolithic people in the Mysore-Bellary Doab, several carbonised seeds of which have been discovered at Tekkalkota. The Neolithic in South India was also characterised by Millet culture since *Eleusine coracana* has been discovered at Hallur in Karnatak [25].

From the north west indirect evidence of the cultivation of wheat has been found in the archaeo-botanical material discovered from the Neolithic site at Burzahom [26]. Should the indirect evidence of Neolithic Wheat culture in Kashmir be ascertained in future, it will be interesting to infer that during the Neolithic times India had Wheat culture prevailing in the north west. About the species of wheat (*Triticum*) cultivated by the Neolithic Indians in the NW, we have no idea and we shall eagerly look forward to the archaeologists working in this part of India to unearth and provide the material. Was it *T. sphaerococcum* which is also known to occur wild in this part ? Or was it a progenitor of *T. sphaerococcum* ?

The Neolithic rice from Orissa [27], however, has been referred to *Oryza sativa* which also occurs wild in marshes of Rajasthan, Sikkim, Bengal, Khasia Hills, central India and the Circars [28]. It is of course easy to presume that it was this wild species which was brought under cultivation. But the earlier experiments of the Neolithic folk in determining the suitability of the grain of wild rice for human consumption and transplanting it from its wild habitat to the prepared one must be interesting and fascinating, if they could be known.

The Neolithic plant economy in India was characterised by three separate cultures viz., the Rice Culture, the Millet Culture and the Wheat Culture. It is yet to be established through fresh excavations as to which of these cultures was dominant over the others. Our knowledge of the Neolithic plant economy is still incomplete since besides the three cereals and a legume we know nothing of the other plants used by the Indian Neolithic folk.

The Wheat, Rice and Millet Cultures comprise mature phases of plant economy of the Neolithic and may be assigned to the mid-or late-Neolithic. The early Neolithic, a period of trial and experimentation and the transition between the late Mesolithic and early Neolithic, should serve as a delimitation between the commencement of Neolithic and the end of Mesolithic. The precise recognition of this transition through typology or sections exposed in excavations may be difficult owing to considerable mixing or passing over of the Mesolithic traits into the Neolithic in India. Botany, however, provides precise evidence of this transitional phase through that part of the pollen diagrams where the sporadic occurrence of culture pollen and Cerealia is indicated. The part of the diagram preceding this obviously represents the Mesolithic period and the part succeeding it the early Neolithic. If plant economy is a measure for such a delimitation then the pollen diagrams constructed from NW Himalayas viz., Kashmir [29] and Kumaon [30] have already provided this information. The radio-carbon assay of the corresponding sediments will, however, attest the validity of the delimitation recognised in pollen diagrams. In both Kumaon and Kashmir it reveals the same environment and hence it is of equal antiquity.

Pollen analyses in India may suffer from serious limitations, since the pollen of rice and millets do not fall in the category of Cerealia pollen. It is yet to be seen if the pollen of associated weeds can throw light on their cultivation. This limitation may also affect the distinction between the pastoral activity and farming. The inference of commencement of farming preceded by a long period of pastoral activity from the pollen diagrams constructed from Ootacamund [31] and suggesting the origin of farming in the Nilgiris in the post-Neolithic period, may not be free from pitfalls.

In the succeeding Copper-Bronze Age—the Chalcolithic period—the pattern of plant economy seen in the Neolithic, undergoes a considerable change. The Rice Culture continues and dominates, the Wheat Culture spreads to the entire north India with the easternmost limit seen in West Bengal and in large part of central India. It is not clear, however, if the Millet Culture spread north-westward as seen in Rajasthan [32] or had already existed there. The spread of Wheat Culture inland during the Chalcolithic is an outstanding feature of ancient plant economy in India. Perhaps the Harappans and later the Aryans share the responsibility for this.

The Chalcolithic wheat belongs to *Triticum vulgarecompactum* type, of which the centre of origin is outside India. The evidence of melon (*Cucumis melo*) at Mohenjo-daro also points to the same, of which middle Asia is the gene centre. How was this diffused into the Indus Valley and who did it ? Wheat Culture here is accompanied by barley also, although only discovered at Mohenjo-daro. The botanical evidence tends to suggest that the Harappan culture has emerged from an influx from the extreme west. Diffusions from the extreme west are also indicated at Navdatoli-Maheshwar [33] by the finds of *Lens culinaris* and *Linun usitatissinum*.

The records from the Iron Age, though meagre as yet, again give evidence of rice and millets. But the finds of gram (*Cicer arietinum*) from Amraoti are an interesting addition to the ancient plant economy of India. Gram is associated with horses which characterise the Aryans. Perhaps the Amraoti evidence is late in history, we ought to discover records of gram from earlier strata and use it as time-marker for the advent of Aryans in India.

The meagre evidence of cotton and silk is from the Chalcolithic and we need to know more of it to infer anything useful from them. The same applies to the oil seeds, though linseed's significance has already been mentioned above. Likewise we need more and substantial evidences to prove pre-Columbian historical contacts of early Indians with the Mexicans to support the insufficient evidence of pre-Columbian maize in India [34]. Perhaps, as opined by Jeffreys [35], maize was introduced into India by the Arabs long before the Portugese entered the land.

Aegilops is ethe precursor of wheat as established by cytogenetical research. Its remains have now been found in Afghanistan from the site Deh Morasi Ghundai dating to circa 3000 B.C. [36]. At other sites the usual associate of barley is wheat but here barley is associated with an ancestor of it. Deh Morasi Ghundai represents an under-developed culture without any contacts with cultural centres in Asia.

The origin of six-rowed barley is still disputed. Diverse opinions exist : its origin from a two-rowed barley or from an extinct six-rowed barley. The Deh Morasi Ghundai find being six-rowed and from culturally isolated site perhaps suggests its development from a wild six-rowed form now extinct. Archaeology thus provides valuable information to solve some riddles in botany and agriculture. We can hopefully look forward to archaeological excavations in the extreme NW of India to recover material of this alongwith that of wheat. The discovery of early and wild cultivated plants will be of added interest to both botany and archaeology.

Although the New Stone Age is accredited for the commencement of agriculture, the Old Stone Age must be accorded due credit for the evidences although indirect for vegetative propagation preceding seed growing. The digging of rhizomes, tubers and other underground parts to provide supply of carbohydrates is the Palaeolithic mode of agriculture. This according to Sauer [37] " assured and increased the reproduction of such plants and did not involve the time-limit for harvest, problem of storage and it was the simplest form of agriculture to supplement and balance his highly protein and fat rich diet with starches derived from roots. Burning and digging provided reproductive advantage to certain plants useful to Man thus leading to profuse propagation and lateration by individual plant selections by nature producing better and useful varieties which could be selected for desired quality by the early Man ".

Past Cultural Contacts

Like implements, plant remains from archaeological sites also provide information of past cultural contacts of pre-and protohistoric folk. The cultivated plants were carried by the people to wherever they went. The diffusion of Wheat Culture into India has already been mentioned.

The discovery of lentil (*Lens culinaris* Medikus), grass pea (*Lathyrus sativus* L.) and linseed (*Linum usitatissimum* L.) at Navdatoli-Maheshwar [38] is highly suggestive of their diffusion into Central India from the Mediterranean and the extreme west of India. The diffusion of *Zizyphus jujuba* Lamk. has taken place into Arabia and Egypt from India [39].

Outside the cultivated plant remains, evidences of the use of wild plants for timber, implements, pounders and coffins have also been found. Some of the plant species identified do not suggest any possibility of having grown in the near vicinity of the site they are discovered from such as *Cedrus, Ulmus, Dalbergia latifolia* the timber of which was used for coffins. *Cedrus* and *Ulmus* today are restricted to the Himalayas, and no possibility suggests for their former occurrence at the sites of their discovery. *Dalbergia latifolia* occurs in the south and it seems improbable that this tree had extended into the Indus Valley about 4000 years ago. Obviously the timber of these must have been imported from the Himalayas and the south of India. This indirectly suggests the cultural contacts of early Indians with the people in far flung areas within the country and outside.

It seems certain that the knowledge of the property and uses of wood such as the durability, the shock absorbing quality characteristic of *Zizyphus* wood used for making wooden mortars, the high Caloric value and suitability as fuel [40] must have been built up through trial and experience and cultural contacts.

Conclusion

In an outline of areas of mutual interest comprising the dating mechanism, the environmental archaeology, the ancient plant economy, and the past cultural contacts, it has been shown how closely the plant sciences and archaeology are related to each other and how in these areas their aid to each other becomes indispensable. It is needless, therefore, to draw attention to the importance of close collaboration among the specialists of these two disciplines of science. It is hoped that this realization will bring them closer for the progress and advancement of science as a whole and their respective disciplines too. The need for mutual collaborative effort has already been pointed out earlier by Vishnu-Mittre [41].

NOTES

[1] F.E. Zeuner, *Dating the Past,* (London), 1958, 6.

[2] *The Ninth Bridgewater Treatises, A Fragment,* (London), 1837.

[3] The oldest known tree is known to exceed 704 years. See P. Maheshwari, 'Flora' in *The Gazetteer of India,* (Delhi), 1965.

[4] 'The formation of Growth rings in Indian trees I', *Indian Forest Rec.,* **2** (1), 1939, 1-39 and 'The formation of Growth rings in Indian trees II', *Ibid,* **2** (2), 1940, 41-57.

[5] 'The formation of Growth rings in Indian trees', *Ibid,* N.S. **1**(2), 1950, 1-27.

[6] 'The formation of Growth rings in Indian trees', *Ibid,* N.S. **1** (1), 1949, 1-15.

[7] S.T. Andersen, H.De Vries and W.H.Zagwijin, 'Climatic change and radio-carbon dating in the Weichselian Interglacial of Denmark and the Netherlands', *Geol.en Mijub.,* 1960, **39**, and 'Vegetation and its environment in Denmark in the Early Weichselian Glacial (Last Glacial)', *Dan. Geol. Unders,* **11** (75), 1961, 1-175.

[8] Difficulties in the application of C—14 results in Archaeology, *Archaeologia Austriaca,* **24**, 1958, 59-69.

[9] Op cit. (1), 244.

[10] Op cit. (8).

[11] Vishnu-Mittre, 'Some problems concerning Pleistocene stratigraphy of India with remarks on Pollen Stratigraphy', *Indian Prehistory*—1964, (Poona), 1965, 15-34.

[12] Vishnu-Mittre, 'Oaks in the Kashmir Valley with remarks on their history', *Grana Palynologica,* **4** (2), 1963, 306-312 and Vishnu-Mittre and B.D. Sharma, 'Studies of Post-glacial Vegetational history from the KashmirValley—1. Haigam Lake', *Palaeobot.* **15** (1 & 2), 1966, 185-212.

[13] H. P. Gupta, *Studies of the Late Quaternary Vegetational History of the Kumaon Hills and the Nilgiris,* Ph D. thesis Lucknow University, 1966.

[14] H. de Terra and T.T. Paterson, *Studies on the Ice Age in India and Associated Human Cultures,* Carnegie Institute, (Washington), 1939 and F.E. Zuner, *Stone Age and*

Pleistocene Chronology in Gujrat, Deccan College Monograph Series 6, -Poona), 1950, 1-50.

[15] The corresponding rise in maximum temperature during abnormal heat waves is within the range of 5-10° throughout the country. See S.Basu, 'Weather and Climate', *The Gazetteer of India,* I, 1965, 67-116.

[16] Vishnu-Mittre, 'On the Plio-Pleistocene boundary in NW India', *Palaeobot.,* **12** (3), 1963, 270-276 and op.cit. [11].

[17] Vishnu-Mittre, 'Some aspects of pollen-analytical investigations in the Kashmir Valley', *Palaeobot,* **16,** (182), 1966; Vishnu-Mittre and B.D. Sharma, op.cit. [12] and op· cit. [13].

[18] H. de Terra aud G.E. Hutchinson, 'Data on Post-glacial climatic changes in North West India', *Curr. Sci.,* **5**, 1936, 5-10.

[19] K. A. Chowdhury and S.S. Ghosh, 'Plants remains from Harappa', *Ancient India,* **7,** 1951.

[20] K.A. Chowdhry and S.S. Ghosh, 'Plant remains from Hastinapura', *Ibid,* **10-11**, 1954-55.

[21] S.S. Ghosh and K.S. Chowdhury, 'Plant remains', *Ancient India* ,**13,** 1957, 133-142.

[22] K.A. Chowdhury and S.S. Ghosh, 'Wood remains from Sisupalgarh', *Ancient India,* **8,** 1952.

[23] N.I. Vavilov, 'The origin, variation, immunity and breeding of cultivated plants', *Chronica Bot.,* **13,** 1950.

[24] Vishnu-Mittre, *History of Agriculture in India,* Deccan College Postgraduate and Research Institute, Poona, (in press).

[25] Vishnu-Mittre, 'Ancient Plant Economy in Hallur', *Report on Excavations at Hallur* by Nagraj Rao, (in press).

[26] Vishnu-Mittre, 'Plant remains from Burzahom', *Report on excavations at Burzahom* by T.N. Khazanchi, (in press).

[27] Op.cit., [24].

[28] J.D. Hooker, *Flora of British India,* **7,** Kent, England, 1895, 92.

[29] Vishnu-Mittre and B.D. Sharma, op.cit. [12].

[30] Op.cit. [13] and Vishnu-Mittre, H.P. Gupta and R. Robert, 'Studies of the Late Quaternary Vegetational History of Kumaon Himalya', *Curr. sci.,* 36 (20), 1967, 539-540.

[31] Op.cit. [13].

[32] Vishnu-Mittre, 'Plant Economy' in *Ancient Ahar, Copper Age city of Tambavati, Udaipur,* by H.D. Sankalia et al, (in press).

[33] Vishnu-Mittre, 'Plant economy from Navadatoli-Maheshwar', *Bulletin of the Deccan College Post-graduate and Research Institute,* (Poona), 1962.

[34] Vishnu-Mittre, 'Kaundinyapur plant economy in prehistoric and historic times', *Palaeobot.,* **15,** (1 & 2), 1966, 152-156.

[35] M.D.W. Jeffreys, 'Plants diffusion. "Hand off America ! A texonomist versus the Rest", *Anthrop. J. Canada,* **3** (1), 1965, 5-15.

[36] K.A. Chowdhury, 'Plant remains from Deh Morasi Ghundai, Afghanistan', *Anthorpol, Papers Amer. Mus. Nat. Hist.,* **50** (2), (New York), 1965, 126-131.

[37] Cultural factors in plant domestication as illustrated from the New World, *Abstract Proc. Tenth Internat. Bop. Congr.,* (Edinburgh), 1964, 127.

[38] Op.cit. [33].

[39] Op.cit. [33].

[40] K.A.Chowdhury, 'Plant remains from Pre-and Proto historic sites and their scientific significance', *Science & Culture,* **31**, 1965, 177,178.

[41] Op.cit. [11].

A Further Note on the Direction of Writing in the Harappan Script

by B. B. LAL

In the March-1966 issue of *Antiquity* (pp. 52-55) I published a note on the above-mentioned topic. To recapitulate, the note, with the help of the illustrations that accompanied it, showed that the direction of writing in the Harappan script was from the right to the left. The conclusion was based on the evidence of overlap of symbols which had been inscribed on some potsherds.

Accompanying the present note also is a photograph (Pl. I) of an inscribed potsherd, but with a difference. Whereas in the case of the potsherds published in *Antiquity* the symbols were inscribed *after* firing, in the present case they were inscribed *before* firing. Thus, as the clay was only leather-hard at the time of the inscribing of the present specimen, the incisions are bold and deep. This makes it much easier to determine the overlap in the present case than it was in the case of the potsherds illustrated with the earlier note.

The potsherd being broken, it is not known if there were any more symbols in the inscription (cf. Pl. I). As it is, the inscription comprises four symbols. Beginning from the right, the first symbol consists of two vertical strokes, the second resembles an arrow, the third resembles a fish, and the fourth comprises three vertical strokes.

As there is no overlap between the first and second symbols, it is difficult to say anything about the sequence *inter se* of their incision. The same applies to the relationship between the third and fourth symbols. It is only in the case of the second and third symbols that there is an overlap. We shall see a little later what this overlap signifies.

The second symbol, resembling an arrow, consists of four strokes, of which three form a triangle and the fourth cuts the base vertically down. Of the three strokes forming the triangle, it is clearly seen that the basal stroke was drawn later than the one on the left, for the former overrides the latter, though only to a very limited extent, at the junction of the two. As to the relationship between the two oblique strokes of the triangle, it is unfortunate that the photograph does not bring out the overlap clearly. From the original, however, it is clear that it is the left-hand stroke that cuts the top-end of the right-hand one, showing thereby that the former was incised after the latter. That the vertical stroke cuts the basal stroke of the triangle is patently clear. Thus, the sequence of incision of the four strokes comprising the 'arrow' would be : the right-hand oblique stroke, the left-hand oblique stroke, the basal stroke, and the vertical stroke.

Now to the third symbol, resembling a fish. It consists of four parts : two arcs, meeting each other at the top but intersecting lower down, and two oblique strokes forming the two 'fins' of the 'fish'. Of the two arcs, the left-hand one overrides the other, as can be seen clearly at the point of their intersection. That the two 'fins' cut across the two respective arcs is also very clear. As to the interrelationship between the two 'fins', it is seen that the left-hand one overrides, though only partially, the top-end of the right-hand one. The sequence *inter se* of the incision of the four parts of the symbol would thus be : the right-hand arc, the left-hand arc, the right 'fin', and the left 'fin'.

Now to the most important point of the discussion, viz., the interrelationship of the second and third symbols, which provides the clue for determining the direction of writing of the inscription. It is clear from the photograph that the horizontal stroke forming a part of the second symbol *is cut* by the right-hand oblique stroke (the 'fin' of the 'fish') of the third symbol. This evidence establishes that the second symbol was incised *before* the third. It would thus mean that the direction of writing of the inscription was from the right to the left.

Here, thus, is one more example to confirm the conclusion arrived at in the note published in *Antiquity*, viz., that the direction of writing in the Harappan script was from the right to the left. In fact, *the sequence of incision even of the individual parts* of the second and third symbols as detailed above, *also demonstrates a behaviour which is normal only to a system in which the direction of writing is from the right to the left.* This second observation has been possible only because the present specimen had been inscribed *before* firing, which resulted in bold and deep incisions.

An inscribed potsherd.

Paunar Mound.

Protohistoric Chronology and Technology and Ecological Factors : A Synthesis

by D. P. AGRAWAL

We propose a model here which adequately explains available evidence on protohistoric archaeology. An attempt has been made to integrate technological, archaeological and ecological evidence. Any model to explain evidence of a period devoid of decipherable written records has admittedly to be largely conjectural. However, an absolute chronology, based on C-14 dates, provides a firm framework.

India had two main phases of urbanisation : first, based upon copper metallurgy and Indus plains ; second, depended upon iron metallurgy and Indo-Gangetic plains. Doab, because of its impregnable forests, had to await advent of iron to colonise it. First wave of intruders (Aryans ?) could not colonise Doab; only second wave could do it, as it had iron. The conclusions, though subjective, seem, in view of the objective evidence enumerated below, inescapable.

Ecology

In the Indus region neither climate nor ecology seems to have changed much [1, 2]. Indus alluvium was quite soft which would yield to even wooden hoe. Copper and bronze hoes were quite sufficient for agriculture. Rainfall was poor. Even now Panjab has 10″ to 20″ of annual rainfall, though it has an immense sea of underground fresh water. The lower Indus plain has much less rainfall : in Sind it is less than 5″ [3]. Such a climate and soil could support only a sparse scrub jungle and at best a gallery forest [1]. Such an ecology was the right ground to sow the seeds of civilisation. Knowledge of copper metallurgy combined with pliable alluvial plains produced large scale surplus in agriculture which led to the granaries and the cities of Indus, viz., urbanisation and state.

In Rajasthan there is evidence for change in climate and continuous advancement of desert. Three distinct breaks between pre-Harappan-cum-Harappan and P. G. Ware, and Rangmahal are of the order of a milleninum. It possibly agrees with the pattern of climatic change [4].

Ecology of the Gangetic plain has however suffered drastic changes at the hands of man. Constant denudation of forests have resulted in vast alluvial plains.

This region has a good rainfall as it falls within the contours 25″-40″ of annual rainfall. " The soil is meadow type and tropical and sub-tropical-dry steppe on older alluvium and hard rocks with solonets " [5]. Naturally, a monsoon fed forest grew up. Most of it was covered with sal and other Terai and Bhabur like forests [6]. There is plenty of evidence to show the original vegetation of these plains [7, 8]. More work on Gangetic fossil pollens is afoot [9]. Even as late as Moghal times there were sizeable forests as is evidenced by their hunting expeditions. The fauna included carnivores, monkeys, elephants and ungulates [6].

Literary evidence of the Epics also confirms the presence of primeval forests in the Doab [10]. *Satpath Brahmana* [11] mentions the advance of *Agni* eastwards upto *Sadānirā* (modern Gandaka) enabling Aryanisation of Videha. Basham [12] says, " the main line of Aryan penetration was not down the river, the banks of which were then probably thick swampy jungles, but along the Himalayan foot hills ". Forest clearance by fire is possible only in the foot hills. Iron was needed for clearance and agriculture in monsoon forests [13].

Thus we see that evidence of flora, fauna, soil, climate and literature point to the thick monsoonal primeval forests in the Doab. Unlike the Indus which flowed largely through a desert, Ganges and Yamuna passed through thick and deep forests and swamps. The Doab alluvial plains are a result of man-made deforestation in the course of several millennia. We would see the role of this primeval forest barrier in the spread of black-and-red ware.

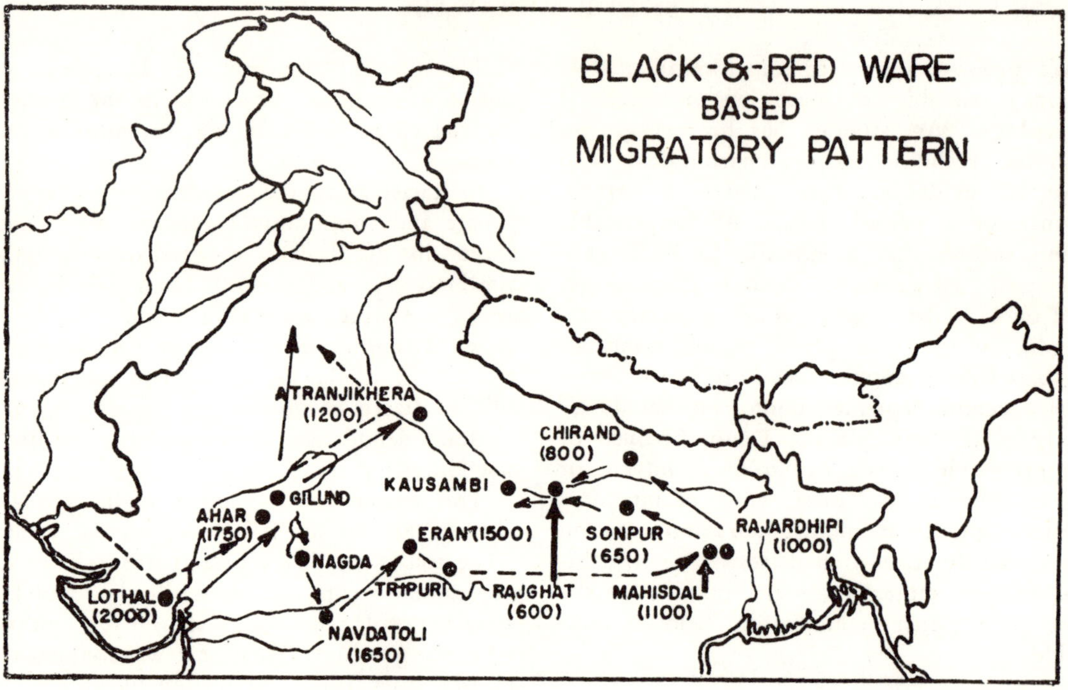

Fig. 1. Probable routes of migration of black-and-red ware. Numbers within brackets are average radiocarbon dates in years B. C. based on 5730 years Value. Younger dates of Rajghat show that they received the impulse from the east rather than the west.

C-14 Dates and Chronology

Before we discuss technology, let us define the chronological framework. To date, about 300 C-14 dates are available [14, 15]. Problems of chronology have been discussed by several workers [16 to 22]. We can safely infer now from the available C-14 dates and archaeological data that there is a clear temporal succession of Pre-Harappan, Harappan, Banas, Malwa, Jorwe, P. G. Ware and N. B. P. Ware cultures. Neolithic of the South, as also of Kashmir, in their start, are roughly contemporary with Harappa culture. Megalithic culture of the South, from the few C-14 dates so far, appears to emerge around c. 900 B.C. However, we know practically nothing about the chronology of the northern and eastern megaliths, nor about the eastern neolithic.

Still, finer points of chronology need more work. Recent dates [23] from the latest phase of HR area of Mohenjodaro and Kalibangan[24], though conforming to shorter time-spreads of Harappans, may indicate, different—though overlapping—brackets for nuclear and peripheral zones. In this light, Raikes' [16] idea of succession of Harappan capitals looks quite plausible. However, with errors as large as± 100 years and probable C-14/C-12 minor variations in the third millennium B. C., greater precision at this stage would not be warranted. These problems will be discussed elsewhere [25].

The germane point to our discussion here is the following of Banas culture in the wake of the Harappans. Though a coexistence in point of time of Harappans in north Rajasthan and Banasians in the south—at least for some time—is not improbable. What is more interesting is the distribution of C-14 dates of these early black-and-red ware sites. A look at Fig. 1 will show that a wave is going northwards to the fringes of west U.P. and east Panjab. The other spreads through central India to West Bengal. This pattern is delineated by the gradually younger C-14 dates on the northern and eastern routes. Such a spread would readily explain the late dates of east U.P. and Bihar. As discussed earlier, the dense forests came, in the way of both these waves as a result of which they recoiled westwards (Fig. 1).

P G ware appears around c. 1000 B.C. (we have only one C-14 date for the early phase though) and overlaps with N B P ware (c. 500-50 B.C.).

We will discuss technological factors below and then we will see how this chronology helps to understand the protohistoric migrations.

Technology

It is agreed that copper metallurgy was quite advanced in Harappa culture [26]. There are several chemical analyses available which show that they did deliberate tin and antimony alloying. They had developed techniques to extract pure copper (upto 99%) from probably chalcopyrites. Problem of correlation with ores is much more complex than the facile claims made by analysts so far. The author is trying to use modern statistical approach to ascertain the types of ores used. Pinpointing of actual mines will require much more work by many workers and willing co-operation of the collectors.* Metallographic analyses are also underway and show definitely that annealing, cold and hot working, closed casting etc. were known to the Harappans. Probably techniques of raising, hollowing, riveting and "running-on" were also known. Copper was never a cheap metal and never in abundance at least in India. Continued use of chert blades indicates costliness of metal. But the prolific copper-bronze repertoire of Harappans does show their access to rich ore deposits for the demand of those times. They even had a true saw which does not appear elsewhere till Iron Age. For agriculture on the pliable fertile Indus alluvium, however, copper hoes, sickles and knives were sufficient.

As pointed out by Fairservis [2] a symbiotic balance was attained which led to proliferation of cattle. The preponderance of bulls on seals and terracottas is a reflection of the recognition of cattle-power. The origin of sacredness of cattle in India may have an origin in the Indus. Harnessing of energy is an essential factor for growth of cultures. Use of cattle-power for agriculture and transport on a large scale was certainly an intensifying factor in the Harappa culture. Rivers too were used for nevigation. Sites like Sutkagendor and Lothal do point to maritime trade.

* For any meaningful and valid conclusions about ore-correlations, it is necessary to have a large number of analyses. With the present techniques available in India, it is possible to do chemical and metallographic analyses without disfiguring or cutting chunks from artifacts. Even milligram quantities are enough to permit full chemical analysis. Spot-polishing enables metallographic analysis without cutting an artifact. It is hoped that Inidan museums would also follow British Museum where such analyses are not only permitted but encouraged.

The surplus produced led to the development of specialised crafts ; because the society could now provide food for their skills. A technological base for the first phase of urbanisation was ready. Evolution of classes, state and civic life were natural concomitants.

Ghosh [27] has seen in many pre-Harappan cultures of Sind, Panjab and Rajasthan a substratum for rise of the Harappans. Quantitative changes were definitely due to these precursors, for these pre-Harappans had the requisite technical knowhow : metallurgy, fortifications, use of cattle and wind power. At some stage this had to give rise to a qualitative change—the urban Harappan society was bound to come. May be it was accelerated by a foreign impulse or an " idea-stimulus ".

Again, the story in Doab was much different. A sprinkling of Harappan sites on the fringes of Doab may indicate either their outposts for importing timber or may be refugee-settlements. What is pertinent is that they failed to colonise Doab to grow into cities. Harappans could survive all their migrations upto Doab, because western India was ecologically one unit; but their socio-economy, their urban culture, withered as soon as it entered an alien ecology of Doab. Despite large number of known Ochre Coloured ware sites, they have nothing of urbanism. In fact, Ochre Colour ware deposits so far encountered have consistently been of a detrital nature. Was it due to a huge deluge ? If yes, any red pottery after the deluge would look like O. C. ware.

Copper Hoards [28, 29] are still an enigma. They are a conglomerate of ill-assorted artifacts. How many tools belong to a particular culture, with definite space-time-spread, is a moot point still. Their tools, however, have a hunting bias with their developed harpoons, heavy axes and even anthropomorphic figures which could have served as missiles or boomerangs (?) (their structure, blunted heads, and externally sharp wings clearly indicate it). Their harpoons are hallmarks of their developed casting skill as also their knowledge of alloying copper with tin [30]. However, many more analyses of tools and ores are necessary before we can say something definite about them. But for large-scale agriculture and clearance of thick forests copper artifacts were no answer. Absence of large settlements of Copper Hoard and O.C. ware cultures are a pointer. In fact, most of the reported Copper Hoard sites are marked by lack of any mounds. Complete absence of any pots or pans of metal, out of more than a thousand Copper Hoard artifacts, may indicate hunting-nomadic life.

To break kankry soil of Doab and to clear monsoon jungle what was needed was use of iron artifacts on a mass scale. It is not surprising therefore that first colonisation of Doab is due to iron using PG ware people around the beginning of I millennium B.C. Whether they used local ores for fabricating iron tools only further work on technology of Iron Age in India will tell. Alternatively, they could have brought their tool kit along with them. Forging and reshaping of old tools could be done by a smith but extraction of metal was an involved process. And how long it took for the PG ware people to acquaint themselves with the terrain and look for local ores is a moot point again. And when did carburization of iron to make steel start. To answer these questions we need technological studies and not only typological catalogues of metal artifacts. A large number of PG ware sites in Doab bears eloquent testimony to the successful colonisation of Doab by these people. Iron technology alone was an answer to Doab colonisation.

Problems of Iron Age in India have been dealt with exhaustively by Banerjee [31]. However, complete absence of technological studies therein leaves many problems where they were. Tandon [32] in his recent paper has laid emphasis on the technological aspect of the problem.

Unless we can prove that PG ware people were smelting local iron ores to forge their tools, one cannot hold that Iron Age in India was brought by them. The real superiority of iron on bronze does not lie in hardness and strength, but in its abundance. Advent of real Iron Age should be dependent upon smelting of local ores and its impact on the economy. To us it appears that the advent of real Iron Age coincides with the second phase of urbanisation with its locale in the Doab. Iron, when it was plentiful, could be used for large-scale jungle clearance and ploughing of the tough Doab soil. This naturally meant surplus food production, increase in cattle-power, quicker transport, river-navigation—all leading to growth of cities.

NBP ware has an epicentre probably in Magadha, an area where iron was available in abundance in an easily smeltable form [33]. PG ware in the Doab is entering from the West. But the transition between the two is smooth, in fact many of the NBP shapes follow PG ware. Besides, many red ware shapes are commonly associated with PG and NBP wares [34]. And growth of cities coincides with the emergence of NBP ware. To us this evidence suggests that use of Bihar iron ores alone could make the use of iron on a mass-scale feasible for complete urbanisation of Doab which gave rise to the first cities. Despite the iron tools of PG ware people and long time-spread, their settlements are very poor. Urbanisation was a far cry. It could probably be due to non-utilisation of local ores by PG ware people. The revolutionary power of iron lies only in the fact that it is most abundant and cheap material which could be used by common man. Comparatively, copper and bronze were never very abundant, especially in India.

These questions will remain in the realm of speculation so long the excavators do not encourage analyses of excavated metal artifacts. Today, technologically-biased investigations can go a long way towards the re-construction of protohistory; in fact, they are a desideratum.

Finally, a few words about Banas Culture technology.

Hegde's excellent work [35] on Chalcolithic metallurgy has given us a fund of information. Such studies on much larger scale and by many more workers are required. Banas Culture people might have sed Khetri ores as agreement in impurity patterns of the ore and the artifacts shows. Though they know smelting of ores, their casting is very poor. Knowledge of tin and antimony alloying is also not attested. Their copper tool-repertoire is of an inferior variety and obviously no match to the challenges of Doab colonisation.

Black-and-red ware is produced by an inverted firing technique. This technique in India is first observed amongst Saurashtra Harappans. From there it seems to have gone to Banas region. One wave of it goes to the north (in Panjab also black-and-red ware has been reported from several sites [36]). But they cannot penetrate deeper in the Doab. The other wave goes via central Chalcolithic sites to West Bengal and then recoils back to Bihar and eastern U.P. Bases of assuming this route for black-and-red ware are two : first it is suggested by radiocarbon dates (Fig. 1); second, specialised techniques have greater probability of diffusion than independent invention every where. A look at Fig. 1 will show that some barrier had to be faced both by the northern wave and the eastern wave. That barrier could only be monsoon-fed dense forests. That explains the late dates of Rajghat, Chirand, Sonepur black-and-red ware, as this impulse covered a longer way (from west to east, then after recoil, from east to west) both in terms of time and space.

There is a sprinkling of black-and-red ware in some late neolithic sites too. Like black-on-red ware, black-and-red ware too was wheel-thrown and technologically is an alien trait in a hand-made pottery-complex. So both these wares are obviously intrusive in a neolithic milieu. In fact, in Tekklakota black-and-red ware has been called an import by the excavator [37] though the ware appears to him as made on a tournette.

So in a neolithic milieu occurrence of black-and-red ware shows at best contacts with Chalcolithic cultures of the north.

The equation of Banas culture with early intruders (Aryans) was based on their geographical and chronological vicinity with the Harappans, as also cultural borrowal from the latter [38]. Their west Asian affinities have been discussed by Sankalia in detail [39]. So if this was the first wave of Aryans, it never penetrated deep into Doab. Gaur [40] has raised interesting questions and seems to agree with the view that black-and-red wave were the early Aryans and P.G. ware later post-Ṛgvedic Aryans. Lallanji Gopal [41] has convincingly shown that "Ayas" in Ṛgveda only means metal and not iron.

Synthesis

Wheeler [42] in his characteristic lucid style has described three inevitable stages in all scientific investigation : "The first stage is one of limited knowledge and restricted inference (often wrong). Upon this follows the accumulation of scarps of evidence which tend to constitute an untidy and incoherent heap. Only, later, when this heap has sufficiently grown and matured, does it begin to take an assured place in the landscape." In 1958 he described Indian archaeological investigation in the "untidy heap stage". But in 1967, we can safely continue the great efforts of the late Subbarao in giving shape to this now grown-up heap of data. Attempts in this direction have already been started by Ghosh [27], Wheeler [21], Sankalia [43], Lal [20], Kosambi [33], and others [31, 32, 38, 44].

About interpretations, Piggot [45] said "The model will be a 'true' one in so far as it does satisfactorily account for the phenomena, but you can have more than one model at a time, all 'true', and the devising of a new model does not mean that all the others have to be scrapped, though some may have to be abandoned or drastically modified in the light of new thought". This is true of the model proposed here too.

There are still many obscure points, apparently contradictory evidence even. But to bring order into the chaos—the "untidy heap"—of data one has to put forth their synthesis—models—which could be precursors of more 'true' ones.

To summarise : India has witnessed two major phases of urbanisations : one about the middle of the third millennium B.C.; the second about the middle of the first millennium B.C. For the first phase the stage is set by the pre-Harappans which culminates in the Harappan civilization. Whether the Harappans represented an exotic impulse which accelerated the process of urbanisation is still a moot point. Its technology is copper and bronze based : and the fertile land is provided by the tender Indus plains.

Harappans did not have a far-flung empire for a millennium. It is probably a gradually shifting empire from west to the east and the south under pressure both of folk migrations and natural agencies.

Black-and-red ware migration may indicate the spread of early Aryans, typified by Banas culture. They could not penetrate and colonise Doab or Sunderbans because of thick monsoonal forests for which the copper supply and technology was no equal. They spread in two waves: one going to north which deflects from the western Doab to spread into east Panjab, the second goes to West Bengal via central India and recoils back from the Sunderbans to spread to Bihar and east U.P. There is a possibility of early Aryans and Kalibangan Harappans partly coexisting in time without interaction. Such a migratory pattern is supported by C-14 dates and ecological considerations.

Copper Hoard problem is still an enigma. But their hunting tool kit, abundance of metal and developed alloying and casting technology shows that they may be much later in time. Unless authorities allow more analyses of Copper Hoards, this problem will indefinitely be discussed subjectively.

PG ware, possibly representing the second wave of Aryans, started the colonisation of Daob with their iron technology. To clear thick forests and cultivate the kankry land only iron tools were an answer. But due to either the lack of ore extraction technology or ignorance of Indian iron ores, real Iron Age had to await till NBP times when plentiful supply of easily smeltable Bihar iron ore was available. Iron when used on mass-scale alone could produce requisite surplus to usher in the second phase of urbanisation resulting in the growth of the first cities in north and east India towards c. 500 B.C. If the foregoing is correct, then occurrence of cities in Doab at c. 1000 B.C. or before would be both incongruous and improbable.

NOTES

[1] R. L. Raikes and R. H. Dyson, *American Anthropologist*, 63, 1961, 265.

[2] W. A. Fairservis, *American Museum Novitates*, *No.* 2055, 1961, 1

[3] R. Revelle, *New Scientist,* 17, *No.* 326, 1963, 340.

[4] R.A. Bryson and D. A. Baerries, *Bulletin of American Meteorological Society*, 48, *No.* 3, 1967, 136.

[5] O. H. K. Spate, *India and Pakistan* (1963).

[6] D. D. Pant, Prof. of Botany, Allahabad University, private communication.

[7] C. C. Calder, in *An Outline of Field Sciences in India*, ed. S. L. Hora, 1937, 83.

[8] E. P. Stebbing, *The Forests of India*, I, 1922, 29.

[9] Gurdeep Singh, Sahni Institute of Palaeobotany, Lucknow, private communication.

[10] K. M. Panikkar, *Geographical Factors in Indian History*, 1959, 50.

[11] *Satpatha Brahmana*, *i*, 4, 1.

[12] A. L. Basham, *The Wonder that was India* , 1963, 40.

[13] D. D. Kosambi, *Jour. of Econ. and Social Hist. of the Orient,* VI, Part III, 1963, 309.

[14] S. Kusumgar, D. Lal and R. P. Sarna, *The Proceedings of Indian Academy of Sciences, LVIII*, *No.* 3, 1963, 141.

[15] D. P. Agrawal, S. Kusumgar and R. P. Sarna, *Current Science,* 33, 1964, 40. Other C-14 dates have been published by the C-14 Lab. of Tata Institute of Fundamental Research in *Current Science*, 33, 1964, 266; 34, 1965, 42; 35, 1966, 585; 34, 1965, 394; 35, 1966, 4; 35, 1966, 276.

[16] R. L. Raikes, *American Anthropologist,* 66, 1964, 284.

[17] G. F. Dales, *Proceedings of the American Philosophical Society,* 110, No. 2, 1966, 130.

[18] D. P. Agrawal, *Science,* 143, *No.* 3609, 1964, 950.

[19] D. P. Agrawal, in *Studies in Prehistory,* 1966, 139.

[20] B. B. Lal, *Ancient India*, 18 and 19, 1963, 208.

[21] R. E. M. Wheeler, *Indus Civilisation,* 1960.

[22] R. E. M. Wheeler, *Antiquity*, 38, 1964, 307.

[23] Robert Stuckenrath, *Radiocarbon,* 9, 1967, 333.

[24] D. P. Agrawal and Sheela Kusumgar, Kalibangan C-14 dates, in press.

[25] D. P. Agrawal, paper in preparation.

[26] C. C. Lamberg-Karlovsky, *American Anthropologist,* 69, *No.* 2, 1967, 145.

[27] A. Ghosh, in *Indian Prehistory*—1964, 1965, 113.

[28] B. B. Lal, *Ancient India*, 7, 1951, 20.

[29] S. P. Gupta, *Journal of the Bihar Research Society, XLIX, Parts I and V*, 1963, 147.

[30] V. A. Smith, *The Indian Antiquary, XXXIV*, 1905, 229 and *XXXVI*, 1907, 53.

[31] N. R. Banerjee, *Iron Age in India*, 1965.

[32] O. P. Tandon, this issue.

[33] D. D. Kosambi, *The Culture and Civilisation of Ancient India*, 1965, 89.

[34] K. K. Sinha, *Report on Sravasti Excavations,* in press.

[35] K. T. M. Hegde, unpublished thesis.

[36] K. N. Dikshit, Archl. Survey, private communication.

[37] M. S. Nagaraja Rao, *The Stone Age Hill Dwellers of Tekklakota*, 1965.

[38] D. P. Agrawal, *Current Science*, 35,(5),1966, 114.

[39] H. D. Sankalia, *Artibus Asiae, XXVI*, 1963, 312.

[40] R. C. Gaur, in *Indian Prehistory*—1964, 1965, 145.

[41] Lallanji Gopal, *Uttar Bharati*, IX, 71.

[42] R. E. M. Wheeler, in his Foreword to *Personality of India*, 1958.

[43] H. D. Sankalia, *Prehistory and Protohistory in India and Pakistan*, 1963.

[44] B. K. Thapar, in *Indian Prehistory*—1964, 1965, 157.

[45] S. Piggott, *Approach to Archaeology*, 1966, 15.

The Changing Face of Archaeological Studies

by K. V. SOUNDARA RAJAN

It was in 1863 that Robert Bruce Foote discovered the first palaeolithic tool in India in a quarry pit at Pallavaram, and soon after displayed it to the yet rather sceptical and smug antiquarians of Europe, stirring them out of their complacence and widening their ken. A hundred years later, prehistory—now a *prima donna*, has indeed broken new grounds and, without remorse or recriminations, is divorcing her quondam hero the taxonomist, and plighting her troth with the sociologist-cum-statistician—the refined technical co-respondent. Perhaps it was well, but lest we might be throwing the baby along with the bathwater, we would do well to narrate the pace of events that had led to this rather exciting development.

To begin with, it would be appropriate to outline the primary objective in Prehistoric researches dealing with the origin and early vicissitudes of the human species. The earliest subhuman primate—the hunting man—was undoubtedly the product of the indefatiguable researches of palaeontologists working in close collaboration with archaeologists. Together, they have pieced out the scattered vestiges of bone remains of these early ancestors of ours, and presented them in the best manner that stratigraphic archaeology has taught them. The search had indeed been hard, frustrating and prolonged. Even now, we have a large part of the world practically unmanned—is so far as the original authors of the countless tools found in the implement—bearing strata of valleys, uplands, river banks, cave fronts etc., are concerned. India is one such region. There is not even a promise yet of any fruitful end of the journey in this direction, save for a more concerted attempt in the cave sites. All the same, none denies that the door is wide open yet and given the proper orientation and the tools for attack, the objective could be fulfilled sooner or later. For, it was the tools that created civilization ultimately, and it is in the selection and coordination of the tools of attack that the best chances for survival for archaeologists exist. The tools, that Prehistoric Stone-Age forebears, used have themselves become the subject of a widespread diversity of interpretation. The approach even has differed, one group of scholars addressing itself to the task of refining the typological criteria and differentiae; another, applying the 'functional' norms to the artefact groups; and a third, isolating the vocational or sociological unit from the plethora of tool types to be found in a given site. Of one thing, however, we may be certain. All these three categories of workers do not envisage any divorcing of the tools from their locale, and very strongly prefer *in situ* investigation. The ethnologists and archaeologists are today jointly seeking explanations for the range of cultural differences and similarities documented for the past and present in other countries. The archaeologist perhaps is, *prima facie* not in need of developing methodology for documenting all the formal characteristics of the human groups observed by the ethnologist, since at the distance of time where the former is operating, specific sophistication in 'social order' might not have been well established. But we must at least concede that any observations, which are of a crucial character in interpreting the true ethno-cultural situation of a given tool-using community, are not lost sight of, either by under-documentation of the environment, or the overelaboration of the typology. The problem is essentially one of reconstruction of dependable 'models' for testing the relationship between material and behavioural cultural phenomena. Here perhaps the ethnographer and the orthodox archaeologists and scientific prehistorians can operate on their own individual or specialised spheres, but come to each other for cross-checking the structural terms of the totality of the primitive society they are all seeking to rebuild.

In India, the situation, briefly stated, is that of the Prehistoric archaeologist on the one hand, and the ethnographer and sociologist, on the other, functioning in almost complete isolation, with the result that firstly, the former is totally unfamiliar with the standards of approach and viewpoints of data-processing that the latter is engaged in; and complementarily, as it were, the latter is almost totally unware of the bulk of field investigations and their qualitative character that the former is carrying on. The anthropologist in India is perhaps the one that is likely to overtake (and perhaps overrun) the Prehistoric archaeologist in the task of systematising the rudiments of Stone Age Culture—reconstruction soon, unless the Prehistorian is assiduously widening his parameter, and integrating his inferences with those of the anthropologist. Currently, however, anthropology in India is almost exclusively directed towards ethno-sociological investigation of tribes, races and exclusive groups, both primitive and modern, and Prehistory is only a fringe interest. Correspondingly, a good grounding in palaeontology, Sociology and Botany is not yet considered as the orthodox pabulum of a prehistorian. In fact, collection of tools and a typological categorisation of these, largely often on subjective standards, are the rule, and no basic qualifications have been insisted upon for a serious academic development of Prehistoric studies. Doubtless, geology and its stratigraphical and fossil concomitants have been much fancied as a desideratum, and this is indeed quite realistic. But as we tackle the problem, we are bound to realise more and more that the reconstruction of very ancient Stone Age societies, particularly in a country like India where the largest number of sites are of the open-air station type on the river banks, could be frustrating and, indeed, like venturing into an unchartered ocean without map or compass. There is no need to be unduly pessimistic about it, but as we grow out of our adolescence in these studies, we may as well learn our lesson and improve the 'methodological' problem of accurate data-computation, which would enable us to feed our fellow workers in the ethnographic, and sociological fields with precise observations. While dealing with the pattern of life in old Stone Age, dealing as we do with 'hunting man,' we are left with three varieties of his vestiges : habitational, equipmental and behavoural. The first, where we are provided with a reasonably convincing accumulation of his occupational rubbish and trivia, would involve a conscious assessment of the importance of each of these items, *per se* as well as in a probably mutually coordinated or isolated relationship. We shall come to this aspect again later.

The second deals almost entirely with his tools, their variety and intensity of incidence. It is here that the archaeologist particularly had his greatest wealth of data, and the functional classification of the tools permitted also comparison in space and time, by their own technological refinement and stylistic bias, as related to the environment that has been deduced or presumed for the hunting man from Early to Middle Stone Age. It is here that the raw material also played a significant role and allowed valid investigation into the nearest useful sources for the same, apart from the reflection they cast upon the geographical and ecological factors. But stylistic attributes could not be read into early Stone Age tools always, because of the limitations of the technique of tool-making implicit in the context, when we realise that almost the entire span of nearly 200,000 years of early Stone Age, the range of techniques involved in tool-artifice was a'direct knock' and 'resolved flaking' in so far as a body-trimming is concerned. The Middle Stone Age, however, markedly differed from the early, by the diversification of stylistic as well as technical criteria, and a differentiation of task-performance could be recongnised in the process. What more, there appears also a fixed locus for the varieties of functions performed namely skinning, scraping, roasting, eating etc., as reflected in the grouping of the vestigeal remnants in a given site. This standardization of the diurnal pursuit of man was not evident in Old Stone Age where man—like the animal he hunted—apparently did not have a customary or habitual habitat and also traversed long distances, stalking, trapping, killing and collecting his food and was thus primarily peripatetic and unstable in daily routine. All the more so in India. Further, the great scatter of his tools and other personal and hunted objects introduce a minimum of probability of a well ordered survival of his activities in a given tool deposit of a river. Lacustrine deposits are,doubtless, the most ideal in this respect but the very recurrence of lacustrine deposits has a direct significance in the character of the climate and topography where he lived, and would be sharply variant from the category of other open air riparian sites. The dispersal element in his remains,thus,is a great disadvantage and in a tropical country like India, the chances of survival of animal and human bones, even under the ideal conditions of preservation are meagre. On an African analogy, experiments made in a deliberately well preserved animal skeleton packed in a wire-netting (to prevent consumption by carnivora) and allowed to be exposed, showed almost total decay of the bones within a few years. Thus, the open-air sites of India have a slender chance of preserving the old Stone Age skeletal vestiges alike of the predatory man as of the animal, not to mention his wooden or bone equipment. We do have, however, fossils of the Bos and Rhino, Elephas etc. in the mid Pleistocene fluviatile deposits, and if they mean anything, their anteriority in age to human remains will have to be presumed. The chances, of course, are least in a lateritic area due to the destructive nature of the ferruginous matrix. Ultimately, our main sources of fossil human and animal remains associated with the tool-making early Man or his own anscestor, should be in the calcarious deposits in the cemented gravels of fossil river beds, not subjected to water movement and having had prolonged subareal as well as sub-terranean consolidation.

The third mode of investigation, namely, behavoural largely made possible in Europe owing to extraordinarily well preserved sites of early human habitation, mostly in caves but elsewhere as well, comprises the scrutiny of the behavoural pattern of activity of the hunting man in his habitat. This study, may it be said, is yet in its formative stages, because the data that it uses, for the time being, are the mass of materials that orthodox prehistorians have unearthed from these sites. The difficulty in excavating intensively a fresh site is explicit and thus it has been accepted on all hands that a wide sampling of all the sites already located and extensively but not totally excavated, should yield a more educative, and wider perspective of the space-time-function co-efficients could be arrived at. Bordes, the French Prehistorian, made a significant contribution in this direction in the 'Mousterian' complex. This itself has been more empirically widened for a consideration of the nature of the socialization process by American specialists and the stylistic differentiation of socio-cultural groups and sub-groups attempts at the definition of the number and nature of tasks undertaken by prehistoric groups.

However, we have yet a lack of systematic 'frame of reference' in organising the artifactual materials for formulating the cultural pattern of these ancient societies. In this connection, it is significant to remind that certain inconsistencies exist in the fundamentals of our way of treatment of the materials on hand. A tradition had been established since early this century wherein the archaeological materials have been defined and ordered in terms of the so-called 'fossils directeurs'—qualitatively, wherein, the restricted stratigraphic distributions over time were considered as *ipso facto* delineating major cultural divisions, with evolutionary stages implicit in the process. This is particularly true of India where we have still to depend largely upon stratigraphic succession of certain tool materials in even those adventitious localities where a reasonably workable stratigraphy exists. The fact that even in proto-historic or historic archaeology, vertical digging has never been, truly speaking, believed to be a dependable substitute for, horizontal or spacial correlations, is equally applicable in Pre-historic Stone Age contexts as well.

Thus, Stone Age stratigraphy could not, directly lead to an understanding of the evolutionary cycle of artifact techniques, stylistic growth, or functional diversification. We have ultimately to fall back upon spatially well preserved sites and in this respect perhaps the terrace gravels have a greater potential for statistical assessment than strata materials. Further, we have had no beginning yet made in India, in a spacial assessment of a given area of gravel and tool scatter, not to mention, other functional correlates of the tool-types involved. A well organised team with a balanced representation of the archaeologist, geologist, ethnographer and statistician is truly the desideratum, in undertaking field studies in favourable localities. Climatic studies or pure stratigraphic data not involving artifactual remains would be strictly speaking in the sphere of pure research, to be undertaken by universities and specialised laboratories of the Government to emphasise the isolated and particularistic character of these categories of evidences. The archaeological, ethnographic, demographic, functional and social aspects of the study of a given assemblage should be coordinated, on *in situ* localities, while the progress otherwise made from time to time in all these individual disciplines, on their own fundamentals, could be used as a stand-by for eliminating avoidable errors of interpretation or overemphasis. To quote an example, even the palaeontological approach is considered by some of the contemporary Western archaeologists as grossly underestimating the complexity of the archaeological record. This was on the basis that the minimum excavation of the palaeontologist was in a major depositional zone which incorporates a number of distinct occupation levels. The sampling procedure emphasised largely the recovery of the type fossils whose diagnostic value had been predetermined, and in this process the cultural integrity of a given stratum was more or less taken as determined by the presence or absence of such diagnostic type fossils. This has led to the most recent studies as the one instituted by Movius and his associates at Abri Patauda at Les Eyzies, where the excavation is directly oriented towards the isolation of the settlement patterns and reconstruction of the ecological context of the concerned Upper Palaeolithic societies.

'Multivariate' Statistic techniques are employed in such ventures for systematically defining the role of each of the associative materials in a stratum, whether intentional or accidental, to the functional or vocational pattern of activities of the societies which lived there. Such sophisticated techniques which, no doubt, call for the most careful plotting, documentation and retrieval *in situ* of the material, and their gross definition and categorization, would not be possible in India for some time, alike for the lack of adequate sites where they can be checked, as for the lack of the academic climate where such a coordinated endeavour between prehistoric archaeologists and statistician—sociologists could effectively function. But it would perhaps be prudent to adapt our techniques early to the prevailing trends in other countries, in order to get the best assessment of our own cultural material. Science congresses should be the forum that could formulate pioneering investigation of such programmes, and the responsibility perhaps rests equally on the statistician-sociologists as well as the archaeologists themselves.

By and large, analytical methods for establishing correlatable models and standards, both stylistic and functional, should be the best fitted tool in the hands of the Prehistorian for classification and the isolation of attribute-clusters, rather than coordination of stylistically allied assemblages, and such should be the method of assessing any given distribution. It is said, for example, that if a particular type of scraper is said to be popular, it should be measured in terms of the frequency of the other scrapers, and it would be completely unaffected by the other tool-types like burin or points. Thus seriation techniques and what are called goodness-of-fit-tests for determining the role of the sampling error of the frequency variations are to be plotted for each pair of assemblages, and indexed in the seriation matrix.

All these, of course, are scientific analyses applied upon humanistic groups, and their utility has its own limitations. But none can gainsay that the perspectives they open out for an analytical loci and range of diurnal activities of a given hunting or more sophisticated groups would be the most refined and specialised tools for the operation under considerations.

In so far as the Protohistoric period is concerned, we are equally impressed by the advent of new approaches towards not only the refinement of the dating apparatus, but also in the enunciation of the corporate character of the different antiquities unearthed in each stratum. We are giving more attention to the organic pattern of life that should be eked out of the apprantly discrete artefactual and other material remains. Hearths, grain silos or storage jars, and samples for the climato-botanical reconstructions are given specific and expert scrutiny. Of course, in the early years of archaeology too, the excavators showed this particularised location of activities in a given site in the different buildings unearthed. But the rather disorganised character of the basic stratigraphic standards prevented the critical assessment of the very diversified antiquarian remains that the excavators assiduously documented. This defect, however, has been eliminated in standard excavations in recent times and the cautious and sensible method of measuring the loci of antiquities and strucures has been given a high place.

All the same, one of the most recurrent features of excavations in recent years is the unduly heavy emphasis laid on the vertical sequence of cultural vicissitudes, and comparatively lesser implementation of the horizontal distribution of material vestiges, even among the individual trenches of the small scale, slit-system of trenching. No doubt, financial viability and competence of trained technical personnel are at the root of a successfully executed excavation project. But it would not be economical to let slip the highly ephemeral spacial distribution of antiquities in a given stratum and trench—thus permanently missing the 'role' they played in constituting the 'fossils' of the temporal activity of the given trench or area. Certainly, there was nothing in the book that dissuades the excavator from keeping as rigid a documentation, stratum by stratum, of the horizontal spread of vestiges in each trench, as possible. But it is nonetheless true that such records are scarce. Needless to say that in the ultimate count of material remains (of both significant and nondescript categories), these records—or perhaps the lack of these—would matter a great deal. Indeed, the modern method of computer-analysis of the room to room and house to house distribution of material varia of evidentiary character in excavations, followed in the west, notably in the U.S.A., is fundamentally upholding this healthy dictum that a habitation site is, not by any means, an orderly display of certain significant antiquity—categories alone, and that what the eye misses might often be what is the most vital part of the drama enacted in any given trench or locale.

This would only mean that excavations when conducted on a large scale, should follow the rule of hastening slowly and trench to trench documentation should be thorough. Also, it should not be far too unwieldy for the Director of excavation to be physically unable to be a witness to the fresh developments unravelled in the various digs of the site. In point of fact, horizontal digging should not be progressing all over the site simultaneously, but only in specific areas, and this should itself have a strictly controlled proportion to the vertical digging going on elsewhere in the site, the latter being equal to, if not much less, than the former quantitatively. The field programmes of the Archaeological Survey of India are, of course, the best models of well-organised digging. Even here, however, there is infinite scope for presenting the layer by layer physical nexus of the antiquities instead of merely a numerical categorisation and count of them. Obviously, photographic and draftsman's labours in these directions would increase by such an approach, but would be eminently worthwhile if we are not to miss the trees that constitute the wood. It would almost be impossible for us to visualise the total range of material culture of a past society, if we do not discern the pattern of activity which they had left in their habitat. *The material culture of a given site is certainly something much more than the sum total of the materials of that culture.* The greater the mapping of the spacial provenance of the habitational debris and debitage organically, alongside finished or finite vestiges of art or craft or functional activity, the greater is the scope of success in eventually reconstructing the past of such ancient and sometimes dead societies.

The various scientific methods used today for data-processing and date-fixation are : C-14 or Radio carbon dating; Thermo-luminiscence, Potassium-Argon (K^{40}-A^{40}) dating (mainly applicable to ranges of millions of years, due to the long life of K^{40}); fission-track dating used in the dating of the Pleistocene Olduvai Gorge bed I in East Africa); Resistance apparatus like proton-magnetometer or Flux-gate magnetometer, for detecting structural vestiges in a given site before hand (as evolved by E.T. Hall and Aitkin at the Archaeological Research laboratory at Oxford); or analytical techniques like Activation analysis (useful for ancient pottery and metals).

Of these, we know that by far the most popular at present in most countries is the Radio-carbon dating. But recent investigations of the data supplied by this method have revealed that there could be scope for corrections not only for C-13 but also for the reaction of atmospheric constituents like cosmic-ray-intensity-difference in balance between atmosphere and oceans etc., on the sample. Besides, the preference for one half-life unit or the other is also a source of mutation. The half-life 5730 (that of Pennsylvania Institute) is considered by some as the present best estimate. Calculation by this is found to be 3% greater than that based on 5568-year half-life, as preferred by Libby. A serious drawback of this method is that the matter of association of *sample* with the *event* for which the date is wanted. This casts the primary responsibility on the archaeologist alone, to be unusually precise and thorough in its seriation of the data.

The Thermoluminiscence method is reasonably the best for pottery samples, whose horizon-makers they can become, and an obvious advantage of this technique is that, by the very principle on which it is based, recently fired ceramics or freshly cooled lava would show no Thermo-lu miniscence. It has been employed in Iran, Italy and U.S.A.

The Potassium-Argon datings most successful implementation is in the determination of the age of 'Zinjanthropos' discovered by Dr. Leakey at Oldwai, East Africa. It has been well upheld by the other independent evidences like Fission-track dating technique of Oldwai bed I.The limitations of the technique comprise in their applicability only to glasses with high uranium content.

In the Resistance appratuses, one *prima facie* inadequacy is their being unsuitable for detection of features of more than two metres below ground. The Proton-magnetometer and the improved Flux-gate magnetometer based on 'anomalous' readings involve the problem of interpretation of these readings as detected by the instrument. It is also being discovered that on certain types of terrains involving pockets of magnetic soils, these instruments are not suitable.

The other modern techniques like Neutron activation analysis, X-ray fluorescence, optical emission spectrometer, Beta-ray-back-scatter meters etc., are all babies of the post-war nuclear research development era, and it could thus be hoped that these would be rapidly improved for application to archaeology in future, making archaeology grade into its nuclear era, and doubtless, giving a new and sensational face-lift to archaeological research itself. This is not to mention, however, that notwithstanding all these technically advanced tools for absolute chronological computation, a sound, orthodox and thorough-going stratigraphic archaeologist, *with a bias for pdinstaking horizontal digging*, would continue to remain well nigh irreplaceable, but well open to coordination with the contemporary sophisticated scientific advancement.

Burial Practices in the Neolithic Cultures of South India

by PURUSHOTTAM SINGH

Recent archaeological excavations of several neolithic sites in South India have furnished some details about the life of the people inhabiting there.

These neolithic folk were pastoral-cum-agricultural community and occupied sparsely wooded hills. The people live in small circular huts as suggested by the discovery of post-holes at Brahmagiri, Maski, Tekkalakota, Sangankallu and Hallur. The house-floors were plastered with clay, dung and lime. They practised agriculture and tended cow, bull, goat, sheep and buffalo. These people used polished stone tools and pottery made by hand in the initial stages but later they used those made on wheel. Stratigraphically, two stages of neolithic culture have been found. The first stage of this culture is represented by Piklihal IA, Sangankallu IA, and Brahmagiri I A and has been termed 'Lower Neolithic' or 'Pure Neolithic'. It is totally devoid of metal tools. The succeeding phase, represented by Brahmagiri I B, Sankankallu I B, Piklihal I B and Maski I shows intrusion of copper and bronze tools in a limited quantity but without affecting the neolithic economy of the people. The pure neolithic culture has a date-range of 2300 B.C. to 1550 B.C. as derived from the radio-carbon tests. The second stage of this culture has been dated to c. 1550 B.C.—1000 B.C.

Evidence regarding burial practices comes from Brahmagiri, Piklihal, Utnur, Tekkalakota, T. Narasipur, Nagarjunakonda and Hallur. As has been said earlier, there are two phases of the Neolithic culture in South India. Thus the burials obtained from Nagarjunakonda, Piklihal, Utnur and T. Narasipur are ascribable to the pure Neolithic phase while those excavated at Brahmagiri, Tekkalakota and Hallur belong to the succeeding phase of this culture. The details of these burials are as follows :

1. Nagarjunakonda

The earliest evidence of disposal of the dead comes from the Neolithic levels, described as the 'Polished Stone Axe Culture' at this site (a term given by Wheeler after the excavation of Brahmagiri in 1947). So far, six neolithic graves comprising of extended inhumations, and a damaged urn-burial of a child, have been excavated. All the six of them [1] were located in the southern part of the valley. The skeletons were oriented in north-south direction in fully extended position but the articulation was not complete. The funerary objects included earthenware pots of wheel as well as handmade burnished grey ware—a characteristic ceramic industry of South Indian Neolithic Culture. This ceramic has also been found in the habitation area at this site. It is not clear whether these graves are within the habitation area or outside. It is an interesting feature that most of the funerary vessels are spouted pots, although straight-sided bowl with featureless rim was also met with. The earlier shape has also been encountered from the neolithic graves at Piklihal and Brahmagiri. No other funerary object accompanied the skeletons.

The damaged urn-burial of a child [2], noted above, was found in the area to the south west of Nallarallabodu, to the west of the road to the museum. The detail of this urn-burial are not available. Besides, some 'pits' were also opened. They yielded pottery, animal bones (including remains of a deer in association with two intact pots), microliths and flake-tools. In one of these pits were found the remains of an articulated skeleton as in the "Sagging Burials". This is a unique feature of Nagarjunakonda neolithic burials.

2. Piklihal

Piklihal is one of the few sites of south India

which have yielded evidence of extended burials in a pure neolithic context. In all, three skeletons have been found from the present site, one each of a male, female and a child, the last being the earliest. Out of these three skeletons, two were found in layers 6 and 11 in Site VII which is a long narrow cutting, measuring 102×4 ft.

The burial of an adult female in layer 6 of cutting VII noted above, is clearly in the habitation area and near a hearth. The body had been buried in extended position in a shallow coffin-shaped pit, which was subsequently covered with a group of small stones, possibly to mark the place. The body lay on its back, the head being roughly towards the north. The head was slightly inclined to the right. The lower part of the skeleton was disturbed. The skull was mezocephalic and slightly prognathous. Funerary articles included a spouted earthenware jar to the left of the head and a tall vase, both of hand-made burnished grey ware. The contents of these pots are not known. No stone tool or ornament accompanied the skeleton [3]. In the same trench, skeleton of a child was found. In this case, the orientation of the skeleton is not toward the north, as was in the case of the former, but roughly towards the south-east. Again, the skeleton did not lie on its back but was resting on its right side. No grave-goods were encountered in this case [4].

The third skeleton [5], which was of an adult male, was excavated in layer 4 of a small cutting named VIII A. In this case, although the body lay on its back, the orientation of the body was entirely different and the head was towards the south. The burial-pit was a shallow grave, the exact outline of which could not be determined. The skull was mesocephalic and slightly prognathous [6]. After filling up the grave, large boulders were kept on the top, possibly to mark the spot. This feature was also present in case of the female skeleton described above.

This grave was interesting for its funerary objects. The grave-goods included five large well made chert blades on the right hand side of the skull, parallel to each other, and two basalt axes at the feet. A small bowl of unburnished hand-made grey ware was placed near the pelvis. Above the body the scapula of a bovine was discovered in the grave.

3. Utnur

This site has given only one burial. Thus, while digging on site I, Allchin encountered a shallow grave containing the much-damaged bones of a newly born infant [7] in layer 9. The bones were badly decayed and few could be preserved unbroken [8]. The burial came from before the stockade of Period I C.

4. T. Narasipur

The site yielded only one example of neolithic burial [9] found in a pit cut into layer 6. The skeleton was buried in extended position and was oriented east-west, the head being towards the east. The hands were placed over each other on the abdomen part. Funerary offerings included earthenware pots arranged near the head. They comprised of two pots of cream-coloured ware together with a shallow bowl with channel-spout. An interesting object was a pottery-stand with a concave top described as neck-rest. This object was found placed by the right side of the head. The pottery 'neck-rests' have also been found from the Neolithic levels at Tekkalakota and Jhukar levels at Chanhudaro in north-west India [10].

5. Brahmagiri

Evidence for the disposal of the dead comes from the upper sub-phase (i.e. I B) at this site. Here, two kinds of burials [11] were encountered. The adults and grown up children were buried in extended position in reglular grave-pits in the main habitation area. This practice conforms well with the method of burials of Neolithic people in the area. Two burials of this kind were excavated, both coming from the site Br. 17, of which only one could be completely exposed. This grave contained the body of a child, 8-10 years of age. In this case, the dead body was oriented in the east-west direction, the head being towards the east. The skull was observed to have been partially crushed. The body was in fully extended condition and was resting on its back. The left hand was placed near the pelvic-region. Funerary offerings included three earthenware vessels. Of these, two bowls were placed by the side of two femurs and a vessel with a funnel-spout was kept near the head. Wheeler has postulated that this vessel with its small cylindrical funnel may have been used to pour libation into the mouth or ears of the dead [12]. A similar vessel has also been found from a neolithic grave at Piklihal.

Another kind of burial was meant for children and infants who were buried in roughly made urns [13] of uniform type. The dead body was folded up into close compass and inserted into the pot. In all, seventeen urn-burials of children were excavated from various trenches. An eighteenth one comes from a pit coeval with the lowestmost deposit of the succeeding Megalithic culture. All the urn-burials are ascribable to I. B. sub-phase. Of these, four come from the cuttings Br. 16 A and 16 B, and eight from cutting Br. 17, belonging to four floor-levels. Of the remaining ones, five burial urns were found in Br. 21 and one was recorded from Br. 21 A. The burial urns are of dull mottled grey colour, often coarse and grey in fabric and are hand-made. They have a globular body, flaring mouth and rounded base. Their average height is thirteen inches and have a diameter of twelve inches at the mouth. These urns were buried in small pits, just sufficient enough to accommodate them. The urns contained the tightly folded bodies of infants and small children. The bones were in advance stage of decay; so it could not be ascertained whether the bodies had been buried intact or after a deliberate fragmentation [14]. However, skull, ribs and a few long bones were identified in almost all the cases. Funerary offerings were conspicuous by their absence. In one case, a small pin or rod of bronze and two small earthenware pots were found in an urn [15]. The urns were covered either with bowls placed upright or inverted or with the lower half of a broken urn.

6. Tekkalakota

Evidence of the disposal of the dead came from both the periods [16]. The burials of Period I comprised of two graves embedded in the red *morum*. These have been supposed to be of the 'fractional' type. However, the detailed description given by the excavators could entitle one to argue for 'incomplete' burials as well. This point has been treated in detail towards the end of the paper. The skulls and long bones were buried in south-north orientation, the head usually being towards the south. In one fractional burial of this period, remains of three individuals were found buried indicating possibly a 'community burial'. In the other case, remains of only one individual were found. The details of these burials are not available, but from the scanty evidence it is clear that it comprised of skull. Some pottery fragments indicating the vestiges of funerary offerings were found placed to the left of the skull. These included a fine goblet of ashy-grey colour.

In contradistinction to the practice of 'fractional burials' in the preceding period, the usual mode of the disposal of the dead in Period II was extended inhumation in the case of adult and urn-burial in the case of children. In the large-scale excavation on this site, as many as twelve extended inhumations of adults were excavated. Of these, eleven were found in a row on the northern side of the locality TKT-1. One extended burial came from TKT-2.

These adult burials were oriented north-south, the head being towards the north. In one case the skeleton was laid in four pots joined together. This is a unique feature of this site and indicates some contacts with the chalcolithic cultures of the Deccan where it was a general practice. The funerary offerings included earthenware pots, the number of which ranges upto seven in one case. These pots include bowls of black-and-red ware painted in white and recall the bowls of the same ceramic industry from a burial at Tekwada [7]. In the case of child-burial, the body was placed in single or double urns joined together. Occasionally, children were buried under the floor of the house. Similar practice was in vogue in the chalcolithic cultures of the Deccan. The children were placed in the embryonic posture in globular urns [18].

7. Hallur

Recently, a small-scale excavation was conducted by M.S. Nagaraja Rao at Hallur [19], situated on the left bank of the river Tungabhadra in Taluk Hirekerur, District Dharwar. A 6.40 m. thick deposit at this site yielded relics of three different cultures, i.e., Pure-Neolithic, Neolithic-Chalcolithic and Megalithic [20].

Two infants' graves have been excavated from phase II (Upper Neolithic) at this site. Of these, a double-pot burial containing the remains of a child was found under the floor of a circular house. The remains of an infant were put in two urns placed mouth-to-mouth. The funerary offerings included three earthen-ware bowls. As is clear from the cultural outfit of this period, it is an intrusion from the contemporary chalcolithic cultures of Godavari-Pravara system where pot-burials are a common feature.

As has already been pointed out earlier, the burials of the neolithic culture of South India fall under two main divisions—those belonging to the Pure Neolithic Period and others ascribable to the succeeding Neolithic-Chalcolithic period. Evidence regarding the burials of the first category is very meagre [21] and any generalization based on this limited data is bound to have its own limitations. However, extended inhumation in regular pits dug in the habitation-area seems to be the general practice during this period. No standard seems to have been followed regarding the orientation of the corpse. Unlike the practice prevalent in the succeeding phase, both adults and childern were buried in regular pits. The funerary offerings include earthenware pots in all cases and a pottery head-rest in the case of the only burial excavated at T. Narasipur.

A marked departure from this practice is seen in the burials of the neolithic-chalcolithic period in this region. Thus, while the adults were buried in extended position, the infants were buried in roughly made urns placed in small pits just sufficient enough to accommodate them. The urns contained the tightly folded bodies of childern placed in embryonic position and were covered with lids. The urn-burials from Tekkalakota and Hallur were found from the house-floors. Funerary offerings were absent in these urns.

Evidence for the complete inhumation of the adults in this sub-phase has been obtained from Brahmagiri and Tekkalakota. The orientation of the corpse at Brahmagiri was in east-west direction, the head being towards the east, but the dead at Tekkalakota were oriented in north-south direction. Funerary offerings were placed in pottery vessels at both the sites. Of special interest is the reported occurrence of 'fractional' burials from the lowestmost levels of Tekkalakota. Implied in this discovery is the suggestion that the same neolithic folks laterly switched over to a new mode of disposal—extended inhumations—without any corresponding change in the cultural material. While it may not be altogether impossible, it has been noted that the change, if it has been, then it has always been the other way round. Furthermore, Tekkalakota is the solitary site in this region which has furnished the evidence of 'fractional' burials of adults. The possibility that these were originally extended inhumations has to be thoroughly ruled out before declaring these to be the case of 'fractional' burials. This point will assume added significance if further field-work in this region fails to produce any other instance of 'fractional' burial in a similar context. The alternative possibility pointed above is also inherent in the description of these burials given by the excavators. In fact, a distinction must be made between 'fractional' and 'fragmentary' burials.

A critical study of the various modes of disposal of the dead, as recorded from the neolithic-chalcolithic sites of South India, establishes beyond doubt that these cultures have borrowed certain traits from the contemporary cultures of the Deccan. That the two cultures were in contact with each other has been proved by the studies of Sankalia [22]. The burial of adults in more than one pot joined together and the urn-burials containing the relics of infants under house-floors were established customs in the chalcolithic cultures of Deccan. A burial of the former class has been found at Tekkalakota and several examples of the latter class have been ditscovered both at Tekkalakota and Hallur.

NOTES

[1] *Indian Archaeology*, 1957-58, *A Review*, 5.

[2] *Indian Archaeology* 1956-57, *A Review*, 36.

[3] F. R. Allchin, *Piklihal Excavations*, Andhra Pradesh Government Archaeological Series No., 1 (Hyderabad) 1960, 22.

[4] Ibid, 23.

[5] Ibid, 24.

[6] Ibid, 113.

[7] F. R. Allchin, *Utnur Excavations*, (Hyderabad) 1961, pl. 5b.

[8] F. R. Allchin, *Neolithic Cattle-keepers of South India* (Cambridge) 1963, 45.

[9] *Indian Archaeology* 1961-62, *A Review*, 35-36.

[10] Stuart Piggott, *Prehistoric India* (Harmondsworth) 1952, 224-224. Fig. 27.

The pottery head-rests from this site and other places have recently been studied by Allchin. Cf· F. R. Allchin, 'Pottery head-rest from Narasipur Sangam' in *Studies in Prehistory* (ed.) D. Sen and A. K. Ghosh (Calcutta) 1966, 58-63.

[11] R. E. M. Wheeler 'Brahmagiri and Chandravalli 1947' *Ancient India*, No. 3, 202.

[12] Ibid, 203.

[13] Ibid,. 202.

[14] Ibid, 226.

[15] It was found in Urn No. T. 36 in cutting Br. 21 and is assignable to the early part of sub-phase IB.

[16] *Indian Archaeology* 1963-64, *A Review*, 24-25.

[17] *Indian Archaeology* 1956-57, *A Review*, 18.

[18] M. S. Nagaraja Rao and K. C. Malhotra, *The Stone Age Hill Dwellers of Tekkalakota* (Poona : 1965), 27-33.

Also, M. S. Nagaraia Rao, 'New Evidence for Neolithic Life in India : Excavations in the Southern Deccan' *Archaeology*, XX, No. 1. (January : 1967), 34-35.

[19] *Indian Archaeology* 1964-65 A Review (cyclostyled copy), I-58.

Also M. S. Nagaraja Rao (1967), 30.

[20] *Indian Archaeology* 1964-65 A Review (cyclostyled copy), I-58.

[21] Only six and three burials have been exposed at Nagarjunakonda and Piklihal respectively while Utnur and T. Narasipur have given one example each.

[22] H. D. Sankalia and others, *From History to Prehistory at Nevasa* (Poona : 1960), 498-503.

A New Painted Pottery From Vidarbha

by S. B. DEO

The older view advocating that there was no copper age in the Deccan has now been finally discarded. The excavations at Nasik-Jorwe in 1952 by the Deccan College, Poona, gave considerable evidence of fairly large chalcolithic habitations. Explorations and excavations in subsequent years have revealed a very extensive colonisation by the chalcolithic people in Maharashtra with possible cultural contacts with the north and the south.

The picture which has emerged during the last fifteen years gives a clear indication that the valleys of the Krishna, Godavari, Pravara, Ghod, Girna, Tapi, Bhima, and Nira were habitated by chalcolithic period between about 1300 and 1000 B.C.

The characteristic trait of the chalcolithic cultures of the Maharashtra region is the extensive use of the now familiar Jorwe ware which has been named after the type site in Ahmadnagar district. This pottery is distinguished by a metallic ring, mostly matt surfaces, regular striations on the interior, mostly geometric painted designs and two fossil types such as the spouted pot with funnel-shaped mouth and carination at the shoulder and the carinated bowl.

The chalcolithic ceramic industry of the Maharashtra region is essentially the Jorwe. At Nevasa, Nasik and Jorwe, it was the dominant unadulterated trait of chalcolithic horizons, the top levels of which could be dated at Nevasa at least to c. 1100 B.C. on the basis of C-14 dating.

However, this dominance of the Jorwe pottery at the key sites in Maharashtra, with tempting possibilities of assigning its origins to this region, was vitiated by the occurrence of the Jorwe ware in relatively earlier horizons at Navdatoli in Central India and in post-Malwa pottery horizons at Daimabad in Maharashtra itself. The position now is that the Malwa pottery, at least at Daimabad, has a precedence over the Jorwe, and the Jorwe appears to be earlier in period in Madhya Pradesh than that assigned to it in Maharashtra proper.

The picture was further complicated by the association of the Black-and-Red pottery with the Jorwe and the Malwa wares at Chandoli, Songaon, Bahal and Daimabad. The Black-and-Red ware is totally absent in chalcolithic horizons at Nevasa, Jorwe and Nasik. It, however, penetrates further south in a Neolithic-Chalcolithic context.

The Vidarbha region of Maharashtra has not been so far extensively tapped archaeologically. The excavations at Kaundanpur and Junapani are the only two noteworthy contributions so far.

Of the two, Kaundanpur [1] in District Amraoti was excavated on a small scale. Here the first period of occupation was characterised by " a megalithic culture (?) " which gave black-and-red wares which were gritt-tempered and having mostly vases with flaring rims. This ware was associated with etched beads with megalithic decorative pattern which possibly tempted the excavator to designate the period as megalithic. Here, no painted pottery was encountered.

At Junapani [2] in Nagpur Taluk, scientific digging was done by the Archaeological Survey, though the site was tapped as early as 1867. In the excavations done in 1960-61, the excavator found four ceramic fabrics : black-and-red, all black, plain red and a ware tempered with micaceous grit. The excavator also pointedly refers to the find of " a bowl of red ware with a hole-

Section of the main trench at Paunar (Layer 9 yielded the painted pottery).

Painted Pottery, Paunar, Period I.

mouth spout and painted in black pigment with oblique strokes on rim ", associated with the black-and-red pottery picked up in the cairn.

Maharzhari]3], opposite Junapani, contains nearly 300 megaliths of the cairn type. On surface explorations, the site is reported to have given numerous beads, though no ceramic evidence is referred to.

The evidence of the painted ware associated with the black-and-red ware at Paunar [4] in the earliest occupation [5] assumes significance when seen in the light of the black-and-red ware association with the chalcolithic painted pottery at Chandoli, and at a number of sites in Khandesh [6]. At Prakash, the Black-and-Red has been found in horizons earlier than those of the NBP [7], which proves that the Black-and-Red can be dated at least prior to the 5th Cent. B.C. [8].

Nearer Paunar, there have been reports of the find of a " chalcolithic site near Marda " in Distt. Chanda which has yielded black-painted red ware sherds [9]. Reference has also been made to the chalcolithic site at Tuljapur Garhi in Distt. Amaraoti [10].

The painted pottery in the earliest occupation at Paunar has been found in horizons which are devoid of iron. Moreover, the shapes of the associated Black-and-Red are not megalithic. And thirdly, one of the sherds of the Black-and-Red bears traces of paintings in dull white. Thus, the context shows that Paunar painted pottery is essentially non-megalithic and could be chalcolithic. Moreover, the concentration of stone circle, so far reported, falls to the east and south-east of Paunar, so far as Vidarbha region is concerned. Thus the painted ware of Paunar adds a new element to the chalcolithic assemblage of Maharashtra.

The fabric of the painted ware from Paunar is essentially mediocre. It is not metallic like the Jorwe, nor it is well-fired like it. It has a ill-fired smoky blackish core with the clay full of small pieces of hey and particles of lime. The slip applied over the entire external surface and only the rim part internally, is drab Indian red and has an uneven application as one feels it. Over the slip, painting in dull black comes. It covers the rim externally and internally, the neck and the shoulder portion. Whereas the rim has only groups of vertical strokes and the neck a series of bands, the shoulder has either close parallel bands drawn horizontally or drawn haltingly and latticed diamonds and triangles. Though almost entirely geometrical, the designs show quite a range in painting [11], as for instance, strokes, groups of slanting or vertical lines, groups of short slanting strokes, the star design (D5), short slanting dots (D18), slanting strokes (D8), groups of horizontal lines drawn haltingly in vertical piles (D16) and irregularly drawn meshes (D15, 17). Normally the bands are thick, but there are specimens which display finer execution as well (D12, D13). It may be worthwhile to note that D3, D5, D8, D9, D11 and D18 are also to be found associated with the Malwa ware in the second season's excavation [12].

Typologically, there is not a single shape which falls in the Jorwe group. Especially the hooded rims are not to be met with in Jorwe at all. It may, however, be noted that the hundred and odd sherds recovered, only a few could be indicative of any shape. A look at Plate V would show that only two main shapes could be had, to wit, globular vessels with broad mouth with hooded or internally undercut rim [13] (T. 1 to 3C) and a dish-cum-cover (T-4). It may be stated here that anologues can be had for the last from Navdatoli [14].

The occurrence of painted pottery and the black-and-red in a non-megalithic and non-iron context indicates the colonisation of Vidarbha by a people whose antecedants could be chalcolithic. How they came and under what condition cannot be stated precisely. However, these people seem to eke out of their living by fishing as a large number of terracotta net-sinkers indicates. Their houses were of clay and they used circular hearths made of clay. Though no other evidence could be had, it appears that in the earlier half of the first millennium B.C. they settled on the bank of the river Dham practising fishing and possibly farming. The bone remains of this period indicate that they had fairly large herds of domesticated cow, bull and goats. Thus there were possibly the earliest farmers of Vidarbha with chalcolithic set up.

NOTES

[1] *Indian Auchaeology* 1961-62 *A Revlew*, 29-30.
[2] Ibid, 32-34.
[3] Ibid, 1958-59, 21-22.
[4] See Pl. II for mound at Paunar
[5] See Pl. III of main trench at Paunar.
[6] *I.A.R.* 1958-59, 22-24.
[7] Ibid, 1954-55, 13.
[8] Ibid.
[9] Ibid, 1963-64, 39.
[10] Ibid, 1965-66, 53.
[11] See Pl. V.
[12] H. D. Sankalia *et. al.*, *The Excavations at Maheshwar and Navdatoli* (1952-53) Fig. 18, T. 20 m; Fig. 46, designs Ic, f.; Fig. 53, designs c ard f.
[13] See Pl. IV and V.
[14] Sankalia *et. at.* I bid, T. 10, 10c (Fig. 8),; T. 26 (Fig. 25).

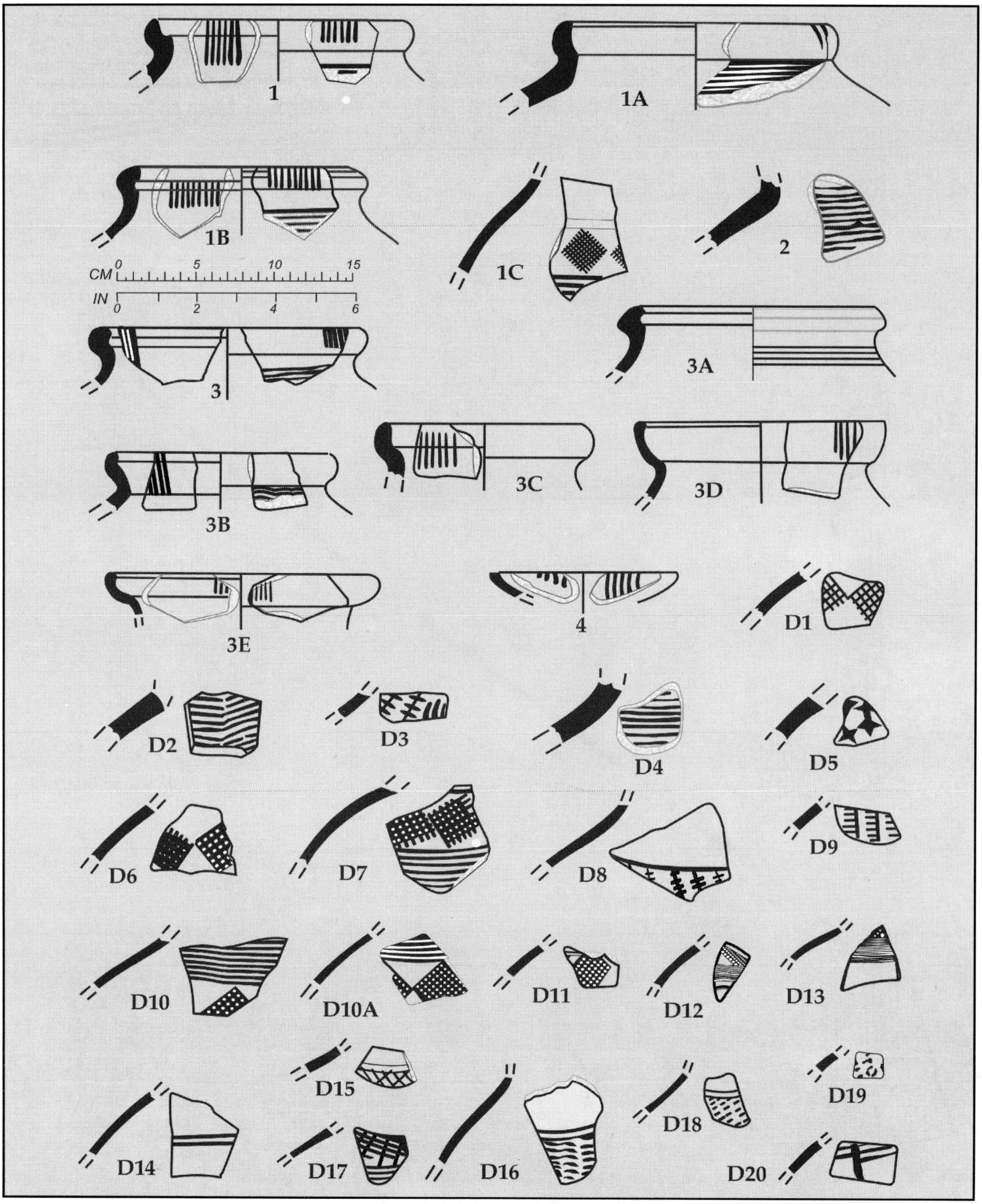

Painted Pottery : shapes and designs.

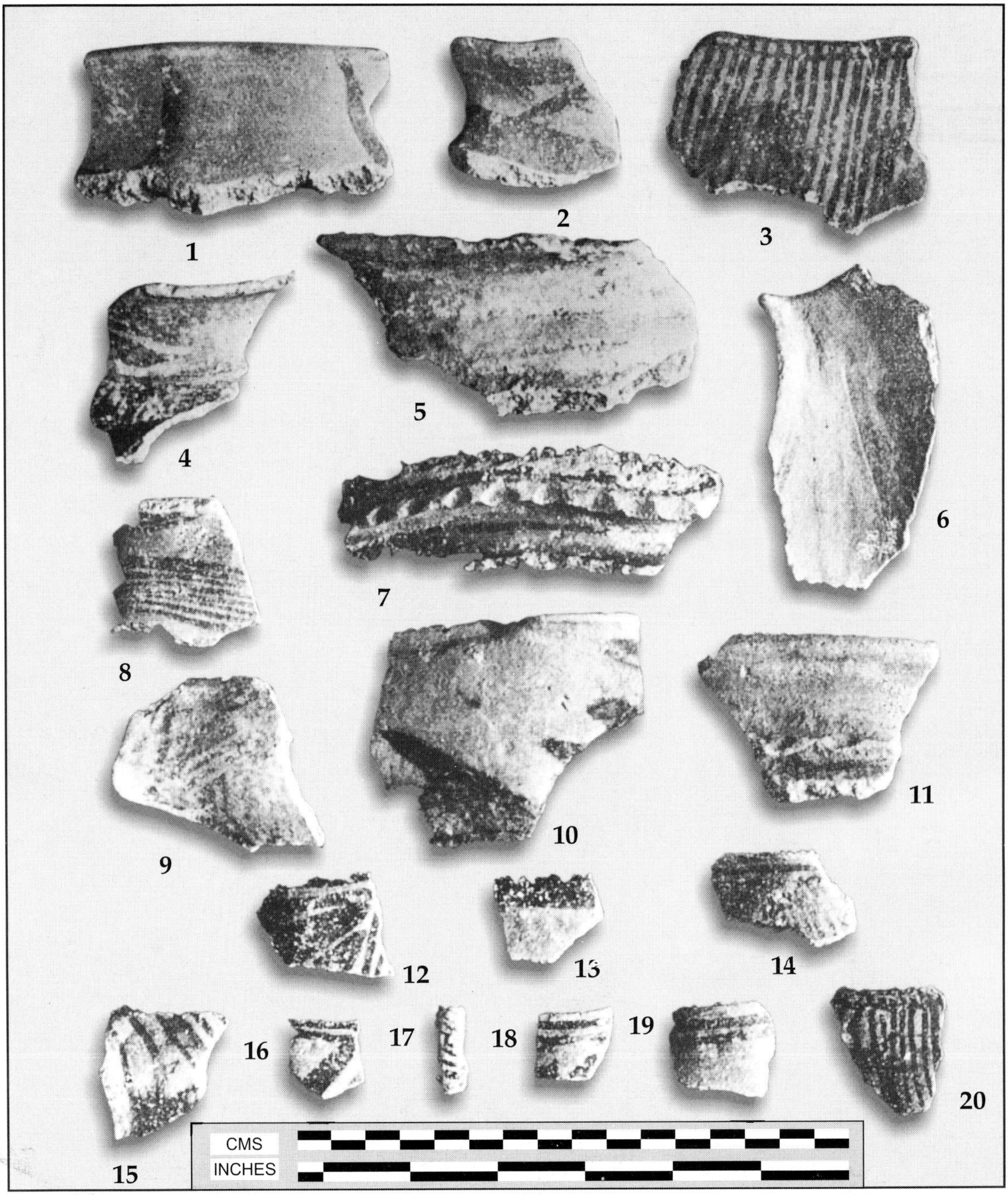

Painted Pottery from explorations : selected types. 1-3, 8-10 and 12-20 from Singanapalle; 4-5, and 11 from Ramapuram; 6-7 Sivavaram.

The Use of the Terms 'Prehistory' & 'Protohistory' in Indian Archaeology*

by K. K. SINHA

There has been a great spurt in archaeological activities during the last twenty years. The result has been a sizable increase in our knowledge of India's hitherto unknown past. It is only natural that more and more of Indian universities are planning to include archaeology in the teaching courses. In this context, there is a need to standardize the scope of the terms 'Prehistory' and 'Protohistory' in Indian archaeology. In this paper it is proposed to examine the alternatives and to suggest modification in the present usage of these terms. But by way of a brief introduction, the current use of the terms in the all-world context may be alluded to.

According to French scholars with whom the word *'la Protohistoire'* is fairly common, prehistory deals with the phase before the history. The latter is said to begin with the advent of writing. In certain restricted areas of the Asia like Egypt, Africa and Mesopotamia, history begins from c. 3000 B.C. According to the french scholars, *'la Prehistoire'* ends *everywhere* in the world with the birth of history in parts of western Asia. All other societies which had no writing or historical records of their own should be grouped under what has been termed as 'Protohistory.' French scholars were apparently obsessed by the fact that there were societies with no writings of their own and which were in close relationship with the historical cultures of western Asia. As these societies could neither be studied under 'prehistoric' nor under 'historic', the French found it expedient to use the word 'protohistory.' If the scope of 'Protohistory' would have been restricted to such societies only as were known to have existed at the fringes of historical people and having close relationship with them, there could not have been much dispute. The complications arise because according to the French usage, 'Protohistory' has a general and wide application and will include all societies existing anywhere in the world after, say, 2500 B.C. The British scholars, on the other hand, are never happy with the word 'protohistory' and in fact, do not use the word at all. According to them, 'Prehistory' should extend right upto the point where the local historical records emerge. They go on to further elaborate the point that the use of the word must not disguise the fact that there are degrees of 'prehistory'. Since once the historical communities were in existence, all non-literate, non-historic and pre-historic communities were necessarily contemporary in time. Some of the British archaeologists, notably Graham Clarke and Christopher Hawkes, have sometimes used the words 'primary' or 'absolute' to distinguish from what has been described as secondary Prehistory. For most of Europe, Prehistory extends right upto the beginning of Roman conquest and accordingly Bronze Age and Iron Age besides Stone Age are very much part of European Prehistory, according to most English-speaking scholars.

At this moment we may consider the position in India. Here the matters are somewhat complicated by the fact that the 'Indus' civilization was a fully literate one and yet non-historic, since its records are not intelligible to us. British archaeologists have no doubt in their mind that the 'Indus' or Harappan civilization should form part of Indian

* The paper was read at the 55 th. Session of Indian Science Congress held in January 1968 at Varanasi.

Prehistory. H. D. Sankalia, on the other hand, thinks that it would not be proper to relegate the Indus civilization which was fully literate to the status of a pre-historic community. According to him, 'it is not their (i.e. Harappan) fault that we cannot decipher their records.' Subba Rao [1] was first to use the tem 'Protohistory,' but its usage gained wide currency in the writings of Sankalia [2]. The present position is that while prehistory is meant to include only Stone Age prehistory, 'Protohistory' is taken to cover a sprawling period from c. 3000 B.C. to 600 B.C. and history begins in India roughly from about 600 B.C.

The present grouping mainly after Sankalia, raises certain basic questions. So far as Palaeolithic archaeology in India is concerned, very little is known and its study and research are unquestionably linked up with palaeontological and environmental studies. In most of the European countries, the emphasis has quite naturally shifted to this aspect of the question. The Indian Middle Stone Age has yet to acquire a definitive status. My point is that if prehistoric Archaeology in India is to restrict itself to Stone Age, there is not much to go by way of a teaching course, let alone for specialized study. Nevertheless, there is quite a lot of spade-work to be done by way of planned and independent field research in close collaboration with palaeontologists and palaeobotanists, but that is another matter. This brings to the question of Neolithic cultures of India. Sometimes they are dubbed under prehistoric and on other occasions under 'Protohistoric.' The confusion is because there were sizable pockets of Neolithic cultures which existed even after the end of the Indus civilization. This anomaly may perhaps be sharpest in the case of neolithic settlement recently discovered at Burzahom in Kashmir. It has a date range of c. 2000 B.C. to 1700 B.C. according to radio-carbon tests. The 'Harappan' had not only come into existence but were not far removed in space as well. The 'pure' Neolithic was succeeded by 'pottery using' people also Neolithic in character. One is also in difficulty to assign particularly many Neolithic, Neolithic-cum-Chalcolithic cultures of central, western and southern India that flourished after the Indus civilization. In a normal situation, these communities with no writing should be studied under prehistory but the present position is vague and no uniform pattern has been devised. There is thus need to rationalize the groupings. We may at this stage examine the validity of Sankalia's objection to Indus civilization being listed under 'Prehistory' which has been briefly referred to above. As pointed, Sankalia feels that we shall not be doing justice to the 'Harappan' if we give them the label of 'Prehistoric community'. Nobody denies the fact that the 'Indus civilization' was fully literate, but the script being undeciphered, the records are no aid to the reconstruction of the past. Prehistory. Protohistory, etc. denotes essentially our conception of past. Implicit in this suggestion is that our understanding of the past will be subject to limitations such as unintelligibility of records. All this need not be mixed up with the achievements or otherwise of the Indus civilization or more precisely whether it was literate or not. Accordingly if we decide to call 'Indus' civilization prehistoric, it is suggestive of the fact that we are expressing primarily our sense of helplessness that the written records have no meaning in deriving our knowledge about that civilization. I am more than inclined to agree with Piggott's view [3] that 'a literate civilization where script cannot be read has to be treated as 'Prehistoric'... I would regard as the essential unifying factor in all prehistory is that our knowledge is based entirely on archaeological evidence as distinct from literary evidence.' Accordingly, 'Indus civilization' about which archaeology alone provides the entire basis of our knowledge should appropriately come under Prehistory. This amended grouping will have the added advantage that there will be no confusion with regard to grouping of post-Harappan cultures of central and western India under 'Prehistoric'. Now we may consider the question: What should be the range of 'Pre-history' in Indian context—whether or not it should extend upto 600 B.C. at which point the history of India is said to begin. The period from 1300 B.C. to 600 B.C. [4] roughly syncronizing with what has been loosely termed as Vedic Age which is neither prehistoric nor fully historic may be given the label of 'Protohistoric.' In this connection, it may be noted that Vedic literature, which is not a historical writing had come into being. To sum up, the suggested divisions will be as follows :

A. Prehistoric Period—pre-1300 B.C., to include Stone Age Prehistory, pre-Harappan cultures, Indus Civilization, Chalcolithic and Neolithic Cultures.

B. Protohistoric Period—1300 B.C. to 600 B.C.

C. Historical Period—600 B.C. and onwards.

NOTES

[1] B. Subba Rao, *The Personality of India,* (Baroda), 1958. p. 38.

[2] H.D. Sankalia, *Prehistory & Protohistory of India and Pakistan.* (Bombay), 1963.

[3] S. Piggott, 'Theory in Prehistory', *Evolution after Darwin,* ed. Sol Tax.

[4] The date 1300 B.C. though arbitrarily taken, has one point to commend. The *Bagazkoy* inscription dated to roughly thereabouts mentions the Vedic gods.

A Note on the Chemical Composition of Some Glass Beads from Rajghat, Varanasi

by H. C. BHARDWAJ

The excavations from Rajghat have yielded about 400 glass beads. The colour variations include from light yellow to different shades of green and blue. There are also beads of buff, red, brown and dark tints amounting to black. There are quite a few beads of black-and-white and black-and-red colour. Most of the beads are translucent, but there are many which are transparent and quite a few are opaque. Among the shades of blue and green, there are pale blue, azure blue, bluish green and pale green beads which approximate the shades of aquamarine, lapis lazuli, turquoise and orient emerald. Blue shades also include variations from light blue to dark blue. Amongst the shade of red, most of the beads are opaque. Majority of these resemble the shade of sealing wax, a few that of coral and jasper. There are also some which are orange in colour.

For the present study, beads have been selected from period I of Rajghat.

Amongst the 400 glass beads, about two dozen come from period I, six of these are black, five are of different shades of blue (mostly light blue), five of green and three are of opaque red glass. For the purpose of detail study (including chemical composition) five beads from this period have been selected.

Description of the Beads

1. Black bead. translucent; in thin section the colour is dirty green ; has a typical conchoidal fracture. It has Sp. gr. 2.41. Under microscope shows air bubbles and a few inclusions. There is no devitrification.
2. Bluish green (approximating the shade of turquoise). translucent; has a typical conchoidal fracture. Sp. gr. 2.397. Under microscope small round and elleptical air bubbles are seen. There are no inclusions. No devitrification.
3. Olive green. It is almost transparent; has a conchoidal fracture. Sp.gr. 2.36; a few air bubbles present. No devitrification.
4. Pale blue. It is translucent. Does not have the typical conchoidal fracture.

TABLE I

General Description of the Glass Beads

Sp. no.	Reg. no.	Period	Date	Colour	Vision	Sp.gr.
1.	825	IB, IC	600 B.C.—200 B.C.	Black	Translucent	2.31
2.	282	IB, IC	—do—	Bluish green	—do—	2.39
3.	2345	IB	600 ,, —400 B.C.	Olive green	Transparent	2.36
4.	876	IB	600 ,, —400 ,,	Pale blue	Translucent	2.37
5.	915	IB	—do—	Reddish-brown	Opaque	2.44

The surface is riddled with cracks. Sp. gr. 2.37.

5. Opaque reddish brown. resembles sealing wax in colour and appearance. It has conchoidal fracture; has sp. gr. 2.49.

The glass beads are in good state of preservation except the sp. no. 4 (pale blue bead), the surface of which is riddled with minute cracks, and none of these is decomposed. The hardness of these beads approaches that of orthoclase (hardness on Moh's scale-6). While some scratch the orthoclase, others are scratched by it. Most of these are translucent. Though their lack of transparency might have been preferred so as to imitate precious stones, yet it might be observed, it is due to defective fabrication that they lack transparency. This might have resulted because the melt was not heated enough, so as to be completely molten. The examination under microscope reveals inclusions and air bubbles of the following description.

Inclusions or Stones. These are probably of non vitreous nature, (non discernible to the naked eye, mostly opaque). This could be due to pieces of material which have broken away from the melting pot or might be batch stones which have escaped melting. These inclusions are responsible for the lack of transparency.

Air bubbles or Vacuoles. Under microscope the translucent glass shows that the general matrix is transparent but in it are embedded vacuoles of different shapes and sizes. This can be explained by the fact that during the first stage of melting (founding period) gases are given off in large volumes and bubbles are formed, which might have been embedded in the vitreous matrix. To remove these bubbles in the glass, plaining or fining is necessary and requires higher temperature, which might not have been attained. The bubbles might also be responsible for general lack of transparency.

Chemical Composition of the Glass Beads

Out of the five samples analysed, three specimens nos. 1, 3 and 4 are Soda-Lime Silica glasses (Table II). Specimen no. 2 is Potash-cum-Soda-Lime-Silica glass. The alkalies could not be determined in specimen no. 5 on account of paucity of the sample.

The silica content is in the range of 64.68 to 70.09%. The variation in their silica content and its comparative high percentage could be due to certain amount of weathering during burial [1]. From the content of alkalies it might be said that soda was more popular alkali used

TABLE II

Table Showing the Chemical Composition of Glass Beads from Rajghat.

SPECIMEN	1	2	3	4	5
	%	%	%	%	%
SiO_2	64.68	70.09	67.07	68.05	65.01
Fe_2O_3	4.20	1.26	2.58	1.84	9.67
Al_2O_3	7.89	3.34	9.95	2.76	2.28
CuO	—	1.13	—	2.40	—
Cu_2O	—	—	—	—	5.27
NiO	—	—	—	—	0.15
CaO	5.42	8.90	6.35	8.04	4.08
MgO	0.86	1.10	0.44	0.98	0.49
Na_2O	17.54	5.25	13.81	16.03	13.05 (by difference)
K_2O	0.30	9.74	0.36	0.62	
TOTAL :	100.89	100.81	100.56	100.72	100.00

by the craftsmen but potash was used at least in conjunction with soda.[2]. Since all the glasses contain iron oxide (1.26% to 9.67%) it is quite likely that it might be present on account of impurities in the batch materials, e.g. sand and alkalies etc. However, when the content of iron oxide is about 2% or higher iron oxide could have been added separately to the melt. High content of alumina 7.81 and 9.95 in specimen nos. 1 and 3 respectively suggests the use of felspathic material, while in other samples, alumina is present as an impurity and might have been derived from the melting pot [3]. Lime is present in moderately good amount and might have been obtained by use of lime stone. The presence of magnesia is probably on account of impurity. This may rule out the possibility of the use of either calcite or dolomite. The absence of lead from these glasses is also of some significance [4]. Though these are multi-component glasses yet it is possible that sand and alkalies were the only batch materials and all the iron oxide, alumina, lime and magnesia were derived from the impurities present in the sand, the alkalies and the refractory materials (arising through corrosive action during melting) [5]. Copper compounds look to be the main colouring agent added to the melt.

Specimen no. 5 has a composition to be classed as haematinum [6] or copper aventurine [7]. Batch formula of this opaque red glass does not show any resemblance to other glasses of the class (Table III). Further the presence of nickel oxide suggests its indigenous manufacture.

In addition to these analyses the author is not aware of any other analysis of opaque red glass beads from India. In connection with opaque red glass bead from Nalanda, Lal [8] points out that no such material has been discovered elsewhere in India. It might be concluded that the percentage compositions of the various constituents of glass, as revealed by the analyses, are quite compatible for producing glass scientifically and this accounts for their good condition after centuries of burial.

Colouring Agents

Black. The glass, as stated earlier, is black due to the thickness of the bead. Further the presence of inclusions has also made it look dark. In thin section the glass is dirty green. The only colouring agent present in this case (sp. no. 1) is iron oxide (4.20%) (Table III) which probably occurs partly in the ferrous form and partly in the ferric condition. The greenish tint, as seen in the thin section, is due to ferrous iron [9]. Ferric iron is liable to impart only weak yellow colour.

Blue. The specimen nos. 2 and 4 contain 1.13 and 2.4 percent copper oxide (CuO) respectively and 1.26% and 1.84% ferric oxide respectively. Blue colour of these glasses is due to the cupric copper. The presence of ferric oxide (in the absence of manganese oxide or other decolouriser) might have added yellowish tint, which is not intense. Further the colour might have been also affected by the base of the glass and temperature.

TABLE III

Table Showing Chemical Content of Opaque Red Glass Beads from Other Sites.

S.No.	Description of the specimen.	SiO_2	Al_2O_3	Fe_2O_3	FeO	Cu	Cu_2O	CaO	MgO	Na_2O & K_2O
		%	%	%	%	%	%	%	%	%
1.	Opaque red glass bead from Nalanda.	61.05	9.82		7.01	—	0.49	4.20	0.6	15.90
2.	Coral glass bead from Assam	53.25	9.16	6.12	—	9.13	—	9.18	1.47	11.69

Green. The specimen no. 3 has a total content of 2.58% of iron oxide which is present partly in ferrous and partly in the ferric condition. It is the combined effect of ferrous (green colour) and ferric (yellow tint) iron that the bead is coloured olive green.

Opaque reddish brown. The reddish brown colour of the specimen no. 5 resembles the colour of sealing wax. The glass of this bead has a typical composition. Among the colouring agents 5.27% of cuprous oxide, 9.67% of iron oxide, and 0.15% of nickel oxide are present.

Under microscope, crystals of cuprous oxide on a transparent back ground are revealed. It is a type of haematinum (blood glass). Regarding its colour and opacity it may be pointed out, when copper is added (either as metal or in the form of a compound) to the melt in ordinary way, it always produces green or blue colour. However, when the oxidation of copper is prevented by the presence of a reducing body and the glass is cooled gradually an intense ruby colouration is produced. But when the content of copper (Cu_2O) is high, the glass assumes a browner colour and becomes opaque. The opacity is probably due to the fact that cuprous oxide has been driven out of silica combination on account of the weak chemical affinity between silica and cuprous oxide [10].

The presence of high percentage (9.67%) of iron oxide is noteworthy. Some of it might be in ferrous condition which might have contributed, in conjunction with cuprous oxide, to the shade of the glass. The presence of 0.15% of NiO looks to be on account of impurity. Though it is supposed to exert a powerful colouring influence in glass, usually greenish brown colour is produced. It has also been advocated as a decolouriser [11]. However, when more than one colourant is present, the interaction of various factors causes the actual absorption effect produced to be too complex to be predicted in simple terms [12]. So it is very difficult to attribute the effect of 9.67% iron oxide and 0.15% of NiO. The presence of nickel oxide, which often occurs as an impurity associated with Indian copper, may point out to the indigenous manufacture of this opaque red glass bead.

Lal [13] attributes the red colour of the Nalanda bead (Table III) to the presence of ferrous silicate and cuprous oxide. The brownish colour of this bead may be due to the high percentage of cuprous oxide. Neuberg states that as the proportion of cuprous oxide is increased, the red colour assumes a browner shade and finally becomes opaque.

TABLE IV

Table Showing the Colouring Agents & Melting Conditions

Specimen No.	Chief colouring constituent	Percentage of colouring constituent	Batch Material	Colour Produced	Melting condition.
1.	Ferrous oxide	4.20	Ferric oxide	Dirty green Becoming dark due to the thickness of bead.	Reducing
2.	Cupric oxide	1.13	Copper oxide	Bluish green	Oxidizing
3.	Ferrous oxide, Ferric oxide	2.58	Ferric oxide	Olive green	Reducing
4.	Cupric oxide	2.40	Copper oxide	Pale blue	Oxidizing
5.	Cuprous oxide	5.27	Copper oxide	Reddish brown	Reducing

Archaeological Value

Amongst these specimens, sp. no. 5 needs special mention. Beads of red opaque glass—the shades of coral and jasper as also in various nuances of red, have been reported from many archaeological sites all over the world [14]. Neuburg [15] states that during the course of centuries, the process of making this type of glass was repeatedly forgotten only to be discovered fresh.

Though, so far the glass beads have not been assigned any particular dating value, yet they do have some potentiality, provided stratified glass beads were chemically analysed and the analyses appended to the excavation reports. Further the beads might have been exchanged by the people in antiquity, and their analyses could throw light on human movement and contact.

Five opaque glass beads of dark red colour have been reported from Ahichchhatra (distributed in Strata VIII-to II). At Kauśāmbī this glass is common in 2nd century A.D., though one specimen is dated about 200 B.C. This type of beads have also been reported from Kumarāhar, Mason Dih etc. In South also, such beads are known from Maski, Kondapur, Arikamedu etc. though in a later sequence [16].

According to Dikshit [17], among the earliest beads of this glass, one is from Ahichchhatra Stratum VIII, (300-200 B.C.) and another from Kauśāmbī (200 B.C.). Here it may be pointed out that sp. no. 5 comes from period IB of Rajghat which is dated (circa 600 B.C. to 400 B.C.), and so might be even earlier than those.

The author is thankful to Professor A. K. Narain, Principal, College of Indology, Banaras Hindu University for giving facilities and encouragement throughout the work.

NOTES

[1] Turner has shown that the weathering of glass results in changes in its composition, the increase for instance of its silica content. Further, even in the confines of a single site, there does not apply an absolutely constant weathering process. W. E. S. Turner, ' Studies in Ancient Glass and Glass Making Processes Pt. II : The Composition, weathering characteristics and historical significance of some Assyrian Glasses of the 8th to 6th century B. C. from Nimrud ', *J. Soc. Glass Technology*, XXXVIII, 1954, 453 T.

[2] Alkalies might have been obtained from the extract of crude natron (Reh), which is essentially a mixture of Na_2CO_3, $NaHCO_3$, Na_2SO_4 and NaCl, together with traces of calcium and magnesium salts. Reh abounds in this area, and it is stated that about 2,000 tons of *Sajji matti* (reh with high proportion of carbonates) used to be sent annually to Calcutta from Banaras, Azamgarh and Ghazipur (*Rec. Geol. Surv. India*, 1930, 64, 432).

[3] R. J. Forbes, *Studies in Ancient Technology*, V, 116.

[4] Lead has been reported from Taxila glasses. *An. Rep. Arch. Surv. Ind.* 1922-23 (1925), 158.

[5] W. E. S. Turner, 'Studies in Ancient Glass and Glass Making Processes', *J. Soc. Glass Technology*, XL, 1956, 297 T.

[6] Haematinum or blood glass is opaque and if greatly magnified, reveals crystals of cuprous oxide on a colourless base. F. Neuburg, *Glass in Antiquity*, (English-translation),1949, 3.

[7] Aventurine glasses are those which have become supersaturated with colouring oxides and on cooling under suitable conditions the colouring oxide crystalizes out and remains scattered as suspended particles in the glass. Copper aventurine is produced when in 100 parts of sand, six to eight parts of copper oxide are incorporated. (R. Charan. *Handbook of Glass Technology*, 1956, 55).

[8] B. B. Lal, 'Examination of some Ancient Indian Glass Specimens, *A. I.*, 8, 1952, 24.

[9] G. W. Morey, *Properties of Glass*, 1954, 457-458.

[10] R. Charan, op. cit., [7] P. 49.

[11] W. Rosenhain, *Glass Manufacture*, 191.

[12] *Op. cit.* [9], 458.

[13] *Op. cit.* [8], 24.

[14] This type of glass beads have been reported from early period of Egypt and Roman Imperial epoch. *Op. cit* [6], 3.

[15] Ibid.

[16] M. G. Dikshit, ' Beads from Ahichchhatra (U. P.)' *A.I.* 8, 1952. 56-58.

[17] *Op. cit.* [16], 59

The Relationship Between the Chalcolithic Culture of India and the Chust Culture of the Farghana Valley, U. S. S. R.

by S. P. GUPTA

The Chalcolithic culture of Malwa and Maharastra in India is probably the most discussed topic of the present day Indian archaeology. Not that it embodies in it the remains of any great material culture, but there are some enigmatic traits in it which need clear understanding. Right now, we are more confused than clear, at least about the origin and the extra-territorial contacts of this culture.

On these issues, scholars in India are divided in two clear-cut camps. One holds that its roots go deep into the Harappa culture and there is little relationship of this culture with any culture flourishing outside India. The other maintains that although it is indigenous in origin, its roots merely touch some of the Harappan elements and it had quite close relations with some of the west Asian towns.

Recently, on these issues almost the same controversy and the same division of scholars have cropped up in the Soviet Union also. The Russian archaeologist Y. A. Zadneprovsky [1] is strongly of the opinion that the Chalocolithic culture of India had definite relations with the cultures existing west of this country. Without refuting Sankalia's theory of the Iranian influence over the Indian Chalcolithic culture, he presents the Chust culture of the Farghana Valley as a strong centre with which the former maintained a close contact. As against this A. V. Shchetenko [2], another noted Russian archaeologist, holds the view that the Chalcolithic culture of India is purely indigeneous, both in origin and development. He strikes a note of dis-agreement with Sankalia and Zadneprovsky that there was any significant influence from Iran, or contact with the Farghana Valley.

In the following pages an attempt has been made to introduce the Chust culture and examine its claim of being another complex with which the Chalcolithic culture of India shared some common features.

The Chust Culture

The Farghana Valley is some 300 km. long area on the upper reaches of the Syr Darya. It is surrounded by the mountain ranges of the Chatkal, Farghana, Alay and Turkestan. The western half of this cup-shaped valley is arid and desert, while the eastern half is fairly green. The valley occupies a central position amongst the Central Asian republics of Kirgizia, Uzbekistan and Tadjikistan.

The sites

In 1950 an ancient habitational mound was explored about 2 km. north of the modern town of Chust on the right bank of the Syr Darya. It was excavated by Voronetz and Sprishevsky for nearly a decade. In the meantime the valley was systematically explored and more than 40 sites of the culture encountered at Chust were found, mainly in the eastern half of the valley. One of these mounds, called Dulvergine, is being very ably excavated by Zadneprovsky for the last nine years. The site, 33 km. from Chust, is situated on the left bank of the river Kara Darya, a tributary of the Syr.

Cultural Deposit

The entire thickness of the deposit, about 4

metres, has been divided into three structural levels. However, the culture does not show any significant change either in pattern or in details in any of these levels.

Fort and House

Dulvergine was a large fortified town with 4 to 6 m. thick walls, the extant height of which is upto 2.5 m. at places. The houses consisted of rectangular rooms, having floors plastered with clay. The walls were made of mud-bricks of 52×22×8 cm. size.

Metallurgy

Within the habitation were also found remains of furnaces for smelting bronze ; on one earthen pot there were small lumps of molten bronze still sticking. The presence of a number of stone moulds with designs of ear-rings, handled mirror, knife, etc. conclusively prove the existence of a developed stage of metallurgy. It is important to note that the metallurgy of iron, along with that of copper and bronze, was known to the people, although, it was used in a very restricted quantity.

Storage pit

One of the most interesting features of the pattern of habitation was the presence of numerous storage-pits, many of them were a metre and more deep. The base of such a pit was flat and the sides were tapering—the whole thing looked like an inverted funnel. They at once remind us of the so called Neolithic 'Pit-Dwellings' of Burzahom, Kashmir Valley, and incidently raise a doubt in our minds, if they were really meant to be underground houses.

Domestication of Animals and Cereals

The economy of the people was mixed which included the cultivation of wheat, barley and millet, and stock raising of cattle,camel, sheep and goat. It is important to note that horse was also domesticated as is evidenced from the presence of 20 pieces of different bones of this animal in the habitation area and the stone-moulds for horse-bits.

The small antiquities used in everyday life of the people included the following :

Stone objects

(*i*) Crescentic harvesters of slate stone or natural pebble, usually pecked and groud to bring out the desired shape of the tool and sharpness of the cutting edge. The concave edge prominently shows areas of sheen and polish, resulting from considerably long use of the tool.

(*ii*) Ring stones of flat pebbles having hour-glass perforation. Sometimes, these are slightly ground.

(*iii*) Shouldered axe-shaped hammer-stones with dent-marks on the broad surface.

(*iv*) Ground stone peckers.

(*v*) Flat oval pebbles with constricted sides produced by bifacially notching the central part of the two longitudinal sides and by removing two or four deep flakes. Probably, these were used as net-sinkers.

(*vi*) Quern and pestle.

(*vii*) Long rectangular pendant with a neck or hole at the top.

Bone objects :

(*i*) Long comb with 3 to 5 teeth at both the ends ; probably, used in weaving.

(*ii*) Perforated disc.

(*iii*) Pieces of long bone with one surface polished ; probably, used for skating.

Terracotta objects :

(*i*) Perforated disc made out of pot-sherds.

(*ii*) Spindle whorls.

(*iii*) Beads, barrel-shaped.

(*iv*) Cones.

(*v*) Ear-rings.

Copper objects :

(*i*) Socketed spearhead.

(*ii*) Convex edged knife with knobbed handle.

(*iii*) Perforated needle.
(*iv*) Barbed and leaf shaped arrowheads; socketed.

Iron objects :
(*i*) Knife.

Pottery

The pottery of the Chust culture is to be considered in greater detail since according to Zadneprovsky, it shows some unmistakable similarity with the Indian Chalcolithic pottery, particularly, of the Malwa fabric [3]. The following observations are mainly based upon the collection from Dulvergine which I had the opportunity of handling personally at Leningrad by the courtesy of Zadneprovsky.

The Chust pottery is rich and varied. The pots are usually well shaped, although all are hand made. They present a variety of coloured slips : red, dark red, orange, grey, dark grey, whitish and their several shades. When the surface is thoroughly burnished and the slip is consistently applied, the pots show some brightness, extra gloss, and a little oily feel. But, by and large, the surface is dull, matt and crackled. When the thickness of the walls is from thin to medium, the core is completely red, indicating perfect firing, but when it is thick, the core is grey in its central portion, showing the effects of incomplete firing. Usually the pots are well-backed. The texture of the clay is always slightly rough due to the presence of observable sand grains. The majority of the pots are plain, but those painted use black or rarely, blackish white pigments. All the designs are geometric, except one showing a man with a raised hand. We do not know the whole composition of this panel since the sherd on which it appears is broken from the middle. The designs are well executed and the panels are crisp and clear. First the outline of each item is delineated with a thick brush, and then the bounded space is filled either by hatching or by solid filling with the help of a thin brush. Sometimes this work is done rather swiftly, with the result that the lines trespass the boundary. On the whole, however, the painted pottery of the Chust culture is fine and exhibits a good taste and variety.

The pottery types which are compared with those found at Navdatoli are :

(*a*) High necked vessels with concave neck and flaring rim.
(*b*) Hemispherical bowls with everted rims.
(*c*) Sub-oval bowls.
(*d*) Carinated bowls with straight sides.
(*e*) Solid stems with flattish base (probably, belonging to pedestalled wine cups).
(*f*) Spouted bowls (with very short tubular and obliquely cut spouts). One painted spout is spoon shaped.
(*g*) Storage jars.
(*h*) Flat dough plates.

Zadneprovsky particularly stresses the importance of the everted rim bowls, high-necked vessels, carinated bowls and spouted bowls.

The comparative painted designs are as follows :

(*i*) Horizontal bands.
(*ii*) Horizontal straight lines.
(*iii*) Triangles forming a net pattern, vertically arranged.
(*iv*) Rhombs.
(*v*) Chess-board pattern.
(*vi*) Opposed triangles (double-axe design),
(*vii*) Filled triangles.
(*viii*) Circles into rhombs.
(*ix*) Simple decoration of the inner ring.
(*x*) Parallel wavy lines.
(*xi*) Groups of vertical or oblique strokes (4 to 5 strokes).
(*xii*) Cross.
(*xiii*) Human figure (only one example).

Burial custom

The people buried their dead under the floor of the house in the flexed position. Apart from these, some separate skulls were recovered from different cultural strata.

Physical Type

The skulls show that the people belonged to the Europeroid long headed Mediterranean type. This type was common in South Turkmenia during the Bronze Age. It is on this score that Zadneprovsky visualizes the migration of a people from South Turkmenia to the Farghana Valley. These people eventually formed the Chust culture during the late 2nd millennium B.C.

Evaluation

To begin with, the Chust pottery does show some similarity with the Malwa ware. The colours of the slip ranging from orange to deep red, in shades common with the Chalcolithic pottery, show a striking similarity. The appearance of dull matt surface with traces of cracklings is conspicuously present in both the potteries. Similarly, individual items of painted designs as listed by Zadneprovsky also show similarity. About commonness in pottery shapes at least bowls with everted rim and carinated neck do show identity. The other shapes listed above also reflect some distant resemblance. So much in favour of Zadneprovsky.

Now, let us examine these points from all angles and also consider some other aspects not raised by him.

Let it be stated at the very outset that the two potteries basically differ in the mode of manufacture. The Indian pottery is largely wheel-turned while the Uzbekian is completely hand made. The similarity in the shades of the red slip is such which does not call for a common source of emergence. So is also the case with the crackled and matt appearance of the surface. In cases where the surface is not burnished or the clay is not well-levigated, crackling may appear in the course of firing itself; in some cases even while the pots are being sun-dried. This happens because of the readjustment of the clay particles when the moisture evaporates. However, mixing salt in the slip, or throwing salt in the kiln during firing, also leads to the similar result. Whatever might have been the reason, none can be considered as a tangible ground for a common source, or origin.

The similarity shown in the painted designs ignores one of the fundamental principles of archaeological studies. A painted panel or a painted design is a complete unit in itself. It is the outcome of a unified thought or imagination in which the component items are meaningfully joined. Each panel is like a complete word consisting of individual items which serve as letters. A whole design is like a sentence expected to convey a complete idea. As the two words are identical only when their spellings are identical, so also the two panels are comparable when the placement of their individual items is identical. Similarly, when we have to compare a sentence with another sentence, we have not only to see the presence of identical words but also the identity in the order of their arrangement. The same rule should be applied in the case of deigns. A design should be compared with another design only when there exists an identity in the arrangement of the panels. As at no stage can we break a word or a sentence in individual letters for purposes of comparison, so also at no stage should we break the panels and the designs into individual items for comparison.

A deviation from this principle is possible in the case of representational art involving faunal and floral motifs. The reason for this shift in principle is simple. In the case of figure, it is the style involved in the portrayal that is specialized and passed on, or imitated, in the course of time. Due consideration should, therefore, be paid to the subject matter and the style of its delineation when the problem of comparison is raised.

Applying this principle, the long list of the comparable geometric designs proposed by Zadneprovsky is reduced to a very short one. It might, at best, include solid or hatched triangles and lozenges arranged in a row around the neck, opposed triangles placed apex to apex in a frieze, and vertical or horizontal lanes or ladders with trellis hatching.

However, even this comparison raises a very vital question for the protohistorians :

What is the distribution of even the comparable designs during the 2nd and early 1st millennia B.C. ? These geometric designs can be seen at several places in Iraq, Iran, Central Asia, China and India. Therefore, they do not seem to be so specialized as to warrant a common source of origin or contact. In fact, reliance should be placed more in the case of floral and faunal motifs found in identical styles. The geometric designs, unless these are of rare type, should not be used as a good evidence of cultural contacts. They are usually more generalized in character and widespread in time and space. In fact, the same objection stands against E.A. Ansari's work in which he has tried to show the Iranian influence on the Chalcolithic pottery of India. Not that such an evidence is no evidence but it is only of a circumstantial nature which is always of second rate value. Judging from this angle the forms of the Chust earthen pots and pans also show only a general similarity, except in the case of bowls with everted rim and bowls with carinated neck. The high necked jar does not show overall similarity. The similarity in neck and dissimilarity in the body profile in the examples of the two assemblages would vouch for their non-comparable character than for their comparableness. The spouted vessels from the Chust sites have extremely short spouts, hardly 2 to 3 cm. long. The spouts are of tubular and obliquely cut varieties, found slightly below the rim. Although such spouts are also found in the Chalcolithic sites of India, their real source lies in the neighbouring Keltminar Neolithic culture of Kazkhastan. In fact when Sankalia talks of comparable spouted bowls and vessels of India and Iran he means long channel-spouted bowls where the spout emerges from the rim itself, and the long tubular spouted vessels where the spout is about $\frac{1}{3}$ of the height of the vessel. The short spouts and lips existed in India in the southern Neolithic culture, their origin need not be traced to any outside contacts. In the absence of real channel spout or long tubular spout in the Chust complex, one would hesitate to produce the spouted pots for comparison with the Indian types. Short-spouted pots seem to be of local origin in both the regions.

There is a disc based solid stem in the Chust collection which is supposed to be identical with the stem of wine cups found in hundreds from the lowest levels of Navdatoli. In the absence of a complete example, or a cup having at its base the remains of a stem, the question remains open.

The comparison shown in the case of shallow flat dough plates and storage jars also suffers from the lack of traits of any specialized character. They are quite common in ancient Asia.

But can we say the same thing about the identity that exists in the shape of the bowls ? The fact of the matter is that these shapes are very simple and basic, and are found from the 3rd millennium B.C. onwards from Egypt to China and from China to India. Recently, similar bowls with everted rim have been discovered in the Persian Gulf sites excavated by a Danish Expedition [4]. Therefore, even though the existing identity cannot be denied, their simple character coupled with their wide distribution in time and space would relegate this evidence also a little in the background.

The overall image that emerges out of this discussion is simple : so far the evidence of pottery is not very convincing in establishing any real contact between the Chust culture of the Farghana Valley and the Chalcolithic culture of India, although some similarity in the non-specialized pot forms and painted designs does exist. But this can only show that these two cultures shared the general tendencies of the time prevalent in this part of the world. However the diffusion of individual items cannot be pin-pointed with any amount of certainty and, therefore, at the present state of our knowledge any real contact between the two potteries is not in the sight.

A close scrutiny of the other items of the

Chust complex also does not help us in visualizing such a contact. The two cultures significantly differ not only in their material elements but also in their moral behaviour. No doubt, both bury their dead under the floor of the house, but in India multiple pot-burial and extended burial were adopted while in the Farghana Valley it was the crouched burial which held the sway.

Since the pattern of economy was agro-pastroal in both the cases, their tool-kits show a few common items, e.g., perforated ring, quern and pestle, net-sinker, spindle whorls, perforated disc, but these are also of wide distribution among the Neolithic-Chalcolithic cultures of the Old World. So is also the case with the domesticated animals and cereals. However, it may again be noted that only the Chust culture had horse-breeding and not the Indian Chalcolithic.

The two complexes also differ in metallurgical achievements. While the Indian complex is devoid of any knowledge of iron, the Chust complex presents the evidence of the use of iron implements, right from the very beginning.

The two cultures also differ in their habitation-pattern. All the Indian sites, known so far, are open villages while, Dulvergine, the site opened by Zadneprovsky is definitely fortified.

About the racial connections of the two peoples, it may be stated that the people with Mediterranean features were present in South Turkmenia from the 4th millennium B.C. onwards. These were also present in Khorezm (Northern Turkistan and western parts of Kazkhastan) in the Neolithic Keltminar culture of the 3rd-2nd millennium B.C., and they are also found in India from the 3rd millennium B.C. (Harappa culture) onwards. With this antiquity of the Mediterranean stock in both the countries, the argument of racial affinity to prove the cultural contact in the early 1st millennium B. C. is not well founded.

The two aspects of time and space also do not help us very much in visualizing the proposed contact. There are two dates for Dulvergine :

(*i*) circa 2720 ± 120B.P., i. e. 770 ± 120B.C.

(*ii*) circa 3050 ± 120 B.P., i.e., 1100 ± 120 B.C.
(B.P. is counted from 1950)

Without twisting these dates in one way or the other, the Chust culture is to be bracketed between circa 1100 and 770 B.C. which coincides not only with the fag end of the Chalcolithic culture in India (bracketed c. 1800-1000 B.C.) but also with the Early Iron stage of this country. During this period the tradition of painted ware had already come to an end, what remained was the plain Black-and-Red ware with its associates of plain wares of dull red and grey colours. This is the stage of Nagada II, Bahal II, Eran II and Prakash II. The time-scale shows that the Chust culture is also contemporaneous with the Sialk VI stage. In this period iron was in common use in Iran. Its early stage also coincides with the end of the Namazga VI stage and the whole of the Yaz Depe I stage of South Turkmenian chronology. This was the time when iron had been introduced in Turkmenia also. It, therefore, appears quite reasonable that the Chust culture should be placed within the general framework of the early Iron stage cultures of Iran, South Turkmenia and India and not in the pool of the Chalcolithic culture of the Indian peninsula.

The factor of gap in space is also worth noting, although it may be argued that in future it might be filled up. The spatial gap between the Farghana Valley and Central India in which the Chust or the Indian Chalcolithic sites have not been found is very vast. The Chust culture is in fact a Valley cutlure with a definite local bias. Whatever traces of foreign elements are seen in it they seem to be from the areas a few hundred kilometres around the Valley, and not from thousands of kilometres away. As mentioned above, so far, more than forty sites of this culture have been located, but not even one outside the valley. That again shows the strong localized character of the culture, and simultaneously raises a doubt in our minds if the Central Indian Chalcolithic culture and the Chust culture could possibly have maintained the physical contact, directly or indirectly, as has been visualized by Zadneprovsky.

NOTES

[1] Y. A. Zadneprovsky, *Ancient Agricultural Chust Culture of Farghana*, (Moscow), 1962, (In Russian).

[2a] A. V. Shchetenko, 'The Problem of Origin of the Aneolithic of Central India', Ancient India, (Moscow), 1964, 31-43 (In Russian).

[2b] 'The question of Indo-Iranian Relation of Post-Harappan time', *The Reports and Informations of the U.S.S.R. Archaeologists*, (Moscow), 1966. The booklet published on the occasion of the VIIth International Congress of the Pre-historic and Proto-historic Sciences, Prague. (In Russian).

[3] Ibid, 102-107.

[4a] P. V. Glob and T. G. Bibby, 'Arabian Gulf Archaeology, *Kuml*, 1964, 90, Fig. 3.

[4b] A Neo-Babylonian Burial from Bahrain's Prehis toric Capital, *Kuml*, 1956, 165, Fig. 2.

Alamgirpur and the Iron Age in India*

by O. P. TANDON

The purpose of this paper is to discuss afresh, the beginning of iron in India in the light of the evidence from Alamgirpur, and analyse the implications related with the ushering of the Iron Age in India.

Archaeological Evidence—Alamgirpur

With the discovery of Alamgirpur [1] in 1958, the Harappan [2] culture was seen for the first time to have entered Ganga-Yamuna Doab. The subsequent excavation of the site in 1959 revealed yet another significant detail for the first time—the association of iron objects with the PGW deposit. As we shall presently see, the deposit was found overlying the earlier Harappan culture remains. The Harappa, the PGW and the post-PGW deposits at the site show three distinct cultural entities with no possibility of overlap. The excavators [3] were also fortunate in discovering that the above-noted cultural periods were separated from each other by a thin sterile layer signifying desertion following both the Harappan and the PGW occupation of the site. This circumstance of the PGW deposit at Alamgirpur together with its association with iron may have an important bearing on the chronology of the Iron Age in India. It is, therefore, proposed to examine the stratigraphy at Alamgirpur in greater detail. The total cultural deposit at Alamgirpur is about 3.66 m. in thickness. The Harappan levels are represented by a 1.83 m. thick deposit of compact and brownish earth. On the other hand the PGW levels with an average thickness of 1.37 m. were loose with frequent bands of burnt earth and ash. The break between the two periods (I and II), besides being cultural, was demonstrated by a thin stratum of a hard and whitish deposit, signifying a long exposure. Over a large portion of the mound this surface was found strewn with small weather-worn potsherds. The deposits of Period III with an average thickness of less than 30 cms. were confined to certain areas of the mound. The gap between this and Period II was again very clear, represented both by the cultural complex as well as the composition of the deposits. An intervening exposed surface was also marked at some places. The ceramic of Period III did not include NBP, a ware which has been commonly following the PGW at other sites in the Upper Gangetic Basin, but was dominated by the Early Historical Red Wares. The deposits of Period IV belonged to very late medieval times and were characterised by 'glazed' ware pottery and structures built of *Lakhauri* bricks. We thus find that the four cultural periods noticed here bearing unmistakable traits of their respective cultures, were separated from each other in similar unmistakable terms.

The sequence of the cultures at Alamgirpur, as seen above, provides a very significant position to the PGW deposit, as these levels are very distinctly defined. Certain ceramic types in red ware found at Hastinapur and Rupar in association with the NBP ware are found to occur in the Period II at Alamgirpur. Then there is a low percentage of the PGW as compared to the plain grey ware and red wares. These occurrences, when taken together with the discovery of iron objects throughout Period II deposits, place this PGW assemblage to a late phase of this culture. The iron objects include a spear-head, arrowheads and few nails and pins. (Details of objects are given at the end of this paper).

* The author records gratefully his acknowledgement to Dr. K. K. Sinha and Shri D. P. Agrawal for various suggestions in writing this paper and their helpful discussions on the problem of the interpretation of radiocarbon determinations.

Evidence from other sites

Having discussed the cultural compositions and the stratigraphy at Alamgirpur, let us now compare the results from other sites yielding PGW and iron objects. Earlier to the evidence from Alamgirpur, Hastinapur [4] was the only site from where iron was suspected in the form of slag from the uppermost levels of the Period II [5], i.e. the PGW deposit. The deposit of Period II follows the levels of Ochre-Coloured ware, the identity and age of which is yet to be established. Then, due to floods, Period II people deserted this site. The site was again inhabited after an appreciable lapse of time in Period III, which is characterised by the NBP and its associated wares.

The next important evidence is from Atranjikhera [6]. Although in all six cultural periods are reported, we shall examine in the present context the three pre-NBP periods. The earliest cultural level at Atranjikhera is represented by Ochre-coloured ware, similar to that obtained from the lowest levels of Hastinapur [7] and Bahadrabad [8], according to the excavator. The Period II, is marked by the occurrence of the black-and-red ware along with black-slipped ware showing almost common techniques and shapes and red slipped and unslipped wares. The Period III is represented by the PGW. Though PGW is the characteristic pottery, it occurs along with plain grey,black-and-red, black slipped, and slipped as well as unslipped wares. The incidence of PGW is reported to be between 3% to 10% of the total pottery complex which does not seem to be much. This ware and the thin plain grey ware show a remarkable similarity in shape, fabric and technique to the black-and-red and black slipped pottery. In the post-PGW Period, both PGW as well as plain grey ware show degeneration. Gradually PGW disappears but plain grey ware continues for a much longer time. On the other hand, the black-slipped ware shows a continuous process of improvement, particularly in fineness and lustre and perhaps develops directly into the NBP ware. In view of the complex evidence only a critical study of the associated red ware types in various cultural periods will present a clearer picture. Iron tools and implements have been found in all the sub-phases of the period. These include spear-heads, arrowheads, knives, an axe, a pair of kitchen tongs (the latter two from the late sub-phases) and two, probably, fish hooks. As there is an overlap of the cultural material it would also be important to work out the frequency and the distribution of tool types in the sub-phases to enable us to work out a better chronological sequence. The overall picture that emerges from the brief interim notes of Atranjikhera excavation is not so clear as that of Alamgirpur where all the levels are distinctly separated from each other.

In recent years further evidence of iron in association with the PGW has come from Ahichchhatra [9] Distt. Bareilly, U.P., Bairat [10] in Distt. Jaipur, and Non [11] in Distt. Bharatpur of Rajasthan. So far, there is no evidence of the occurrence of iron being found stratigraphically below the PGW deposits anywhere [12].

Chronology

Archaeologically speaking, the users of the PGW were, therefore, the earliest people to introduce iron in India. Lal [13] worked out a chronology of c. 1100-800 B.C. for the PGW levels at Hastinapur. The excavators of Atranjikhera, working on the basis of a solitary C-14 date of 1025 B.C. [14] relating to the early phase of PGW culture, inferred that the users of this ceramic settled down in the Ganga Valley around 1200 B.C. [15] Samples from other sites have given much later dates. We have to guard against the tendency of depending too much on stray radio-carbon determinations [16] particularly for sites like Atranjikhera where cultural levels both preceding and following the PGW deposit do not appear very firmly defined. In this respect the evidence from Alamgirpur is much better placed. Now, even if Lal's chronology of Hastinapur is accepted, the upper levels of PGW which yielded iron cannot be dated to c. 1000 B.C. A post 800 B.C. context is indicated for PGW both at Alamgirpur and Sravasti [17]. Having begun round 1000 B.C. the PGW may have survived upto 500 B.C., if not later. It will, therefore, be not logical to assume that wherever there is PGW, the deposit must be dated to 1000 B.C.

The above brief resume of the recent archaeological work would indicate that there is no good evidence to believe that the earliest occurrence of iron can be pushed to c. 1000 B.C. Perhaps a date of *circa* 800 B.C. for the earliest known use of iron seems more appropriate.

Chronological Controversy

Discussing the antiquity of iron, Gordon [18] stated that there is no iron earlier than 400 B.C. in the Indian deposits. Wheeler [19] suggests that iron came into Northern India with the Achaemenids towards the end of the 6th century B.C. and the beginning of the 5th (as indeed in distant Britain). Kosambi [20] collating both literary and archaeological evidence, however, held, "Remembering that food gathering was so easy that less metal was needed, the date 800-700 B.C., therefore, seems to me a reasonable beginning for the Iron Age in India, meaning thereby specifically the Gangetic Basin where iron was most needed and most likely to have been worked". Banerjee [21] fixed the beginning of Iron Age in India to c. 1000 B.C. and made the Aryan endeavour responsible for spreading Iron far and wide within the sub-continent.

It may not perhaps be very much out of place to refer here that Banerjee and others have maintained that the Aryans were responsible for both introducing iron and PGW about 1200 B.C. (We have already questioned this early date). In the light of the Radio-Carbon determinations and other evidences it does not appear probable that Harappa Culture survived much beyond 1750 B.C. [22]. The commonly held belief that the 'Aryans' followed in the wake of the end of Harappan Culture (c. 1750 B.C.) needs to be reconciled with the supposition that the users of PGW were Aryans. But Banerjee does not answer the question, "What was happening in the period between 1750 B.C. and 1200 B.C. in India ?". Agrawal's [23] observations that the authors of the PGW belong to the second wave of the Aryan movement into our sub-continent deserves consideration.

The above critical study of the archaeological evidence of the PGW deposits from Alamgirpur and other sites in the Ganga-Yamuna Doab has shown that the beginning of iron in India does not go beyond c. 800 B.C. and to push it back further new evidence will be required which at present is lacking. The ushering of Iron Age in India invokes far greater horizons which have to be studied on a much broader canvas to be able to present a more complete picture.

Studies On The Iron Age

Recently there has been a good deal of writing on the problem of Iron Age, more precisely of the antiquity of iron in India, particularly in the direction of correlating the literary and archaeological evidence by Gopal [24], Singh [25], Kosambi [26] and Banerjee [27]. The discussion on literary evidence has mainly centred round the interpretation of the word *Ayas*, while the archaeological evidence has been rather uncritically utilized to push back the antiquity of iron to 1000 B.C. or earlier as by Singh [28], who says, "The Archaeological discovery and the literary evidence seem to be mutually corroborative, and 1000 B.C. may be suggested as the *provisional* date for the introduction of iron smelting in India." Attention in this connection may be drawn to D.D. Kosambi's scientific study of the problem wherein he has made a plea that the problem was to be viewed from the social and economic angle to assess the totality of impact of the use of iron in India [29]. One would have wished that Banerjee's [30] latest work, "Iron Age in India", which is a monumental reference work, had contained an analytical interpretation of the problems linked with the total impact of Iron Age in India and answered the technological problems involved. The ushering of Iron Age is far more a complex problem for the simple treatment given to it by Banerjee.

Iron age and its implications

The problem of Iron Age is altogether different from the problem of the beginning or the introduction of iron in India. A distinction between the stage of mere occurrence of iron and the introduction of an Iron Age has to be made. The impact of Indian Iron Age has to be studied under the following headings :—

I. When did the smelting and exploitation of Indian iron ores start ?

II. The metal's role in the means of production; and,

III. The revolutionary impact that it had on the society, economy, and the polity.

These implications of the Iron Age have to be understood clearly so that its tremendous impact is properly appreciated. Mere possession of the iron objects—mainly weapons of war—and lack of a metallurgical know-how, will tend one to look for the source of the introduction of iron beyond the frontiers of this sub-continent. The present evidence or perhaps the lack of it points towards a foreign source [31]. The 'Aryans', the users of iron, might have come in contact with West Asian iron-working communities before entering this continent and had in this way gathered the knowledge of the use and smelting of iron. But there is hardly any evidence to show that they knew the Indian iron ores in the northern region and the Doab. The only two important iron ores in the northern region are at Mandi in Himachal Pradesh and Narnaul in Patiala [32]. Did the Aryans explore these as soon as they reached Panjab ? The best northern ores come from Bihar where the Aryans could not have reached so early, as the plains of the Ganga-Yamuna were completely covered with thick forests [33]. The Aryans came as nomadic intruders. They were constantly travelling on horses with their cattle wealth, carrying arms to conquer new lands. The next stage came when they started settling down in small groups. Only after this sedentary stage we can imagine them exploring the mineral wealth of the land and smelting iron from the local ores. From nomadic to sedentary phase of life is a great change. "The Ganges region did not see such a development until the Iron Age, for without iron implements it was impossible to clear its dense jungles". This transition may have taken considerable time.

Mere occurrence of a metal, therefore, is not the sole criterion to judge the ushering of the Age of that metal. Forbes [34] observes, "even areas into which metal objects have been carried by trade need not themselves be in the Metal Age." The discovery of iron heralds only the coming of the dawn. It is only the beginning of the day and not the day itself. The appearance of iron in the PGW levels is, therefore, only the beginning of the use of iron in a very limited sense and not the ushering of Iron Age in India.

(i) Metallurgical knowledge

The knowledge of the metallurgical processes is the most important factor. "No Iron Age could start from the knowledge of meteoric Iron alon." The Iron Age could be initiated only by a people who knew how to reduce Iron ore and had acquired the special knowledge of of working the bloom obtained from the ore. Until it is chemically established that the PGW iron is smelted from Indian iron ores or the evidence of smithies and smelting is found this criterion is not fulfilled in the Indian context. It has been further emphasized by Forbes 35", that only by considering both the chemical-technological aspects as well as the typological ones we can build chronological series and find out the trade-routes of metals".

(II) Iron in the Means of production

At the time when the earliest settlements were coming up in the Ganga Valley the economy was rural, based mainly on agricultural production,

For the cultivation, the land was to be cleared of thick forests and then tilled with such implements which could be effective in the circumstances in the Ganga Valley. Unlike the valley of Euphrates, Nile and Indus, the Ganga Valley was full of thick monsoon jungles. A harrow effective in the silted deposits brought by the floods of Euphrates, Nile and Indus could not be used in the Ganga Basin for the obvious reason of the presence of roots and stones in the soil. It required a plough share far stronger and sharper than the stone or bronze could provide. Only iron could provide such an implement. The metal repertoire of the PGW includes objects which generally come under the category of the weapons of war. But the agricultural implements are conspicuous by their absence. Under the circumstances is it possible to credit these early settlers with the clearance of forests, making trade-routes and introducing agriculture on a scale where it can be termed as a food producing economy ? While with the dawn of 1st millennium B.C. people elsewhere began to use iron widely for weapons and implements, the picture of the society that emerges in India is very poor. The available though scanty evidence shows that the society was still in a pastoral and nomadic economic stage.

(III) **Economic Revolution**

The role of copper and bronze in mobilising the first Urban revolution in the West Asia is for too well known to be discussed here and beyond the scope of this paper but the analogy stands good in the case of the role of Iron that it played in bringing forth an economic revolution of far wider and deeper magnitude. "The iron was the cheap metal and it provided a tool of such hardness and sharpness that no stone, no other known metal could withstand it. Iron made possible field agriculture on a larger scale and the clearing of extensive forest tracts for cultivation" [36]. With agriculture becoming a reputable pursuit during this age, and agriculture production increased due to large-scale cultivation in the plains of Doab, the economy obtained a surplus base. Similarly the efficiency of industry was enormously increased. There was quickening of transport, trade and civic life. This surplus wealth lead to the second urbanisation in the Ganga valley. "This is not the place to trace in detail the growth of cities and monarchies in this valley. It is sufficient to point out that in a short period a transition took place from innumerable scattered, independent tribes, colonies, and city-states to a few large kingdoms which first swallowed up the remaining free settlements and then fought one another for supremacy and universal empire." [37]

The economic changes of the Iron Age also found political expression. In the south-eastern region of Bihar so full of iron ores of a very high grade, he Kingdom of Magadha rose, its political supremacy firmly established over other Kingdoms. The source of the Magadhan supremacy is to be located in its greater technological development. The Magadhans had the control over the supply of iron. This metal was worked out usefully and popularly and traded in abundance in the central Gangetic Basin. "This then, was Magadha's great source of power, for that state used the metal systematically to clear land and to bring it under the plough" [38]. The Hitittes [39] presented a similar example, beyond the frontiers of our sub continent in earlier times. "Its (Hitittes) prosperity was due pre-eminently to its soil's mineral wealth. Iron was particularly abundant there.... They were the masters of the mineral wealth and the "Iron Kings", by virtue of this fact and whether they liked it or not all Empires became tributary to them, and their skill in using the metal increased their wealth and power even further. In a well governed and well organized empire like theirs commercial wealth of this kind could have been the stay of a true hegemony—especially with help of warrior people's arms and the Hitittes came very near to achieving it". It is commonly held that the Aryans, the users of iron in India, had come in contact with the Hitittes before entering this sub-continent and they had acquired the knowledge of the use of iron from them. When these Aryans reached the Ganga Valley and started exploiting the best iron ores in the country, the history was repeated. (We have already discussed the growth of Magadhan empire). The iron is found in abundance in the levels comparable to the period of the Magadhan supremacy and later on. A look into the metal repertoire of the NBP levels shows that the implements now include more agricultural implements than before.

An analysis of the implications of the Iron Age made in the foregoing pages establishes that the answer to the multi-faceted problem lies in chemical-technical-cum-typological studies. [40]

NOTES

[1] *Indian Archaeology* 1958-59 *A Review,* 50-55 (Hence after abbreviated as *I.A.R.*)

[2] R.E.M. Wheeler, *The Indus Civilization* (Supplementary volume to C.H.I.), (London), 1962, 3.

[3] The author was closely associated with the excavations at Alamigrpur conducted by Dr. Y.D. Sharma of the Archaeological Survey of India.

[4] B.B. Lal in *Ancient India* (hence after abbreviated as *A. I.*) No. 10 ;& 11 (Delhi), 1955, 6-150.

[5] Ibid, 13. Further small-scale excavations at Hastinapur in 1962 yielded finished iron objects from the middle levels of the PGW deposit. N.R. Banerjee, *The Iron Age in India* (Delhi), 1965, 216.

[6] R.C. Gaur, *Indian Prehistory,* 1964 (Poona), 1965, 142-145.

[7] Ibid, 10-11.

[8] A. Ghosh, *The Indus Civilization* : Its *origins, Authors, Extent and Chronolog, Indian Prehistory* 1964 (Poona), 1965, 123-124.

[9] N. R. Banerjee, *The Iron Age in India,* (Delhi), 1965, 1965, 216.

[10] *I.A.R.* 1962-63, 31.

[11] *I.A.R.* 1963-94 & 1964-65, Section I.

[12] S. D. Singh, *Ancient Indian warfare with special reference to Vedic Period* (Leiden), 1965, 101. His remarks that the earliest evidence comes from Kausambi is based on a misinterpretation of stratigraphy on that site. A characteristic PGW deposit is missing there.

[13] Ibid, 23.

[14] D.P. Agrawal, *et. al.,* in *Current science,* May 1964, XXXIII-9), 266.

[15] *Op.cit.,* 145.

[16] It has been emphasised by the scientists again and again that to arrive at meaningful chronologies, one should have cluster of dates or internally consistent sequence of dates. Solitary dates can often be deceptive. For Atranjikhera, too, unless we have a sequence of C-14 dates for various periods, no reliable chronology can be built on stray dates.

[17] Information from Dr. K. K. Sinha. A full report of the excavation *o* pending publication.

[18] D.H. Gordon, *The Pre-historic Bakground of Indian Culture* (Bombay), 1958, 155.

[19] R.E.V. Wheeler, *Early India and Pakistan to Asohka* (London), 1959, p. 24.

[20] D.D. Kosambi, 'The beginning of Iron Age in India, *Journal of Economic, Social* Nistory *of the Orient,* **VI (3),** 318.

[21] *Op. cit.,* 9, 239.

[22] D.P. Agrawal, *Harappan Chronology : A re-examination of the Evidence, Studies in Prehistory,* (Robert Bruce Foote Memorial Volume), 1966, 139.

[23] D.P. Agrawal, 'C-14 Dates, Banas Culture And The Aryans,' *Current Science,* March 1966, **5,** 114-117.

[24] Lallanji Gopzal, *'Antiquity of Iron in India',* ***Uttar Bharati,*** **IX** (3), 71-86.

[25] S.D. Singh, 'Iron in Ancient India.,' *Journal of Economic ,Social History of the Orient,* **V** (2), 212-16 and Op.cit. 12.

[26] *Opcit.,* 20, 309-318.

[27] *Op.cit.* 9.

[28] *Op.cit.* 12, 102.

[29] *Op.cit.* 20.

[30] *Op.cit.* 9.

[31] Ibid, The author has discussed at great length the evidence of iron in the Ancient world and the possibility of a foreign source for the early iron objects associated with the PGW deposit.

[32] Ibid, 190.

[33] *Op.cit.,* 19, 118.

[34] R.J. Forbes, *Studies in Ancient Technology,* **VIII,** 7.

[35] Ibid, 15.

[36] K. Marx and F. Engels, *Selected ...orks* (Moscow), 1955, 311.

[37] A.K. Warder, On the Relationship between early Buddhism and other contemporary systems, *'Bull. of school of Oriental and African Studies,* 1956, 48. See also p. 46 for the impact of Iron Age towards the development of a scientific philosophical outlook in about 6th cetnury B.C.

[38] D.D. Kosambi, *The Culture and Civilisation of Anceint India* (London), 1965, 123.

[39] Marcel, Brion, *The world of Archaeology* (London), 1962, 311.

[40] The author is presently engaged in collecting data for the proposde study.

Typology in Prehistory*

by P. C. PANT

Some of the noted prehistorians of India have been saying for the past few years that we have enough of typology in Indian Prehistory and what we require now is to concentrate on stratigraphy with a view to giving proper stratigraphical horizons to different industries. Nobody can deny the importance of stratigraphy in the study of prehistoric cultures, but, at the same time, a question arises—Have we done enough of typological studies in India as compared to the standards followed in other parts of the world specially in Europe ? In fact we have over-simplified typology and our studies are, more or less, limited to very broad classification of implements and that too does not always agree with the patterns internationally followed. We still do not know the typical tool-types of the Middle Palaeolithic Culture or Middle Stone Age in India. We have yet to determine the percentage of Clactonian flakes and Levalloisian cores, flakes, points and blades in the different palaeolithic industries. It is even now a query before us whether all the industries of the different parts of the country, assignable to the second cycle of aggradation of Pleictocene period of India form one single culture or belong to the different cultures. All these questions may be answered with the help of scientific techo-typological studies of various industries.

Stratigraphy and typology are universally accepted as the two basic methods of the study of prehistoric cultures. As far as the former is concerned, a prehistorian has to seek help from geologists, soil chemists, palaeontologists,—palaeobotanists and similar other scientists, unless he combines in himself the qualities of a prehistorian as well as a quaternary geologist. Such prehistorians are of course rare in the world. So there is not much left for a prehistorian to do except to concentrate himself on typology.

Several scholars have attempted to provide proper definitions to different tool-types. The pioneer work on the typology of Palaeolithic period has been done by Bordes [1], Muller-Beck [2], Bosinski [3], Bohmers [4], Tixier [5], Sonneville-Bordes and I. Perrot [6]. The tool-types of the different Mesolithic cultures have been studied in detail by Clarke [7], Scherabedissen [8], Althin [9], Bohmers [10] and Barrière [11]. These prehistorians have given proper footing to the typological studies. The standards presented by them may be followed in India and other parts of the world.

Typological studies have proved to be of great help in solving some of the complex problems of European Prehistory. It is with the help of typology, it was concluded that 'Levalloisian' is not a separate culture, but only a technique which is to be found in all the Middle Palaeolithic cultures. The typological studies have also shown that 'Tayacian' is probably not a culture by itself and the so-called 'Tayac point' not a tool. Again, typology, in collaboration with stratigraphy, has provided the evidences to differentiate between typical Mousterian on one hand and the Mousterian of the Acheulian tradition, Mousterian of La Quina type, Mousterian of La Ferrasie type, Mousterian with toothed implements and Charentian on the other. The typological studies are also of much use in making a comparative study of the different cultures.

At the same time, let it be understood that we do not wish to overemphasise the importance of typological studies. On the contrary, it may be said that the conclusions drawn only on the basis of typology, without taking the stratigra-

*This paper was read in the 55th session of Indian Science Congress held at Varanasi in January, 1968.

phical evidences into consideration, are likely to be incorrect. Such a study is inadequate and unscientific. We have a very good example of such a study made by Burkitt and Camiade [12] in relation to the palaeolithic industries of south eastern India. They differentiated Abbevillian tool-types from Acheulian ones only on the basis of typology. The subsequent workers in the field took this division for granted, as if they were the two different cultures. But our recent studies indicate that nowhere in India they are found in different stratigraphical horizons, and they seem to be the two components of one and the same culture. For all practical purposes, at least in Indian Prehistory, Abbevillian and Acheulian have merely typological value.

Now we propose to summarise some of the general factors which should be taken into consideration while dealing with the typology of an industry.

Typology Versus Functions of Tools

There is a general belief, particularly in India, that typology and the functions of the tools go together and the former is largely based upon the latter. Our contention is that typology has little to do with the functions of the tools and both should be studied separately. The typological, classification of tools is based upon other factors viz., general shape of the tool,technique of manufacture, type, technique and angle of retouch etc. Since Prehistoric Archaeology is a concrete science, we should be objective in our studies. When we talk of the functions of the tools, particularly of the palaeolithic period, we mostly speculate and thus become subjective in our outlook, ignoring the basic requirement of the discipline as there are hardly any evidences to prove the functions of the tools. At the same time, we do not deny the importance of the functional aspect of tool-types. In fact we welcome such scientific studies which throw light on the functions of the implements. But they should be scientific and not speculative. The work of the Russian prehistorian Semenov [13] is an ideal before us.

Shape of the Tool

General shape of the implement is one of the factors which is taken into account in typological studies. For example a pear-shaped handaxe is differentiated from a triangular one and a 'U' shaped cleaver from that of 'V' shape. This phenomenon plays a very important part in the classification of microliths.

Technique of Manufacture

The particular type of technique, which has been employed in manufacturing the tool, is one of the deciding factor in typological classification. It is on this basis that a simple point is differentiated from a Mousterian Point and an Abbevillian Handaxe from an Acheulian one.

Retouch

With the exception of handaxe, cleaver, chopper and chopping tool, no artefact comes in the category of a tool unless it is also retouched. Then one has to take into consideration the type of retouch. For example, a flake or blade is an End Scraper only when it is steeply retouched to produce a convex working end.

Measurements

The measurements of length and width of the tools, the angle of percussion and that of retouch are very much helpful in making the comparative study of different industries. On the basis of these measurements one can prepare the different indices. For instance, if a tool measures 4×2 cms., the index will be 3. Such a study may lead an investigator to observe that a particular industry has a preference for a particular tool-type of a certain group of indices as compared to the other industry. The same is true about the measurements of the angle of percussion and that of retouch.

Statistics

The statistical studies have been recently introduced in Prehistory and have been fruitfully used

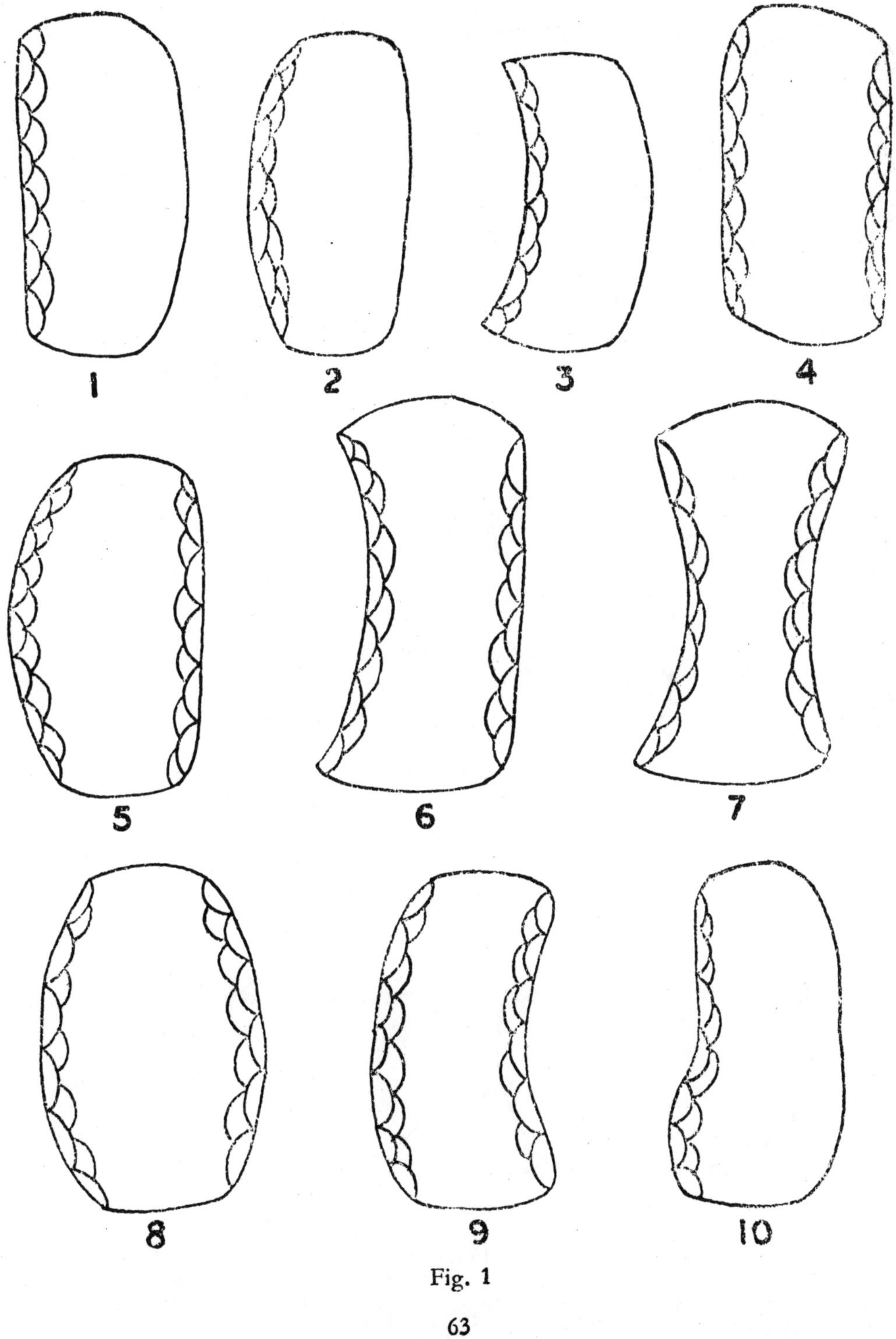

Fig. 1

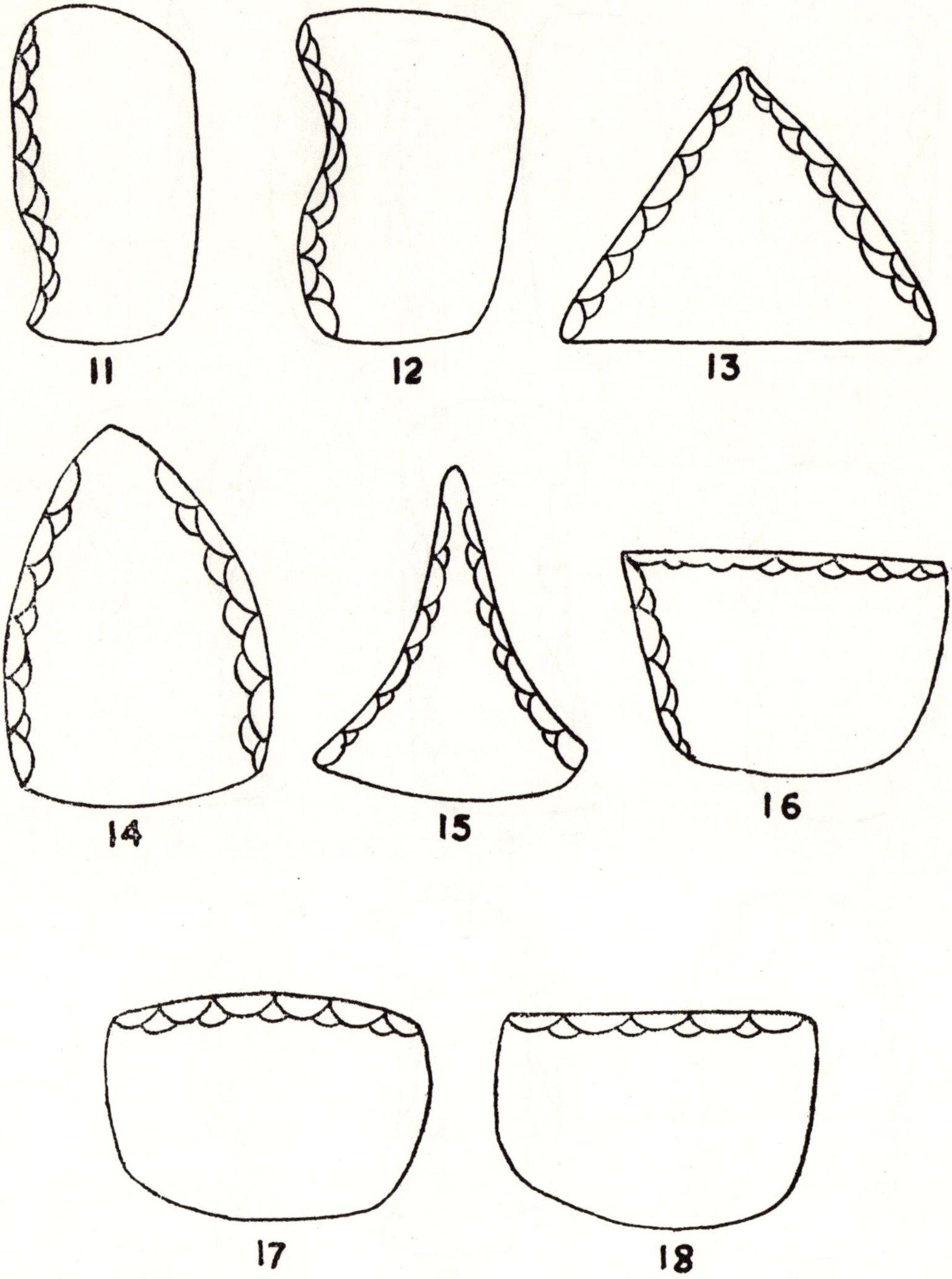

Fig. 2

by some of the European scholars [14]. For the purpose, one should calculate the percentage of each tool-type and notice the preference for one as compared to the other in an industry. The same can be presented in graphs, diagrams and tables. These methods are well suited for making a comparative study and enable us to present the results both concisely and legibly. The hollow or concave side scraper, for example is one of the important tool-type in the Middle Palaeolithic culture of India. The percentage can be calculated in the following two ways :—

$$\text{A. } \frac{\text{Number of hollow side scraper} \times 100}{\text{Total number of side scrapers.}}$$

$$\text{B. } \frac{\text{Number of hollow side scraper} \times 100}{\text{Total number of implements}}$$

Although different methods should be employed to different industries, depending upon their nature, the above mentioned are the general factors, which, in our opinion, should be taken into account in the classification of tools.

Types of Side-Scraper

If some of these methods are applied, we can classify the side-scraper into following main types. Ofcourse some more types may be recognised if we also consider the size of the tool and type and angle of retouch.

1. *Straight Side-scraper.* A flake retouched on one of the long sides resulting in a convex working edge (Fig. 1, 1).
2. *Convex Side-scraper.* A flake retouched on one of the long sides resulting in a convex working edge (Fig. 1, 2).
3. *Hollow or Concave Side-scraper.* A flake retouched on one of the long sides resulting in a concave or hollow working edge (Fig. 1, 3).
4. *Side-scraper, straight-convex.* A flake retouched on one of the long sides producing partly straight and partly convex working edge (Fig. 1, 10).
5. *Side-scraper, straight-concave.* A flake retouched on one of the long sides to produce partly straight and partly concave working edge (Fig. 2, 11).
6. *Side scraper, concavo-convex.* A flake retouched on one of the long sides to produce partly concave and partly convex working edge (Fig. 2, 12).
7. *Double Side-scraper, straight.* A flake retouched on both the long sides producing straight working edges (Fig. 1, 4).
8. *Double Side-scraper, convex-straight.* A flake retouched on both the long sides. One of the working edge is convex and the other straight (Fig. 1, 5).
9. *Double Side-scraper, concave-straight.* A flake retouched on both the long sides. One of the working edges is concave and the other straight (Fig. 1, 6).
10. *Double Side-scraper, biconvex.* A flake retouched on both the long sides. Both the working edges are convex (Fig. 1, 8).
11. *Double Side-scraper, biconcave.* A flake retouched on both the long sides. Both the working edges are concave (Fig. 1, 7).
12. *Double Side-scraper, convexo-concave.* A flake retouched on both the long sides. One of the working edge is convex and the other concave (Fig. 1, 9).
13. *Point cum-side-scraper, straight.* Both sides of a flake are retouched to make a point opposite the bulb end. The angle between the two straight sides is more than 45° (Fig. 2, 13).
14. *Point-cum-side-scraper, convex.* Similar to No. 13, but both the sides are convex (Fig. 2, 14).
15. *Point-cum-side-scraper, concave.* Similar to No. 13, but both the sides are concave (Fig. 2, 15).
16. *Angled side-scraper.* One of the long sides and the other lying opposite the bulb-end retouched to produce an angle (Fig. 2, 16).
17. *Wide Side-scraper, straight.* A flake retouched on the top side lying opposite

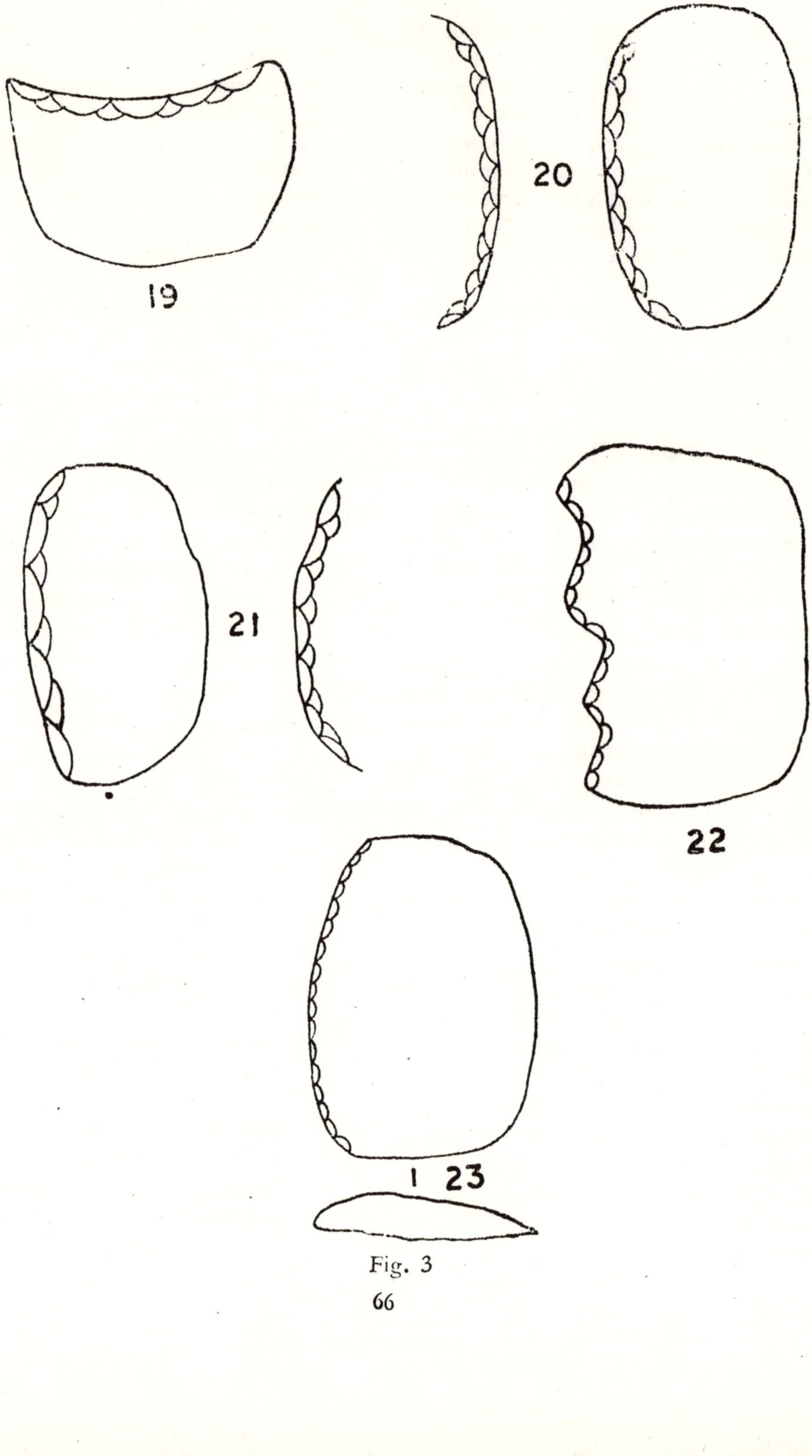

Fig. 3

the bulb-end, producing a straight working edge (Fig. 2, 18).

18. *Wide Side-scraper, convex.* Similar to No. 17, but the working edge is convex (Fig. 2, 17).
19. *Wide Side-scraper, concave.* Similar to No. 17, but the working edge is concave (Fig. 3, 19).
20. *Side-scraper with retouch on ventral surfacel* A flake retouched on one of the long side from the ventral surface.
21. *Side-scraper with retouch on both the sides from alternate surfaces.* One of the sides of a flake is retouched from the upper surface and the other from the under (Fig. 3, 21).
22. *Side-scraper retouched from both the surfaces.* A flake retouched on one of the sides from both the surfaces (Fig. 3, 20).
23. *Side-scraper with short steep retouch.* A flake retouched on one of the long sides. The retouch is short and steep (Fig. 3, 23).
24. *Toothed Side-scraper.* A flake having more than one notch on one of the long sides, as a result of secondary work (Fig. 3, 22).
25. *Side-scraper on a core.* A side-scraper made on core.

NOTES

[1] F. Bordes, *Typologie du Paleolithique Ancient et Moyen,* (Bordeaux), 1961, two volumes.

[2] H.J. Mueller-Beck, 'Zur Bezeichnung Palaeolithischer Artefakttypen', *Alt Thueringen,* III, 1957-58, 140-200.

[3] G. Bosinski, 'Eine Mittelpalaeolithische Formengruppe und das Problem Ihrer Geochronologischen Einordnung', *Eiszeitalter und Gegenwart,* **XIV,** (Ohringen), 1963, 124-140; and 'Abschlaege mit Fazettierter Schagflaeche in Mittelpalaeolithischen Funden', *Fundberichte aus Schwaben,* (Neue Folge)1,7, 1965, 5-10.

[4] A Bohmers, 'Statistics and Graphs in the Study of Flint Assemblages,' I, II & III, *Palaeohistoria,* **V,** 1956, 1-38; and 'Statistiques et Graphiques dans 1' Etudes des Industries Lithiques Prehistoriques', Ibid, **VIII**, 1961, 15-37.

[5] J. Tixier, 'Le Hachereau dans 1' Acheuleen Nord-Africain; Notes Typologiques', *Congres Prehistorique de France,* (Poitiers), 1956, 914-923; and *Typologie de* 1' *Epipaleolithique du Maghreb,* (Paris), 1963.

[6] D. de Sonneville-Bordes and J. Perrot, 'Lexique Typologique du Paleolithique Superieur, ' *Bulletin de la Societe Prehistorique Francaise,* **51,** 1954, 327-335; **52,** 1955, 76-79; **53**, 1965, 408-412 and 547-559; and D. de Sonneville-Bordes, *Le Paleolithique Superieur en Perigord,* (Bordeaux) 1960, two volumes.

[7] J.G.D. Clarke, *The Mesolithic Settlements of Northern Europe,* (Cambridge), 1935; and *The Excavations at Star Carr,* (Cambridge), 1956.

[8] H. Schwabedissen, *Die Mittelere Steinzeit im Westlischen Norddeutschland,* (Neumuenster), 1944.

[9] C.A. Althin, *The Chronology of the Stone Age Settlement of Scania, Sweden. I : The Mesolithic Settlement,* (Bonn-Lund), 1954.

[10] *Op.cit.* [4]

[11] C., Barriere, *Les Civilizations Tardenoisiennes en Europe Occidentale,* (Bordeaux), 1956.

[12] L.A. Cammiade and M.C. Burkitt, 'Fresh Light on the Stone Ages of South India, '*Antiquity*, IV, 1930.

[13] S.A. Semenov, *Prehistoric Technology,* (London), 1964.

[14] *Op.cit.* [4] and D. de Sonneville-Bordes *op.cit.* [6].

Patapadu Revisited : A New Painted Pottery Culture of South-East India

by I. KARTHIKEYA SARMA

I. Topographical Background

The village of Pātapādu [1] (15° 19′ North Latitude and 78° 10′ East Longitude), is in Banganapalle taluq of Kurnool district. It is about five miles west of Banganapalle itself on the Gooty road.

The village is in a low lying area surrounded by thickly grown fields. A river known as Jurreru flows along the southern fringes of the village with slight curves within the fields, in a west-east direction. A small hill range ' Ravvalakondalu ' by name (ending at Bhanumukkala, near Banganapalle), gaurds its southern extent and another minor hillock projecting from the famous ' Yaganti ' hill abounds the north-east of the village. These hillocks are the offshoots of the ' Erramalai ' ranges and are locally famous for limestone and brown-slate, as also for diamond and copper mines. There is a big bungalow of the earstwhile Nawab of Banganapalle towards north of the present village over a hillock close to the right side of the Banganapalle-Gooty road.

II. Previous Exploration

The site was first visited by Robert Bruce Foote [2] in 1883. His observations were remarkable and in fact paved the way for the present search. Leaving apart the various pottery types and wares of the Megalithic and early historical sequences, his discovery of a milk bowl having a broad channel-lip (which Dr. Sankalia [3] compared to the one at Navdatoli and farther west in bronze age Crete, Anatolia and Iran), deserved much keener attention. Besides, in the same locality, i.e., " in the fields to the east of the Cache site ", as Foote informs us, were found several microliths essentially non-geometric in character and some short serrated blades and flakes of agate, chert and lydian stone. The recent explorations of H. D. Sankalia [4] and N. Issac, seem to have yielded only stone tools, black-and-red ware and other remains of the early historical period. In the year 1962 F. R. Allchin [5] also collected from the same site some painted pottery specimens. Allchin's collections seem to be very meagre and nothing is made clear as to their exact location within Patapadu village. Nevertheless, his observations are worth quoting here. " The almost complete absence of grey ware at Patapadu is accompanied by a dominance of red which superficially at least recalls the pottery from Chalcolithic assemblages in Maharashtra [6] and Malwa. This might lead one to infer that the Patapadu site contains intrusive elements which during the upper Neolithic found their way into this region from the Northern Deccan or beyond. *But this question demands further evidence and field work.* Whatever the precise affinities of the pottery, its general position seems to be well established."

This study constituted a good background coupled with the archaic meaning conveyed by the very name of the village, (Pāta = old and Pāḍu = refuse, heap or mound), tempted a fresh exploration of the site and environs. Besides, the author had studied the Madras Govt. Museum collections of Patapadu and allied sites of Bruce Foote [7]. A brief and general

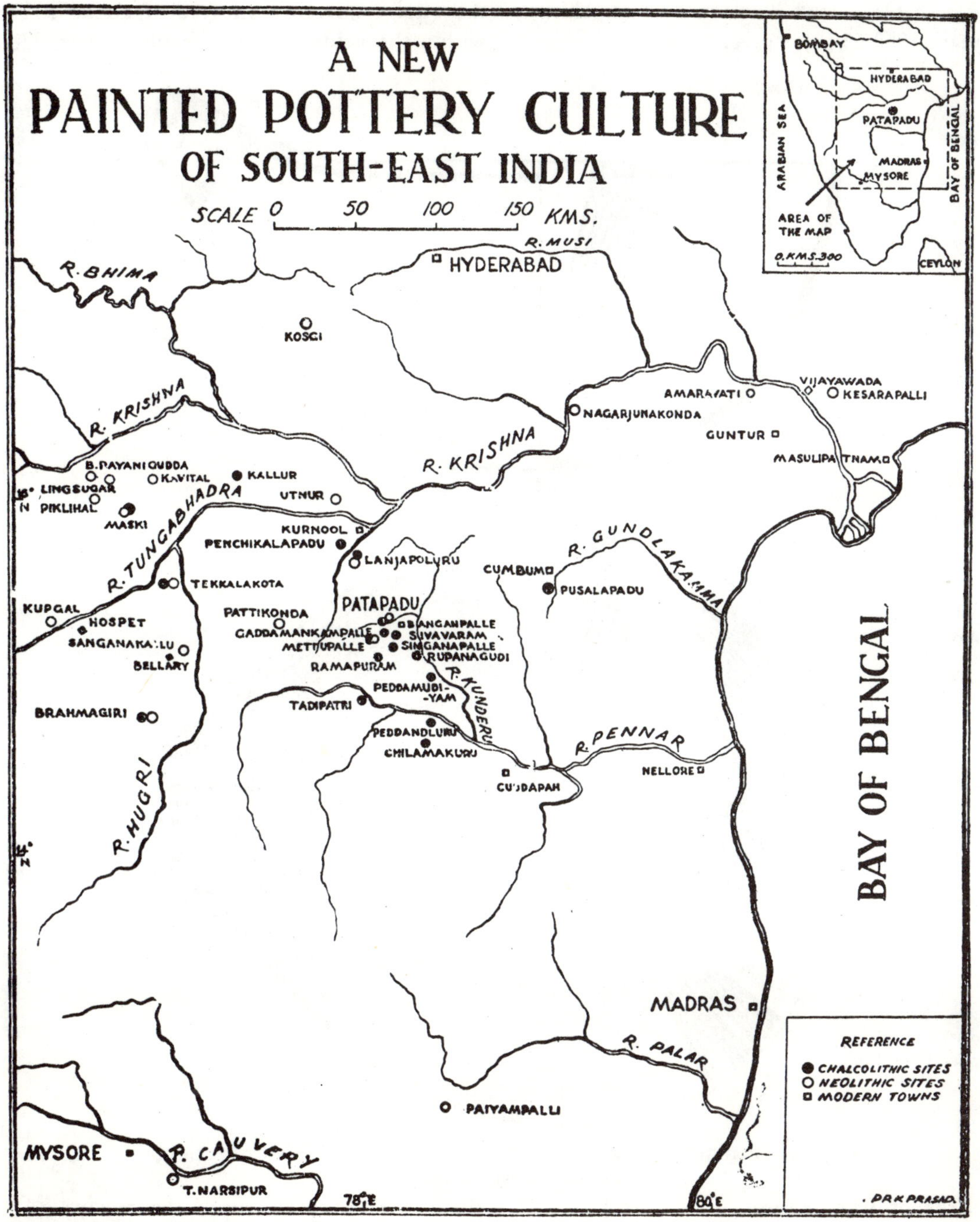
A NEW
PAINTED POTTERY CULTURE
OF SOUTH-EAST INDIA
SCALE 0 50 100 150 KMS.
BOMBAY
HYDERABAD
PATAPADU
MADRAS
MYSORE
ARABIAN SEA
BAY OF BENGAL
AREA OF THE MAP
0 KMS 300
CEYLON
R. MUSI
HYDERABAD
R. BHIMA
KOSGI
R. KRISHNA
AMARAVATI
VIJAYAWADA
KESARAPALLI
NAGARJUNAKONDA
GUNTUR
R. KRISHNA
MASULIPATNAM
B. PAYANI GUDDA
KAVITAL
KALLUR
LINGSUGAR
PIKLIHAL
MASKI
R. TUNGABHADRA
UTNUR
KURNOOL
PENCHIKALAPADU
LANJAPOLURU
R. GUNDLAKAMMA
CUMBUM
PUSALAPADU
TEKKALAKOTA
KUPGAL
HOSPET
SANGANAKALLU
BELLARY
PATTIKONDA
PATAPADU
BANGANPALLE
GADDAMANKAMPALLE
SIVAVARAM
METTUPALLE
SINGANAPALLE
RUPANAGUDI
RAMAPURAM
PEDDAMUDIYAM
R. KUNDERU
BRAHMAGIRI
TADIPATRI
PEDDANDLURU
CHILAMAKURU
R. PENNAR
NELLORE
CUDDAPAH
R. HUGRI
BAY OF BENGAL
MADRAS
R. PALAR
REFERENCE
CHALCOLITHIC SITES
NEOLITHIC SITES
MODERN TOWNS
PAIYAMPALLI
MYSORE
R. CAUVERY
T. NARSIPUR
78° E
80° E
DR K PRASAD

Map 1.

account of the recent discoveries made during the years 1962-63 [8] is given here.

the village covering an area of about 10 acres within the fields, (starting from the left side of

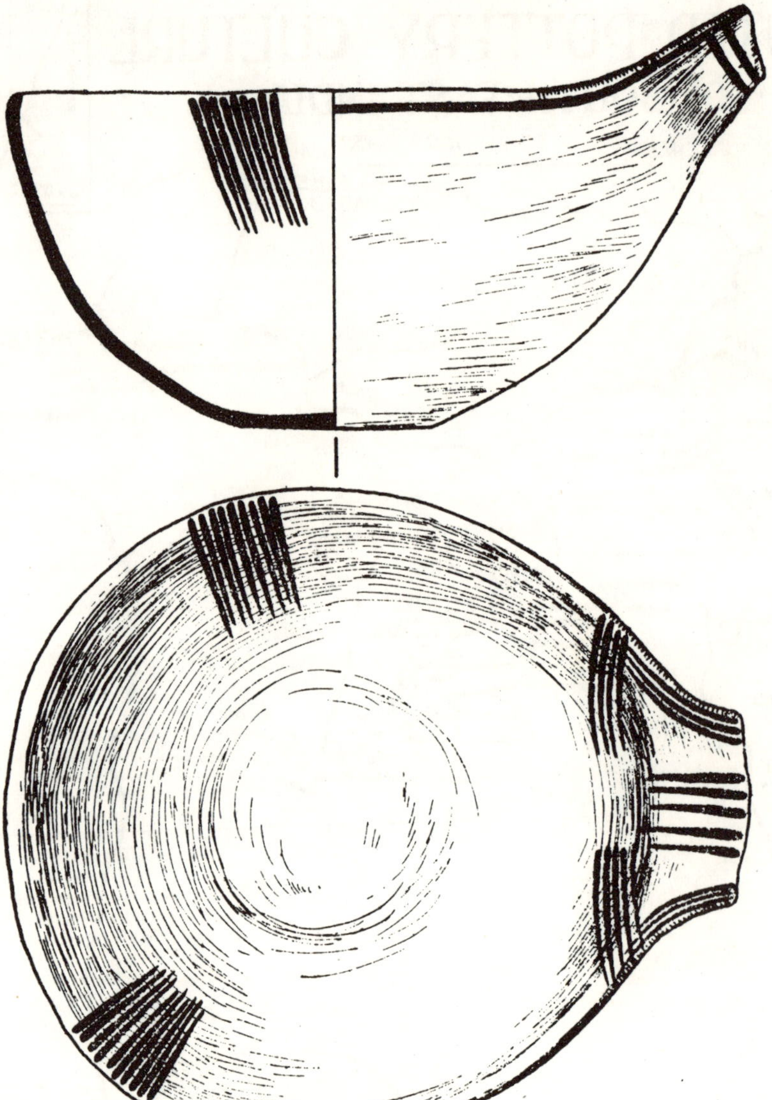

Fig. 1—Channeled Bowl from Patapadu; Bruce Foote's Collection, Madras Govt. Museum (1/3).

III. **Present Exploration**

Two ancient mounds were located within tne village area. (1) On the western side close to the Gooty road and upto the reaches of the Jurreru river on the south), and the other, (2) A mile east of the village covered by the fields and the Banganapalle—Gooty main road, (in between 29/4 and 29/6 mile stones).

1. West Mound

Exploration over and around this extensive mound yielded microliths of late stone age predominantly of jasper in various shades and a few fluted cores of chert and chalcedony. A few potsherds of red slipped, plain coarse red and grey wares pointed out a late historical sequence. A much ruined Śiva temple stood on the eastern edge of this mound where the village ends. This extensive mound is overgrown with vegetation and further search in a dry season may reveal some more finds.

2. East Mound

This is the most promising locality and fits in with the 'Cache' site of Foote [9]. It is about a mile away towards east from the village proper and a few yards south-east of the Nawab's bungalow. The present size of the mound is about 300 metres from east-west and 200 metres north-south and as big as the famous Chalcolithic mounds of Navdatoli. The main road from Banganapalle-Gooty bisects the mound and runs across it covering the apex. The river Jurreru flows past the mound on its south and within the fields. The local P.W.D. often takes resort to this mound for earth required for occasional repair of the road. Thus on either side of the road,it is much distorted by long trenches whereas the northern side is under cultivation, the southern extent left as a waste land owing to its (4 metre), elevation from the surrounding fields. Several rain gulleys yielded large quantities of painted pottery.

The right side extent of the mound is comparatively not much disturbed as the area is under cultivation but a canal cuts along the mound periphery on this side, which is dug by P.W.D. for the Jurreru reservoir.

IV. Results of The Exploration

The various finds encountered from the mound proper and its close vicinity fell under the following groups.

1. Pottery Wares

Though Pusalapadu [10] in Cumbum taluq is credited as the first painted pottery site discovered below the lower Krishna basin, Patapadu stands as the foremost in richness and variety of the pottery forms and fabrics of the Neolithic/ Chalcolithic sequence. The absence of the lower Neolithic pale grey, the meagre quantity of typical burnished grey in the present collections, as well as, in Bruce Foote's and Allchin's [11] the dominance of red ware of coarse to medium fabric with profusely painted surfaces alongwith short blades and ground stone axes etc. gave a fresh impetus for a thorough investigation.

(i) **Painted Black-on-Red Ware**

More than 200 sherds were picked up pertaining to this category. The fabric is from coarse to medium, the former being more common. They are hand made with a few doubtful exceptions for which turn-table may have been employed. The surfaces are dabbered and reveal intensive 'scooping', possibly with the help of a bunch of grass or a piece of cloth. Both the methods have been followed and one could actually distinguish them by seeing the inner surface of the utensil. The 'merge' marks are very distinct in vases and jars, which were made in parts and luted. The thickness of the pot-walls is never uniform. The clay is composed of more grit, sand, and lime specks. It can be said from the majority of the fragments that the ware is subjected to medium firing. The thicker fragments possessed a black or smoky central core region. The slip is generally of dark red colour, (burnished in a few cases), sometimes brown or orange-red, affording a pleasing contrast to the painted black designs. These painted designs extended on the inner surfaces also, particularly in case of cups, bowls and basins.

In this group the unpainted red ware is also present in large quantities having all the characteristic features of the painted counterpart.

Paintings

They are executed in black pigment but rarely in lighter shades. They are most common on the exterior surfaces of the pots either at the neck or shoulder. Certain deep bowls, basins and channeled bowls contained paintings on the inner surfaces also. Both geometrical and naturalistic froms were found on them.

Geometrical Designs

(1) Horizontal bands either singular or in groups, (Pl. VI-18, 19; Pl. VII-10; Fig. 2-2, 9 and 12; Fg. 3-16, 25).

(2) Thick rim bands, (Pl. VI-4, 11, 13; Fig. 2-5, 6, 13).

(3) Close and plain lattice, (Pl. VII-2, 5, 9; Fig. 2-11; Fig. 3—17). Variants of these within horizontal bands and sometimes followed by vertical or diagonal lines (Pl. VII—1, 3, 4).

(4) Simple uprights or oblique lines from horizontal bands, (Pl. VI—3, 4, 14, 15, 20; Pl. VII-11, 21; Fig. 3—18, 19, 33).

(5) Oblique lines on the interiors of bowls and dishes, (Fig. 2—1, 3, 6, 7, 12).

(6) Short vertical strokes with pen-knife edges or buds terminating at the rim interiors of the bowls, small cups and vases with flared rim etc., (Fig. 2—5, 12; Fig. 3—15, 16, 17, 19, 20 and 21).

(7) Groups of thin and short horizontal or vertical lines at the lips interior of the channeled bowls, (Pl. VI—2, 6, 8 and Fig. 1).

(8) Circular bands on the flat interior of the bowl base, (Pl. VII—17).

(9) Cross-hatched segments, (Pl. VII—7), and triangles, (Pl. VII—8).

(10) Miscellaneous designs such as, wavy bands, (Fig. 3—28), irregular horizontals etc. (Fig. 3—29).

Naturalistic Designs

Some of these designs show close affinity to the patterns on the central Indian chalcolithic pottery. Though no complete picture could be made out from the available fragments, it is fairly certain that quite many of them represented animals and birds.

(*i*) Stylized presentations of human figures [13] with loose bunch of wavy hair and solid cone-shaped body, similar to that of Navdatoli. (Pl. VII—14).

(*ii*) Stylized horned animals (Pl. VI—12, 16).

(*iii*) Birds, (Pl. VII—13, 15, 18), snakes or leeches, (Pl. VII—19, 20; Fig. 3—27, 31), creeping insects (Pl. VI—2 and Pl. VII—16), fish (Pl. I—10) etc.

(*iv*) Feather motifs (?) incomplete (Pl. VII—6, 7; Fig. 3—26, 27, 30, 34).

(*v*) Miscellaneous : Triśūla (Pl. VII—12).

Types

Typologically this pottery has nothing new. All the lower Neolithic types of the region are invariably present. Even the decoration, such as applique (finger-press) bands remain the same, (Pl VI-7, 11 ; Pl. VII—1, 3, 5). The difference is therefore mainly in the ware and surface paintings in black. Main types are :

(1) Hemispherical bowls (Fig. 2—6, 8, 10; Fig. 3—16, 20).

(2) Convex sided rimless bowl (Fig. 2—5, 7, 9, 12 : fig. 3-18, 19, 23, 25). Variants (Fig. 2—1, 3) may have a stand also.

(3) Sub-ovaloid or goblet bowls (Fig. 2—2, 4, 6, 14 ; Fig. 3—24).

Instances are also there where the rim tops are either blunted or flattened. The most notable among the pottery types is the channeled bowl,

Fig. 2. *Painted Pottery from Explorations in Cuddapah and Kurnool* 2. 5, 6, 9, 11—13 *from Patapadu*; 1, 3, 7, 10 *from Singanapalle*; 4, 14 *from Kanyathirtham* (1/4). →

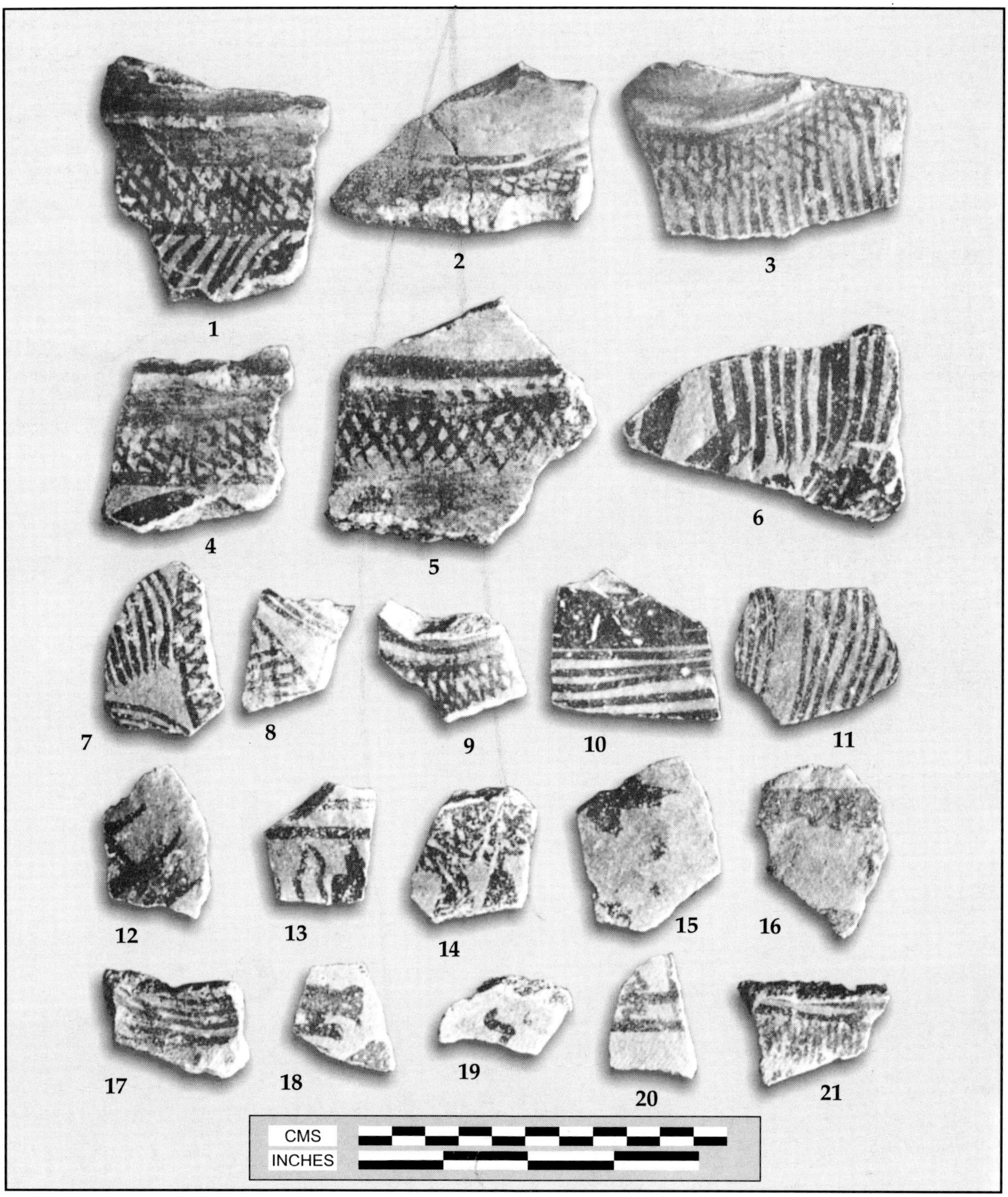

Painted pottery from explorations : design fragments. 2 from Kayathirtham; 7-8 and 11 from Ramapuram; 20 from Sivavaram; rest from Singanapalle.

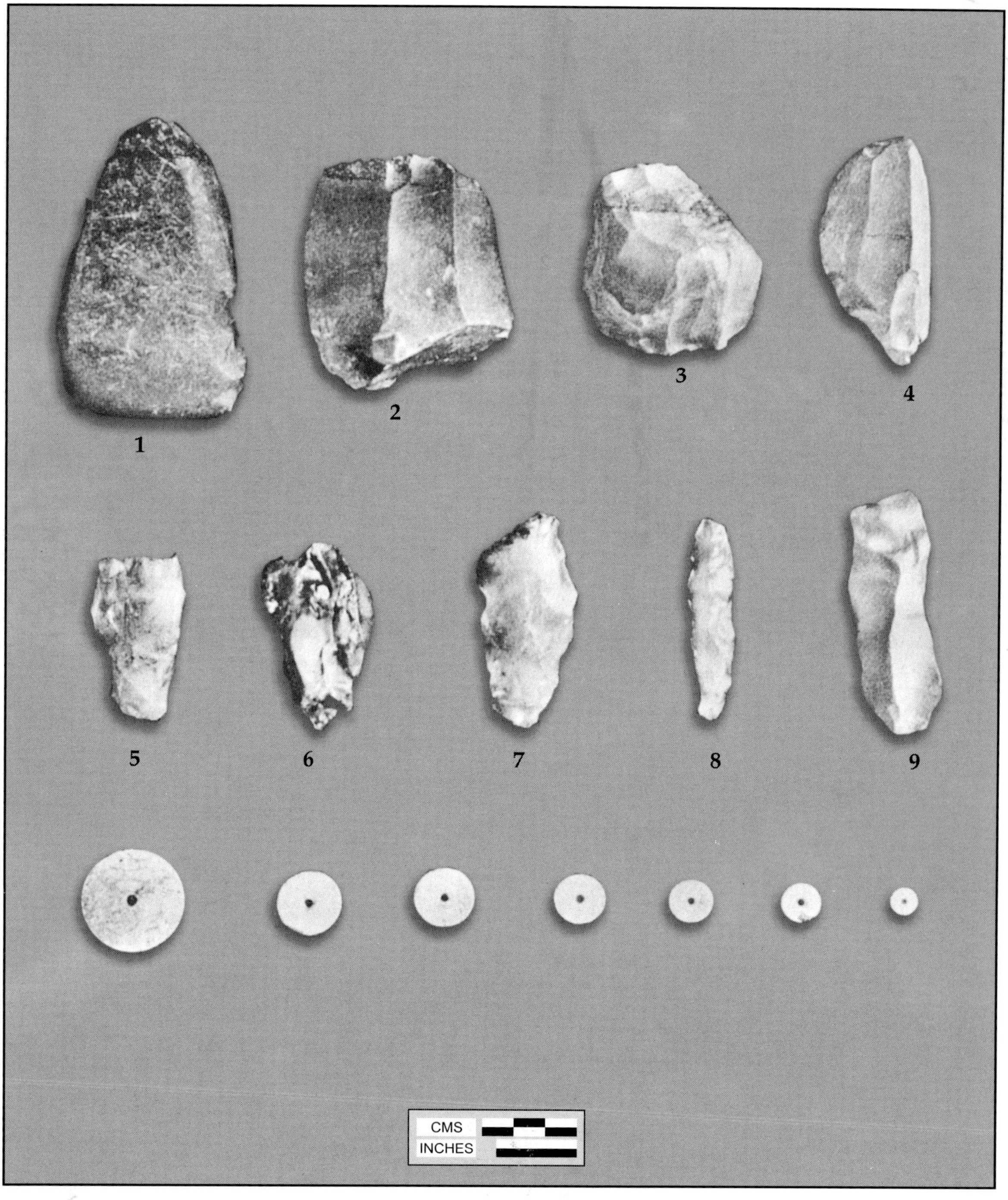

Stone tools etc. 1-4 and 9 from Patapadu; 5-7 from Sivavaram; 8 from Lanjapoluru; last row: steatite discular beads from Ramapuram.

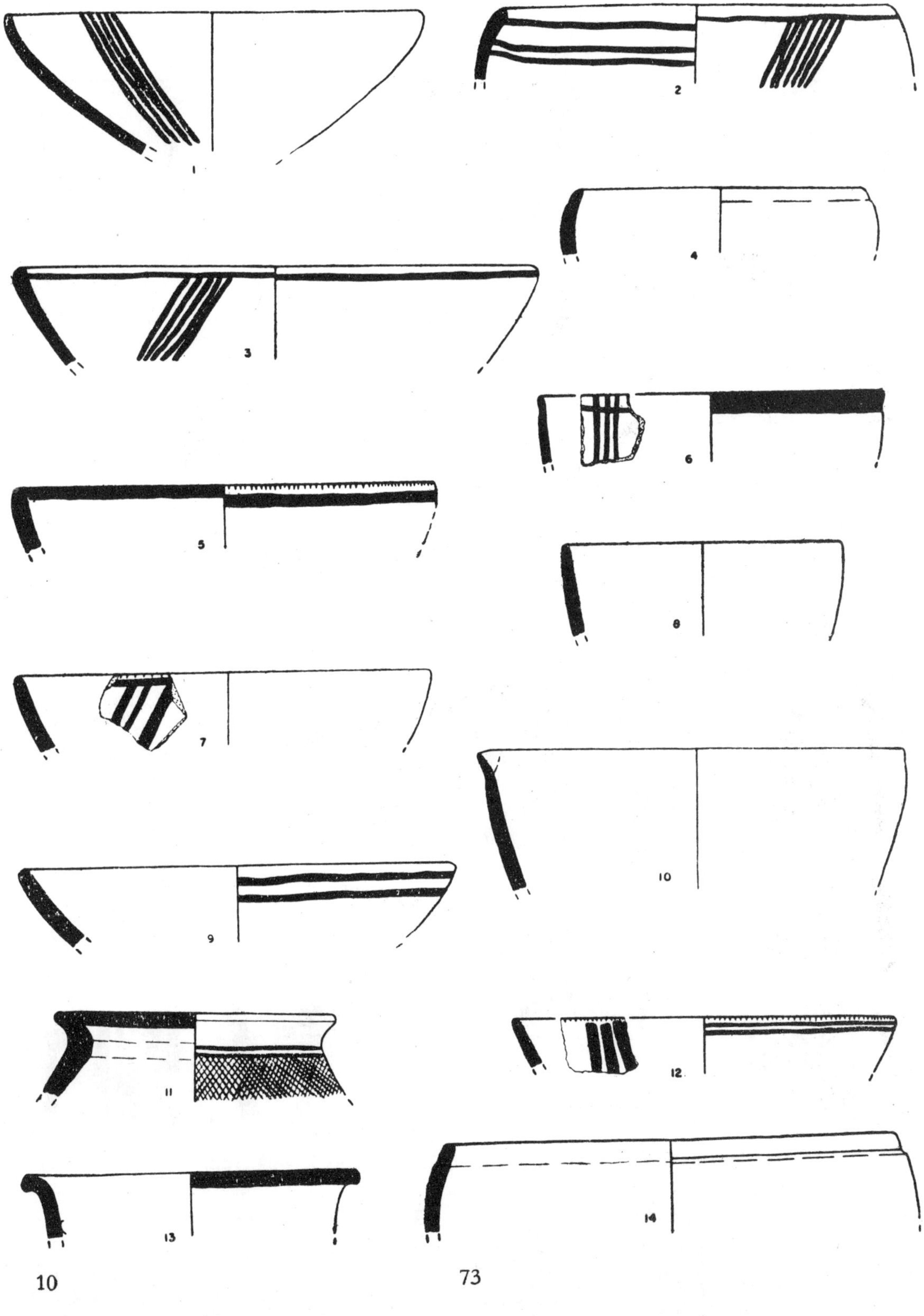

10

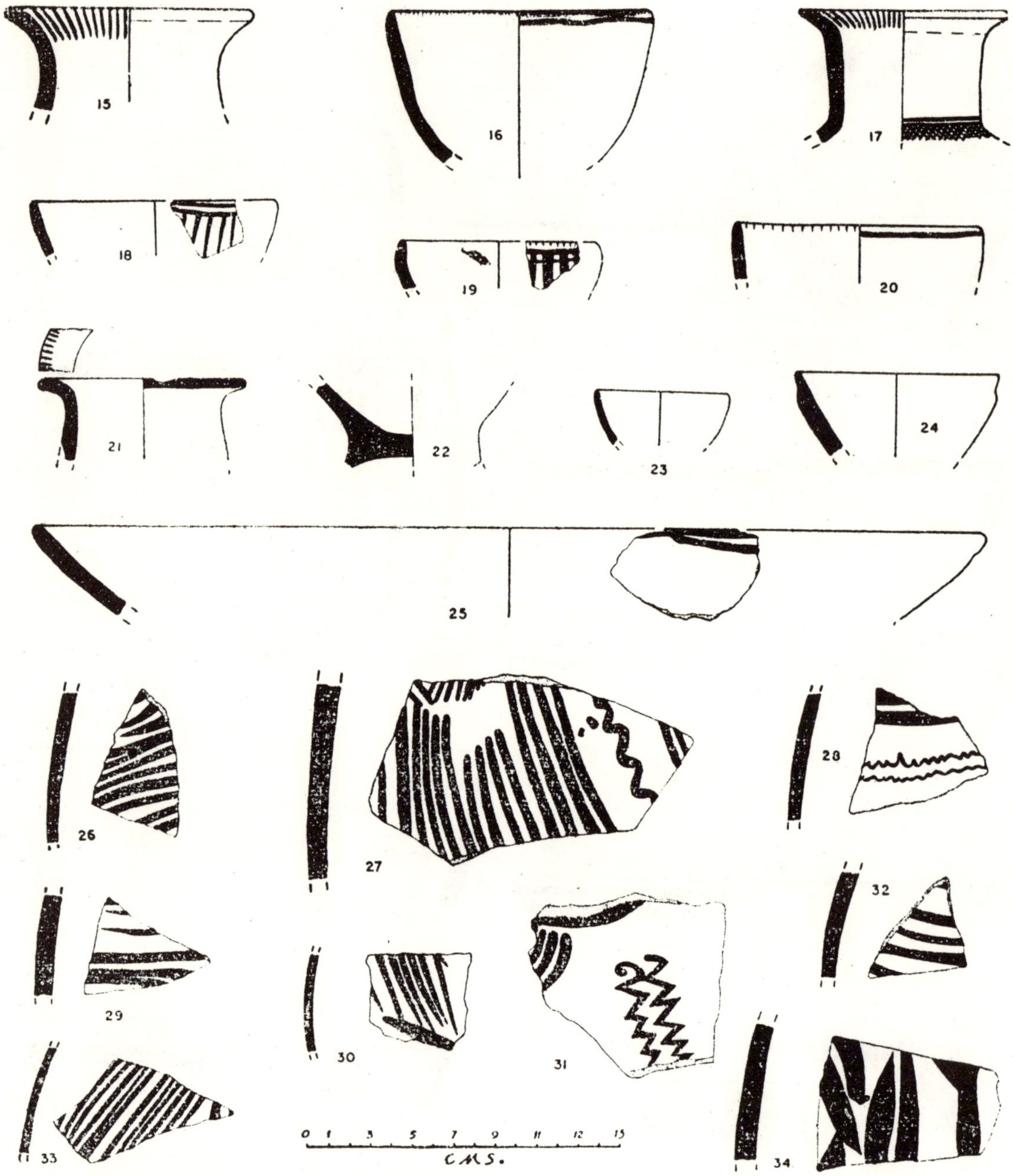

Fig. 3. Painted Pottery from Explorations : 16, 25—30 and 32—34 from Patapadu, Bruce Foote's Collections; Madras Govt. Museum; 17, 19, 21 Author's Collections from Patapadu; 22, 24 and 31 from Kanyathirtham; 15 and 23 from Singanapalle; 18 and 20 from Sivavaram. (1/5).

(Fig. 1) so characteristic of the site that it deserved to be named along with the entire range of pottery as 'Patapadu ware'. Several variants of this form with profusely painted surfaces were encountered (Pl. VI—2, 6, 8, 9, 10 and 15), not only from Patapadu but from a series of sites in this region. Allchin's specimens differ from Navdatoli as " the style of the painting of the Patapadu bowl (Fig. 1) is still without analogues [14]." The fact is that this type [15] is originally found in plain wares from the lower Neolithic levels of Andhra-Karnataka and as this region proved to be the main source it is in the fitness of things that we come across several variants with different painted designs. It may also be noted that the entire painted ware as such is not an isolated development and the author's intensive explorations in Cuddapah and Kurnool districts yielded similar chalcolithic sites containing the very same painted pottery. Among the pots, the globular vessel with constricted neck (Fig. 2—11 and Pl. VI—1,7), vessel with flared mouth(Fig.3—15, 21; Pl. VI—5, 11), pots with narrow straight neck and bulging globular body (Fig. 2-13; Fig. 3-17 and Pl. VI—4) are the most common. In some smaller vases the thin rim is spacious and outcurved (Fig. 3—15, 21), over which series of thin vertical lines resembling the palm leaf pattern are drawn. These are the finest examples, well finished and fired with bright red slip. They can be compared pot by pot to the so called 'Malwa' ware vases of Navdatoli, Nagda and Chandoli. The fragments of tiny cups (Fig. 3—19, 23 and Pl. VII—16, 18, 19, 20) with fine finish and paintings are similar to the stemmed wine cups of Navdatoli but no stem in any case is found. However, a stand of a bowl from Kanyathirtham (Fig. 3—22) and a small loop-handle fragment, of perhaps a cup or bowl, with black bands from Singanapalle (Pl. VI—17), are noteworthy examples.

(ii) Plain Red Ware with Crude Red Slip

This ware stands separated from the black-on-red ware only due to the lack of paintings on its surface. Apart from that, a few other factors favoured a distinction. The potting in general is distinctly poor. The surfaces are not carefully smoothened and rarely the dull red slip is seen, that too peeled off in flakes. The types usually are bowls similar to the painted ones. Large and medium size vases and jars are also in plenty and the base portions contained soot patches.

(iii) Coarse Brown and Crude Black-and-Red Wares

This ware has varied core colours occasionally bringing out blotchy pot surfaces. It has a very coarse fabric, ill burnt and hand made. The main type is represented by vases with thick out-going rim and wide-mouthed pantis with flaring rim. Crude Black-and-Red ware is also present in small quantities. Undoubtedly these sherds indicate the technique of inverted firing by the irregular black tops and totally black interiors. Whether these fragments (a few in number from several excavated Chalcolithic Neolithic sites as well) indicate the knowledge of the potter of this method and resultant effect or they are just freaks—cannot be presently determined.

(iv) Megalithic Black-and-Red ware

This mound has also yielded a few Megalithic and early historical pottery. Bruce Foote collected several pottery fragments and iron objects of this sequence. No evidence of Megalithic burials was to be seen closer or round about the site but an extensive Megalithic burial site was located one mile west of Patapadu close to the village Mirapuram.

The fragments under this group possessed the characteristic fine fabric and finish. A convex sided bowl with flat round base, and straight sided bowl with a sagger base stand as good examples.

(v) Plain Red Slipped Ware

There are two fabrics in this ware, coarse and medium. The former is represented by thick walled vases and the latter by bowls and medium size vases etc. having a bright red slipped exterior. A thick outcurved rim fragment of a jar has lime coating on the exterior. It may well belong to the Chalcolithic sequence.

2. Stone Implements

Associated with the above pottery wares, the stone tools belonged to two known groups.

(*i*) *Microlithic tools* :—Flakes, cores and tools belonging to the two categories were found. The material used is predominantly jasper with various shades, also chert, chalcedony and quartz. Among them fluted cores (Pl. VIII—2, 4) alone numbered twenty, by virtue of which we can say that the site must have been a factory site producing fine short blades. Typologically two tool groups were found. Flake tools of purely Neolithic association, consisted of scrapers and blades. Short blade industry along with fluted cores as noted above.

Though not from this very site a crested guiding ridge blade and cores of chalcedony (PL. VIII nos. 5, 8), along with the painted pottery noted earlier. Bruce Foote also found, " a large and very interesting series of flakes and scrapers, also strike-a-lights. Pygmy flakes and small serrated and biserrated flakes deserve close attention as also does the large series of small cores of agate, chert and lydian stone numbered from 2475 to 2604. Many are objects of great beauty and colour ". All these finds pertain to Cache site, viz., the eastern mound. Not only Patapadu but also the other explored sites shown in Map-I have yielded large number of short blades and fluted cores.

(*ii*) *Neolithic tools* : A single example of a fine Neolithic celt out of diorite was obtained, (PL. VIII no. 1). It is triangular in shape with flat rectangular central cross-section and pointed butt-end and pertained to the so-called ' Eastern type '. Foote collected a similar thin celt and calls it ' childs' toy ', (no. 2364).

V. Further Explorations in Andhra : A New Painted Pottery Culture of South-East India

Leaving aside the Megalithic and later pottery from the mounds the rest of the collections, including the painted pottery, microlithic tools, Neolithic ground stone axes, etc. belonged to an earlier complex and quite significantly Chalcolithic in character. This painted pottery seems to possess close affinities to the Malwa ware group and not to the later Deccan Chalcolithic, (Nevasa-Jorwe), typologically as well as by fabric and surface treatment. The painted designs are also closer to the Malwa wares of Navdatoli, Eran and Nagda in general. The surprising fact is that neither the spouted vases of Jorwe-Nevasa group nor those characteristic carinated bowls could be seen from this collection of painted pottery which is quite representative. For that matter Patapadu is not a solitary example. More than half a dozen similar mounds have now been discovered in the Banganapalle taluq itself and a few more from Giddalur and Kurnool taluqs, as a result of the present explorations. There is no doubt in the fact that future planned explorations may still yield many more sites of a similar sequence. The author's chance visit to the historically famous ancient mounds at Chilamakuru, Peddamudiyam and Peddandluru, (also known as Kanyathirtham), all in Cuddapah district of Andhra Pradesh, also promised the existence of a similar sequence as that of Patapadu [16].

The geographical distribution of these painted pottery sites, (as shown in the Map-1), clearly presupposes a selection on the part of the Neolithic/Chalcolithic communities for their grounds of habitation. Whereas the thickly vegetated castellated hills and rocks and the surrounding fertile valleys were preferred by the lower Neolithic, these painted pottery communities seem to have no doubt continued in older habitations to some extent, but soon moved upto the plainer hills commanding cultivable tracts round their slopes and much less vegetated. Thus we do find sites like Pusalapadu, Mettupalle, (so also Brahmagiri, Sanganakallu, Tekkalakota, Hallur and Piklihal), close to the granatoid hills wherein we get the burnished grey, pale-grey and other lower Neolithic wares along with the black painted ware, but the profusely rich painted pottery sites like Singanapalle, Sivavaram, Ramapuram and Patapadu are situated in plainer hill regions, shooting out from Erramalais. Here the lower Neolithic wares are very meagre and in some places almost absent. Of utmost significance is the occurrence of a few white or cream slipped sherds from the last mentioned sites in particular, whose significance is to be viewed along with the Navdatoli Chalcolithic phase-I, Ahar period-Ia and Ib and Gilund early sequence [17]. In this regard, the meagre evidence of more southerly T. Narsipur [18] is no less important. At Utnur within the lower Neolithic itself cream slipped grey ware sherds [19] among A-2 ware, pointed out to the earliest dating of the ware in this region. At Pusalapadu in Cumbum taluq the painted pottery is comparatively less but the steatite discular beads are too many in number promising the existence of a factory site. Indeed, the very name of the village is striking i. e. Pūsalu meaning beads, and Pāḍu meaning refuse heap or mound of antiquity. At this particular site there are indications for a sequence right from lower Neolithic to Chalcolithic and Megalithic. A similar name is prevalent at Ramapuram in Banganapalle taluq where the Chalcolithic mound is called as 'Banḍipūsala chenu' literally meaning 'a field of wheel shaped beads, (PL. VIII, last row). This site also promised a sequence starting from Neolithic to the painted pottery Chalcolithic and early historical containing the well dated Russet-coated white painted ware.

The most notable and profuse form in all these sites, as also at Patapadu, is the lipped or channeled bowl. Several variants were collected and the channeled lip is mainly of three kinds. (*i*) Short 'V' shaped lip like wick-channel at the featureless rim of the deep bowl or basin, (fig. 2, no. 10), (*ii*) Broadened short channel, (PL. VI, no. 10), (*iii*) Long channeled lips, (PL. VI, nos. 6, 8, 9) the channel being deeper with externally beaded rim feature also in some cases. (PL. VI. nos. 2, 15). The last variety is mostly present in Central Indian Chalcolithic sites.

They bear profusely painted surfaces internally and as well as externally and the designs are monotonus lines, veritcal or horizontal lines, sometimes mixed in groups and drawn interiorly terminating near the channel as in the case of the Patapadu bowl. (fig. 1). The most important factor in all these sites, may it be repeated once again, is the total absence of the later typical 'Nevasa-Jorwe' ware, by virtue of which these sites deserved to be chronologically placed at par with the early phases of Navdatoli, Nagda, and Eran Chalcolithic periods, if not still earlier.

VI. Possible Origins of the Painted Pottery and its Northerly Spread

Here again the distribution pattern of these painted pottery sites posed certain problems. Though coarse red, red slipped and brown plainer wares are present [20] in lower Neolithic itself to a meagre extent, they never dominated the field unlike the typical pale grey, burnished grey and buff wares. Southwards and westwards of these explored sites the evidence from Paiyampalli, T. Narsipur and Tekkalakota-Hallur respectively, did not contain any analogues painted pottery from the digs but plain red ware is present in considerable numbers with all the other characteristic Neolithic traits. This shows that the painted pottery sites of Cuddapah and Kurnool emerged as a result of inter-regional development due to some external stimuli. That such a development did not take place necessarily, in every region and site uniformly, in a particular period is amply attested. It may also be that such a change did not very much cater the taste of several other Neolithic villages closeby. The paucity of this painted ware in most of the excavated Neolithic sites of Andhra-Karnataka can be attributed to any of the above factors. In addition, there seems to be a local specialization of industries, like pottery making, beads etc., based on close availability of raw material, as a result of which a particular Neolithic village specialized in plain or painted pottery and supplied them to the others the desired variety, perhaps on barter. All these factors may have to be taken into account for a comprehensive study of the development of the Neolithic culture. However, it may be noted that there existed already a tradition of painting right from lower Neolithic, though simplest and most primitive as it may seem to be, in the form of ocherous red bands over the rims of the burnished grey ware bowls, lids, and thick jars, etc.

Besides this, at Brahmagiri [21] a wheel made (?) painted pottery and an incised ware was found in very limited quantities from the lowest levels of the stone-axe culture, designated as period-IA. At Sanganakallu also a similar painted pottery was encountered [22]. M. H. krishna in his earlier excavations at Brahmagiri [23] found an analogous painted pottery (also at Maski), and pointed out its similarity to some Indus valley pottery. Wheeler [24] readily discarded the view of Krishna but did not explain what this painted pottery is and where does it fit in within a Neolithic culture. Brahmagiri excavation is no doubt very limited and so also of Sanganakallu. But even the recently excavated [25] Sanganakallu (1965), or Hallur did not give any new data in this regard. It must be said with a caution as these digs are also of a very limited nature.

In the earliest levels of Maski period-I, mostly comprising of pits dug into the natural soil, Thapar found a painted pottery, thin in section, coarse in texture and apparently wheel made and compares it to the Brahmagiri-IA, Sanganakallu-II2 and Kallur painted examples. Further more he states " Indulging for a moment in speculation, one is tempted to feel that the painted pottery of Brahmagiri-IA equated to that of Maski-I, although not remarkably similar to Indus valley, as asserted by M. H. Krishna, may, nevertheless show vague affinities with the Harappan cultures through some unidentified stages " [26]. Of great significance is the fact that even the plain pottery at Maski-I is wheel made, though the types and wares are closer to all the above sites of Andhra-Karnataka. Thus Maski evidenced the sudden introduction of wheel from perhaps the Harappan source, as supported by long ribbon blades, the famous surface find of a cylinder seal etc. Maski Neolithic should be placed to a still early date than what is now conjectured and it would be of great interest if a C-14 date is obtained. Again the absence of Patapadu ware at the sites like Tekkalakota and Hallur, now firmly dated to 1710 B.C. and 1675 B.C. respectively would indicate the terminus *post quem* of this ware.

If so, can we safely attribute the emergence of black painted designing and the switch over to red slipped wares by a group of early Neolithians due to the Harappan contact [27] ? There is no other higher contemporaneous culture existing during this stage of southern Neolithic [28].

VII. Contact and Correlations

We have seen that the types like the spouted vases and bowls, channeled bowls, vases with flaring mouth, deep convex bowls etc. in dull grey, burnished grey, and coarse brown and red wares occur right from the lower Neolithic of Andhra-Karnataka. All these plainer types are typically represented in these explored sites under review and significantly enough both are hand made. Thus there is a basic unity in this painted pottery group with the elderly, precedent lower Neolithic of the same region. But when these types, found to dominate in a different and distant [29] region as that of central India or

Dr. S. B. Deo who has very kindly examined this material is also of the firm opinion that *Nevasa-Jorwe* ware is totally absent in it.

[7] A recent study of the collections of Bruce Foote in the Madras Govt. Museum revealed that the pottery sherds bearing nos. 2605/22 onwards upto 2605/58 pertained to the famous Patapadu east *Cache* site and all of them were painted black-on-red ware sherds. Some selected shapes and design fragments are reproduced here with the kind courtesy of the Director, Madras Govt. Museum. The author is extremely grateful to Dr. S.T. Satya—Murthy, Director and to Sarvashri Devasahayam and Srinivasadesikan, Curators, for their generous help.

[8] *IAR* 1963-64 (cyclostyled copy). These explorations were conducted by the author as an official of the Archaeological Survey of India, under the general guidance of late Shri M. Venkataramayya, Superintendent, S.E. Circle of the Survey. The author is deeply beholden to him and to the Director General of Archaeology in India for their very genrous help at all the stages and in particular to the latter for kindly permitting him to publish this work outside.

[9] Foote calls this site as a *Cache,* or hiding place "due to peculiar make in which the vessels and other objects occured here, it appears to me that the only reasonable way to account for the presence of such a qunatity of what must have been a valuable property to its owners in such a limited space is to regard the find as Cache." *IPPA.* CH. XVI.

[10] I. K. Sarma, 'Painted pottery from Pusalapadu, Andhra Pradesh : And Further Explorations in Cuddapah and Kurnool districts', *India* Sept. 1967, 75-94, figs. 1-2. Pls. I-II.

[11] *Op. Cit.,* [5], 224.

[12] Of significance are some of the applied ring based bowl fragments in this ware. They could be typologically compared to types 66, 67 and 69 of Piklihal lower Neolithic A3 burnished ware. cf. F. R. Allchin, *Piklihal Excavations,* 1961, 56, Pl. 35. Similar ones but painted in black occured at the chalcolithic mounds of Singanapalle and Sivavaram in Banganapalle taluq itself. The painted base fragments of bowls from Chandoli in Malwa ware, (T. XIII and fig. 34), are very much the same. Also see the plainer ones from Maski period-I (T. 33-34) and Sanganakallu (PL. VIII. xiii).

[13] H. D. Sankalia, 'New light on the Indo-Iranian or Western Asiatic relations between 1700-1200 B.C.', *Artibus Asiae* : *XXVI* 3/4 1964,, 312-331. fig. 3. Also see J.S. Nigam, 'Human motifs on the Chalcolithic Black-on-Red ware', *Bharati,* 1962, 1-10. PL. I, compare nos. 1, 2, 12 & 13. Dr. Motichandra has drawn our attention in particular to the grotesque human figure of Navdatoli and compared it to similar representations on the pottery of Cemetry-H at Harappa. He states that "the figure may represent *Rudra.* If that is so the barbed spear held by him should stand for the thunderbolt held in his arm (*Vajrabaho, RV,* II, 33.3). His lightening shaft, *Vidyut* discharged from the sky traverses the earth. (*RV.* VII, 46.3). cf. Motichandra, 'Nidhiśringa. (Cornucopia) : A study in symbolism', *Bulletin Prince of Walse Museum,* 9, 1964-66, 20-21. It may be noted here that we have a *trisula* symbol also in the present collection. PL. II, no. 12.

[14] *Op. Cit.,* [5], 222. fig. 1-nos. 1, 2.

[15] The channeled bowl or vase is known as *Gokarna* (as it resembles the ear of a cow), and is still very much in use in Andhra-Karnataka in metal. This type is entirely different from the spouted vases and bowls, *Kamandal* or or *Kamandalu.* Functionally and typologically both differ very much. In addition the former type has an earlier chronological horizon than the latter, though both emerged from the Neolithic culture, initially in plainer wares as the evidence from various Andhra-Karnataka sites revealed. *Op. cit.* [10], 87. 30 fn. Quite significantly indeed, not a single spouted jar, vase or bowl nor those characteristic carinated bowls of Jorwe-Nevasa type were found in the painted pottery sites under review. This conspicuous absence gives an added meaning for such a typological distinction between the two. While extra-Indian comparisons paving the way for a firmer identification would be welcomed, one should not ignore to classify first and foremost the internal evidence on a sound chronological framework. Sites like Patapadu, Pusalapadu and Singanapalle have yielded profusely painted and unpainted channeled bowls. They exhibit an evolution from the preceding lower Neolithic of the region itself and certainly earlier to the Malwa ware sites. Some scholars are still prone to think of the West-Asiatic origin. (cf. *Indian Prehistory—* 1964, 162-163; 169-173). The Iranian parallels are several centuries later to our southern Neolithic examples. (cf. R. E. M. Wheeler, '*Civilizations of Indus Valley and Beyond*', 1966, 91-92). Even if we consider these distinct types as imports into the Indian *Neolithic,* why should we seek the source from West alone ? Dr. Subba Rao has rightly cautioned us that "we have not adequately looked for the eastern influences which our anthropologists and linguists point out". (cf. B. Subba Rao, 'Asia and India : etc.' *J.M.S.U.* (Baroda) 1962, *XI. no.* 1, 10-13). In this context the Neolithic culture of Phillippines and Formosa is exremely relevant. Subba Rao says that the Harappan dish-on-stand has no satisfactory source in Western Asia. The Neolithic culture of Huangho and Sinkiang have a grey ware dish-on-stand of the Harappan type with hallow stem as well as the corrugated one. This becomes very significant when viewed with the anthropological data of Mangoloid elements in the skeletal remains of Mohenjodaro and Harappa.

In the light of the discovery of so many painted pottery sites in the south-eastern Andhra (though not quite closer to the coast), an early cutlure contact from the South-East Asian Neolithic sites cannot be ruled out. This presupposes a linkage with the Islands of the Indian ocean during 1700-2000 B.C.

[16] Bruce Foote's collections in Madras Museum contained a few sherds of the same painted pottery from *Tadpatri* also. This shows the extent of the ware still southwards. Recently Shri B. Raja Rao of the South-Eastern circle of the Survey, found a site named *Rupanagudi* near Koilkuntla taluq of Kurnool district, which has again yielded large quantities of painted pottery. cf. *IAR* 1964-65, 6 (cyclostyled copy).

[17] H. D. Sankalia, *Prehistory and Protohistory in India and Pakistan* (Bombay) 1962, 196. These cream slipped sherds were represented as at Chandoli by fragments of high necked pots with encircling horizontal bands and globular pots etc. and not of that fine make as at Navadatoli. Also see, S. B. Deo and Z. D. Ansari, *Chalcolithic Chandoli,* 1965, 53. T. XXIII and T. XXIV. fig. 37.

[18] *IAR* 1961-62, 35-36.

[19] F. R. Allchin, *Utnur Excavations* 1961, 23 and 35.. C-14 dating for the lower Neolithic is 4250-115, T. F. cf. *Current Science, 33, no.* 9, May 1964, 219-292.

[20] For that matter the coarse red and brown wares were present at Sanganakallu (cf. B. Subba Raoo, *Stone Age Cultures of Bellary* 1948, 10), at Maski a pinkish dull red ware (cf. *Ancient India,* no 13, 40-47), and at Nagarjunakonda pale red ware in Lower Neolithic itself (cf. *Ancient India,* no. 14, 105). A coarse brown ware and thick gritty red ware was abundantly found at Paiyampalli in district North-Arcot (Madras), and Hallur district Dharwar (Mysore), from an early Neolithic levels wherein blade industry was also found. That this ware has become more prominent in the upper Neolithic as witnessed at Tekkla-kota-II and at Chandoli. (cf. Deo and Ansari, *Ibid,* 52, 103, 104), and developed paintings.

[21] R. E. M. Wheeler, 'Brahmagiri and Chandravalli 1947 : Megalithic and other cultures in Mysore state', *Ancient India No.* 4, 1947-48, 180-310. These sherds seem to be turn table made. Allchin says that this black-painted ware with designs applied over a red or brown ochre dressing of the burnished A-3 ware was also found at Brahmagiri-IA, Sanganakallu-II-1, and Maski pits in the very lowest levels. The prefiring black purple painted designs such as horizontal bands, cross-hatched triangles, etc. over the shoulder fragments of necked jars (similar to Patapadu), in A-3 ware of Piklihal lower Neolithic seem to indicate the origin of this painted ware.

[22] S. Subba Rao, *Stone Age Cultures of Bellary,* (Poona) 1948.

[23] *Mysore Archaeological Department. Annual Report for* 1940. (1941) and *ibid.* 1942 (Mysore) 1943, 1000f. For the account of the excavations conducted at Maski in 1935-37 see *Annual Report of the Archaeological Department, H. E. H. The Nizam's Dominions* 1935-36 and 1936-37, (Calcutta) 1939, 19-31 and 14-16.

[24] *Ancient India no.*4, ibid, 222n.

[25] H. D. Sankalia, 'Stone Age hill dwellers of South-India' *Indica, I no.* 2 Sept 1964, 129-140 and M. S. Nagaraja Rao, 'A New evidence for Neolithic life in India : Excavations in the Southern Deccan' *Archaeology* 20 *no.* 1. Jan 1967, 28-35. From the recent evidences we can say that the Neolithic habitations in Karnataka which started round about 1700 B.C. remained in the same cultural level without any drastic change until the introduction of iron in 1000 B.C.

[26] B. K. Thapar, 'Maski-1954' *Ancient India No.* 13, 1957, 24,38. fig. 9. Dr. S. B. Deo says that this radical change of profusely painting the pot surfaces and the high preference for red slipped wares, (technologically speaking), despite the fact that the types remaining the same, would mean certainly a very firm external stimulus that changed the fashions even in such daily needed pottery utensils.

[27] M. S. Nagaraja Rao and K. C. Malhotra, *Stone Age Hill dwellers of Tekkalakota* (Poona) 1965, 75-76. PL. X. The occurence of highly sophisticated copper objects from the earliest levels of Tekkalakota (phase-I 1675 B.C.), and slightly later in Hallur Neolithic phase-II postulates an established contact with the decadent Harappan or early stages of metal age Ahar culture group of sites. This contact may have been either in the form of obtaining the finished tools as such of a local manufacture by the Harappan or Aharian experts, who sought a rich source for this metal, (along with metal), in Andhra-Karnataka. Further the gold ornaments from the lowest levels of TKT-I, go to proove such a thesis. Allchin postulates the local extraction of metal on a small scale on the surface during the Neolithic period on the evidence of the settlements clustered around Maski, Hutti and Kolar gold fields. A large number of huge crushing and rubbing stones were found by Munn. (cf. F. R. Allchin, 'Upon the Antiquity and Methods of Gold Mining in Ancient India', *Journal of the Economic and Social History of the Orient* 1962, *V. part.* 2, 195-211). In the Bellary district itself gold working is evidenced in the hills near Chitageri south Bellary. Gold coils preferably ornaments were found in phase-III of Daimabad Chalcolithic, (*IAR*1958-59,18), which is undoubtedly later to Tekkalakota. However at Eran (*IAR* 1961-62, 25. PL. XLB), within the Chalcolithic period-I, a signet ring and a thin gold piece were obtained. We cannot be certain as to its earlier date to Tekkalakota examples. So also the steatite beads occuring at TKT-I and other sites starting from late levels of lower Neolithic and Allchin has correctly pointed out to their source from Harappan cultures. (cf. *Piklihal Excavations* 1961, 111). S. R. Rao on the basis of the gold ornaments

obtained from Lothal, a Harappan site in Saurashtra, informs that the analysis of the gold pendants revealed a high percentage of silver and the absence of copper and lead and points out that the gold came from the mines of Hutti and Kolar in South-India. Raw steatite required by the lapidaries and seal engravers at Lothal may have come from Southern Neolithic sites. Such contacts may have resulted in bringing the painted tradition on the vases and sites having steatite bead factories like Pusalapadu and Ramapuram. The author is grateful to Shri S. R. Rao for this information.

[28] The earlier views of B. B. Lal (*Ancient India*, No. 9, P. 102, 2n), and Subba Rao (*Personality of India* 1958, 35), about the possible advent of this painted ware from north as stray intrusions no more holds good in the light of the present discoveries.

[29] Even the plainer Neolithic wares such as coarse grey, thick burnished grey with occasionally post-firing red ochrous paint on the rims, mouth etc. are reported from the earliest phases of the Western and Central Indian Chalcolithic starting from Daimabad, Bahal, Prakash to Navdatoli, Nagda, Eran, Gilund etc. and upto Rangpur in Saurashtra. This shows that either the Neolithic of South reached northwards as a substratum of these chalcolithic cultures or a closely similar Neolithic culture should have been existing in the foot hills of Vindhyas as also supposed by Dr. Subba Rao. (Asia and India, 7).

[30] Spouted vases were found at Navdatoli from Phase-III of the chalcolithic period, from the renewed digs. Information kindly supplied by Dr. S. B. Deo.

[31] Yet Dr. Sankalia says that the 'Jorwe-Nevasa' culture gave "its highly individualistic pottery to the southern brothers, which had given in turn the burial practices, ground stone axes etc." It is becoming abundantly clear that the so termed 'Jorwe-Nevasa' culture is nothing but a regional evolution from the very southern Neolithic, confined to the Maharashtra region. That this typical Jorwe-Nevasa ware did not reach farther south is again of interest. cf. H. D. Sankalia, 'Cultural Divisions of India' *Science Today*. Aug. 67, 13 and 16.

[32] But even here we cannot forget the striking similarity between the 13 dancing figurines with linked hands from Tekkalakota and those on the Navdatoli potsherds. (cf. Nagaraja Rao and Malhotra, *Op. cit.* 1965, 84, 98. fig. 31a compare '*Excavations at Navdatoli*' 1953 fig. 42). And again the terracotta bulls (also blade industry), of the lower Neolithic having a close affinity with the terracotta bulls of Nagda (*IAR* 1955-56, 12-19), and to some of the earliest rock bruised ones from Piklihal (cf. *Piklihal Excavations*, 84), would all go to prove that the origin of these designs lies within the Neolithic sites. Instead Dr. Sankalia attempted to compare with the west-Asiatic painted dancers. (cf. *Antiquity*, *XXIX* 1955, 30. fig. 2).

[33] It has been convincingly demonstrated by S. R. Rao at Rangpur how the pedestalled bowls (or wine cups), are evolved from the Harappan bowls and dishes-on-stand in three stages. (*Ancient India No.* 18-19, 63. fig. 17). At Ahar too the intermediate stages of the large bowls with stand have been found. It is therefore not necessary, as Rao points out (*Indian Prehistory*—1964, 171), to look to any foreign influence to understand the emergence of the wine cup. Similarly, the spouted vases and channeled bowls, as pointed out earlier have certainly emerged out of the Neolithic cultures firstly in plainer wares and subsequently in painted black-on-red wares also.

[34] Wheeler even tried to show how the 'Saurashtrian Indus' itself has "less affinity to Indus fashions than to some of those of the Central Indian chalcolithic (Malwa and Narmada region)". He further states that "there is an inter-regional linkage between Saurashtrian Indus and Central India" and brings forth the long chert blades of Maski, the flat copper axes of Navdatoli and Jorwe and the availability of rice in Lothal phase—A (1700 B.C.), and at Navdatoli phases—II and III of the chalcolithic. Finally he points out the Black-and-Red ware of Saurashtrian Indus variegated by the inverted firing coming into central Indian chalcolithic through Ahar-Gilund sites. cf. Wheeler, *Op. cit.* 1966, 87-90.

[35] H. D. Sankalia, 'Archaeology in India during 1965' *Indica, Vol.* 3 *no.* 2 Sept. 1966, 91. At the chalcolithic site of Kayatha, Ujjain district Shri Wakankar obtained a sturdy Harappan like painted pottery below the Malwa and Ahar fabrics.

[36] *Ibid.*, Ground stone axes have again been found in the chalcolithic deposits at Eran and Dr. Sankalia thinks of their possible source from Banda district of U.P.

[37] S. B. Deo and Z. D. Ansari, Ibid., 1965, 4, 17, 24-25, 47, 106, 138-142.

[38] *IAR* 1954-55, PL. XXB, P. 13.

[39] *IAR* 1958-59, 16-18. fig. 7, Pl. XXXII-A, B.

[40] H. D. Sankalia, 'Spouted vessels' *Antiquity*, *XXIX* 1955, 112-115. Also see *IAR* 1957-58, 30-33. figs. 17-18. and *IAR* 1958-59, 30-31.

[41] *IAR* 1960-61, 17-18. *IAR* 1961-62, 24-25, Pl. XLI-A and *IAR* 1962-63, 11.

[42] *IAR* 1955-56, 11-19. That shows that Nagda-I ended before phase-Ic of Ahar (1550-110 B.C.), and earlier to Navdatoli phase-III dated to 1600 B.C.

[43] Dr. Sankalia pleads that "however the quest might be left open for an independent and indigenous origin for both, though there is no doubt that the south received the chalcolithic elements in its culture from north. Cf. Sankalia, Bombay, 1962, 273.

[44] Bruce Foote held this view in 1887, quite justifiably indeed to his times. But even now some archaeologists still think so. cf. George Dales, F. 'Recent trends in the Pre and Protohistoric Archaeology of South Asia' *Proceedings of the American philosophical Society*. 110. *no.* 2, April 1966, 133.

Acknowledgements

The author is extremely grateful to Shri S. R. Rao, Superintending Archaeologist, Archaeological Survey of India, Nagpur, for his valuable suggestions and for the keen interest shown in the completion of the work. Prof. Deo has read the whole manuscript and enabled the author to improve it very much by his penetrating criticisms. The author is deeply beholden to Dr. Deo for sparing his valuable time very often.

The occompanying illustrations were drawn, arranged and photographed respectively by Sarvashri A. Basheer Khan, P. R. K. Prasad, and M. B. Limayeji, collegues of the author in the Archaeological Survey, Nagpur. The author is thankful to them for their ungrudging help. The copyright of the illustrations rests with the Archaeological Survey of India.

Miscellanea

Sankhu Buddha*

by BALRAM SRIVASTAVA

Nepal is the land where artistic experience finds its manifestations through various media and the bronze and copper are the most popular among them. Bronze or copper images in Nepal, as a matter of fact, are considered more sanctified than stone sculptures and they have certain sacradotal significance. The various *yatras* celibrated throughout in Nepal, are the most significant occasions when metal images are particularly exhibited.

But, in spite of so much popularity and religious significance of metal images, it was observed that stone sculptures represent earlier sculptural traditions than the bronze ones. Thus, Stella Kramrisch writing about the antiquity of Nepal bronzes remarks, "During the rule of Pala Dynasty (750-1150)) the eastern Indian bronze images were made in large numbers in Nalanda and Kurkihar in Bihar and being easily portable found their way to Nepal where their form at once became recast in Nepali tradition.'[1] Here it is to be noted that by 'at once' she probably means the difference of more than one century, for, as it appears from her monograph that the earliest bronze figure she refers to, belongs to ninth or the early tenth century A. D. (Viṣṇu of the Brooklyn Museum, New York and Tara of the collection of Nasli and Alice Heeramaneck, New York city). She does not refer to any metal image, even of this antiquity, still *in situ* in Nepal. But the present image of the Buddha from the village Sankhu, noticed and brought to light for the first time by the author[2], aesthetically and historically is of great significance and throws entirely a new light on the antiquity of the metal images of Nepal.

Sankhu and its Heritage

Sankhu is a small village on the bank of the river Śāli, in the Bagmati *Ancala* of the Kathmandu Valley. It was also an ancient seat of Buddhism and had in the time of Anśumāna Varman (7th century A.D.) a monastic establishment. An inscription[3] of his time, issued by the authorities of the monastery of Sankhu, has been published by Silva lêvi, which not only throws light on the antiquity of the place, but also indicates the significance of Sankhu as the seat of a powerful *sāṅghika* of a *bhikkhusaṅgha*. At present also, Sankhu represents the ancient heritage of its art of different ages and styles.

The present image is found in the corner of a subsidiary shrine in the terraced courtyard of Vajrayogini Tara temple on the Sankhu hill. This image is not in worship and has no connection with the main deity of this shrine. It is simply housed in the shrine along with the other images, which were found by the temple-priests in the locality.

Artistic features of this image

It is unfortunate that this beautiful image has been so badly preserved and has been kept in a neglected corner of a shrine. It is a life-size bronze image of Buddha having a high percen-

* I am much thankful to Dr. P. N. Pant, the Additional Secretary in the ministry of Planning, Sri R. J. Thapa, the Director of Archaeology of His Majesty's Government, the King of Nepal, who have provided me facilities for my journey to Sankhu. I was accompanied in the exploration of the Sankhu region by Dr. H. N. Jha, Head of the Deptt. of History, Trichand college, Kathmandu and Sri B. K. Rizal, a tourist guide.

tage of copper, made through the 'lost wax process'. The features of this image may be described as follows:

The Buddha is represented in *ābhaṅgasthānaka* attitude. The weight of the body is explicitly firmed on the right leg, left being slightly in the advanced position, as if ready to move. This position, as B. Rolland remarks, 'was intended to suggest to worshipper that the Buddha image was actually moving or walking towards the supplant' [5] to offer boon. Hence the right hand is characteristically in the *varada mudrā*. The hand itself rhythmically follows the curve of the body. The left hand of the deity is turned upwards to touch the drapery on the shoulders. This is an unusual mode of holding the drapery (in the other standing Buddha images of Sarnath and Mathura of the Gupta period, the drapery is held by the left hand in a lower position). The drapery covers the whole body from the shoulders to a little over the anklets, entirely diaphanous to reveal the unadorned yet majestic expanse of torso beneath it. Unlike the mesh of strings typical to the Buddhas of Mathura, the parallel folds of the *saṅghātī* are less conventional and conspicuous and represent faithfully the clear delineation of the features of the body, not only in the plane and the outline, but also in the details showing even the nipples on the bust and the *nābhi* on the stomach. The drapery is shown not by the incision of lines, as we find on the image of the Buddha in the Birmingham Museum, but by expressing its natural volume through mouldings. The delineation of the *trivalli* on the *grīvā* is clear.

But much of the impression is derived from the facial expression. The oval face shows fullness and the grace of the deity with the lotiform eyes, the sight being fixed on the tip of the nose (*nāsāgradṛṣṭi*). Like other Gupta images the *Urṇā* is absent, but the bump of the head is charming with the curly hair on the head. The elongation of the ears is typical to Gupta tradition.

Chronological considerations

The image is uninscribed and undated. But, in spite of the fact that the Nepalese artists had skill enough to reproduce the older artistic traditions in later periods also, this particular image, for its perfect balance between the realization of the tensionless plasticity and the delicacy of its execution, seems to be a counterpart of the Buddha stone images of the early Gupta period in India and the Lichchhavi period in Nepal.

NOTES

[1] *The Art of Nepal,* 40.

[2] I have shown the photographs of the image to Stella Kramrisch, Benjamin Rolland and N.R. Banerjee in the month of November 1967, when they were in Varanasi. They found the image interesting and of great antiquity.

[3] *Le Nepal,* **III,** 112.

[4] Due to certain unavoidable and unpleasant circumstances, I could not take better photographs.

[5] *The Art and Architecture of India,* 133.

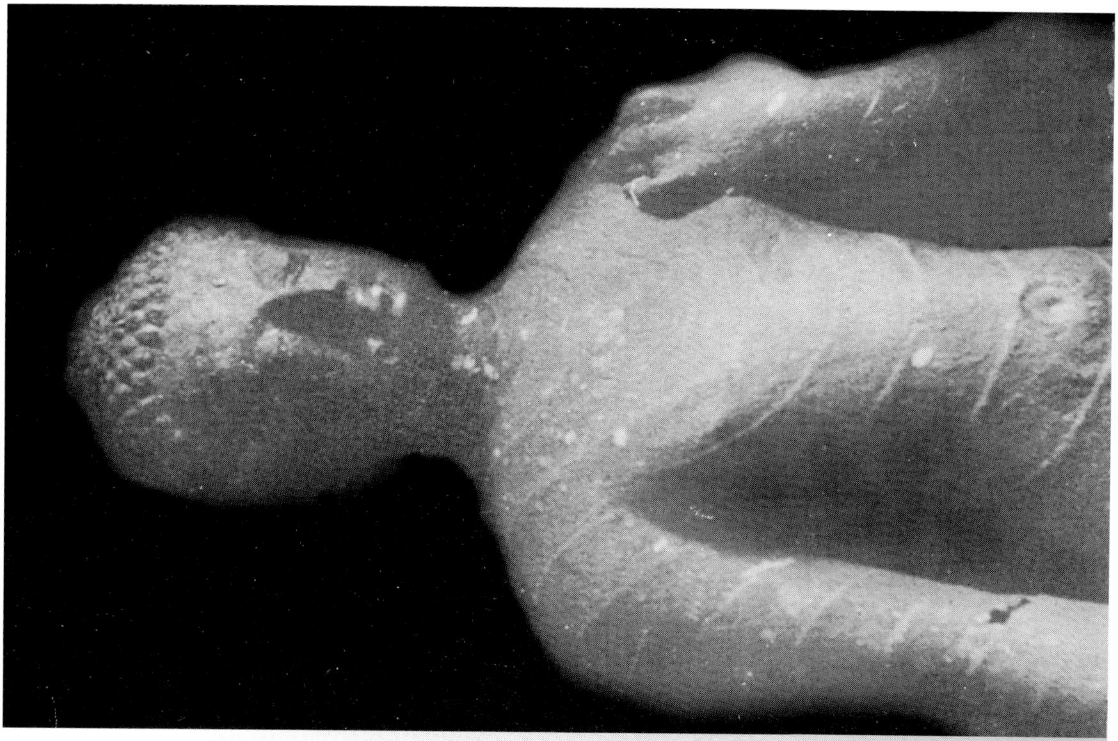

B

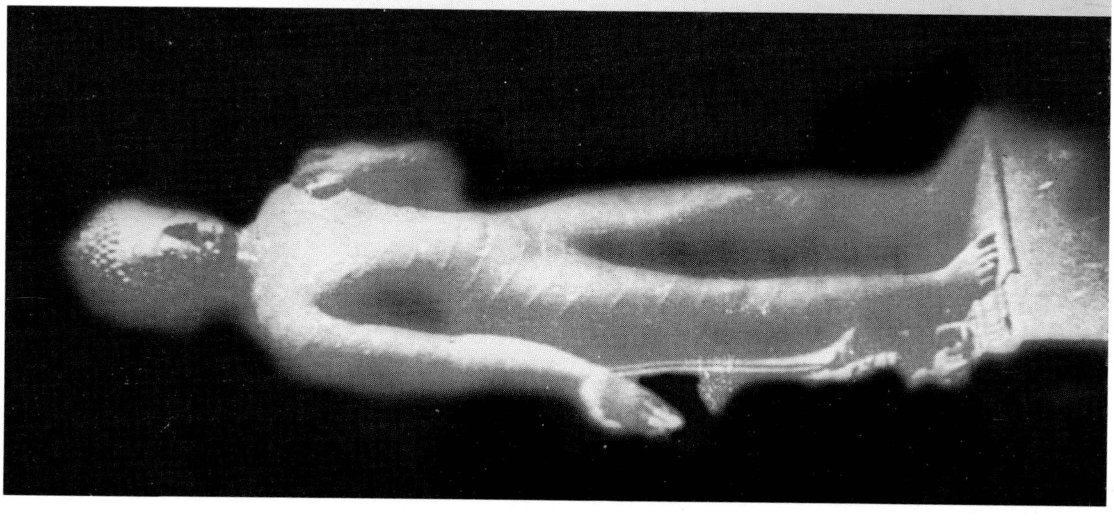

A

Sankhu Buddha (Nepal).

A. Terracotta panel from Śrāvastī.

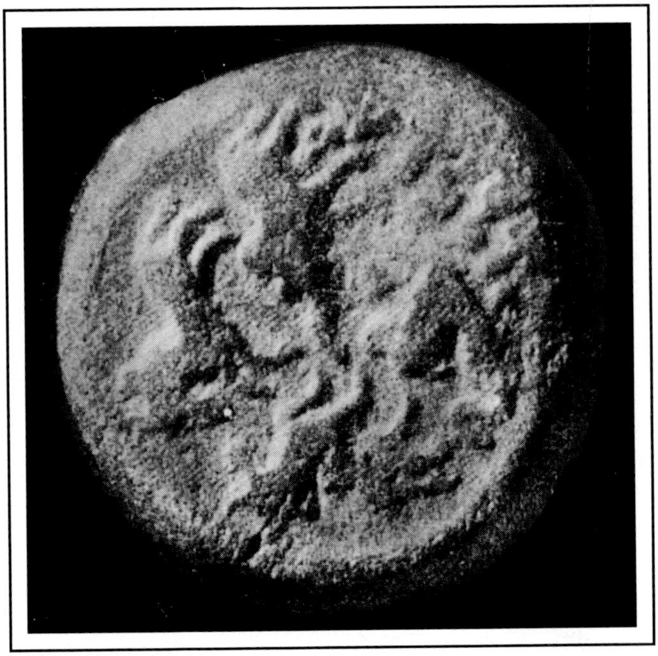

B. Clay tablet in Lucknow Museum.

Two Early Stone Age Sites on River Son in District Bilaspur, M. P.

by NISAR AHMAD

Since the sporadic collection of stone age artifacts by a few antiquaries towards the end of the last century, the Son Valley and its tributaries have largely remained unexplored. It was only in the last decade that this region attracted the attention of prehistorians who located several stone age sites in Rewa and Sidhi districts [1]. In course of his systematic investigations of prehistoric sites, the present author discovered two Early Stone Age sites in the upper reaches of the river Son [2].

The river Son orginates in the Maikal range and flows through the Lower Gondwana formations. The river flows to the north in the western part of Bilaspur district (M.P.) and then takes a turn towards the east in Madhya Pradesh. Flowing through Uttar Pradesh and Bihar, ultimately it joins the Ganges in the Shahabad district of the last named province.

A few kilometres away from the source of this river, two Early Stone Age sites namely Nawatola and Salamtola were located in the western part of district Bilaspur. No Middle and Late Stone Age tools were present on these sites.

Nawatola 22°48′ N., 80°3′ E. [3]

This village is situated on the left bank of the Son, nearly 10 kilometres downstream from its source. Here, the cliff section at the opposite side shows from bottom upwards :

Black brown soil	...	.15 m.
Dark brown sandy silt	...	3.65 m.
Highly compact Kankars mixed with few pebbles.	...	1.52 m.

Four Early Stone Age tools were found *in situ* from the bottom layer.

Salamtota 22° 49′ N., 82° 4′ E. [4]

Downstream on the left bank of the above river is Salamtola. Here the cliff section has the same implementiferous deposits as in the Nawatola section.

Black brown soil.	...	.16 m.
Dark brown sandy silt.	...	4.57 m.
Compact Kankars mixed with few pebbles.	...	1.82 m.

Seven Early Stone Age tools were obtained from the bottom deposit.

In all, eleven tools were found from these sites *in situ*. The principal material of these tools is quartzite which is some times coarse to medium grained but occasionally fine grained as well. One artifact is made of quartz. As has been pointed out earlier, the Son flows through the Lower Gondwana formation in its upper reaches, hence it is quite likely that the material of the artifacts might have been derived from the Lower Gondwana conglomerates. These implements are of various colours such as brown, yellowish and white.

The artifacts may be classified as follows :

Tool-types	Sites		Total
	Nawatola	Salamtola	
Chopping-tools	2	1	3
Handaxes on core	2	1	3
Flakes	...	5	5
	4	7	11

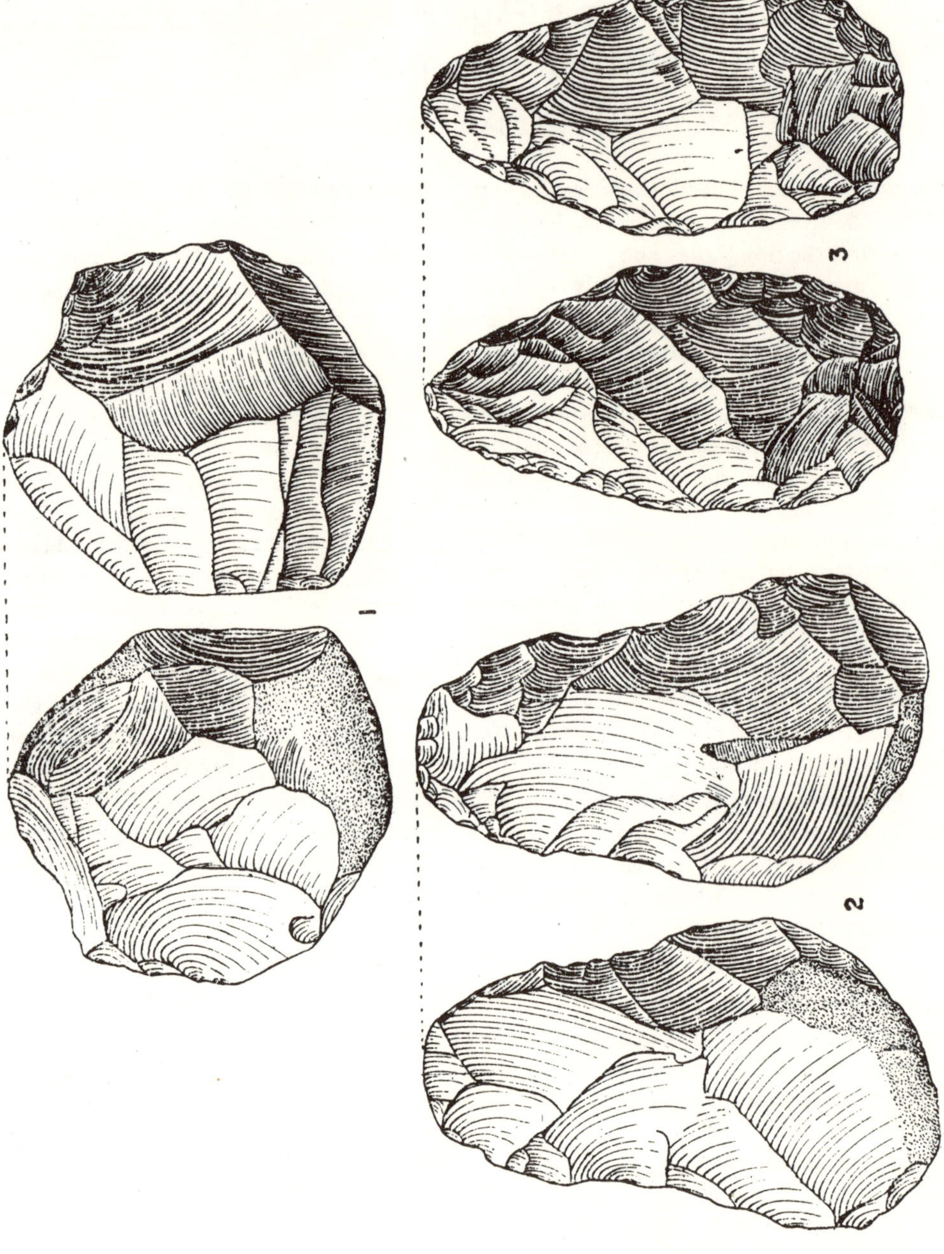

Fig. 1 (Scale 1/2)

All the chopping-tools have been flaked alternatively at one edge of the pebbles producing the wavy convex edge by the intersection of flake scars from both faces. In two of them, under surfaces have been made flat by removing several flakes. The flakes are removed from the edges. Of the three handaxes, two have big deep as well as shallow flake scars. They have also not been fully flaked and cortex is still present in both the specimens. The third one has been fully flaked showing long and shallow flake scars.

The flakes appear to have been detached by a stone hammer. Except in one case, the working is done partly on the surface of the tools, leaving the original cortex. They make a wide angle with the platform.

Chopping tool

NTA-2 [5] (Fig.1,1) : Fresh; on a round pebble of quartzite; a few shallow flake scars on the upper surface; two patches of cortex; under surface shows nine shallow and one steep flake scars; wavy edge produced by the intersection of steep flake scars from the upper surface and the flat-flaked under surface.

Size : 100 x 95 x 70 mm.

Handaxe

STA-2 [6] (Fig. 1,2) Pear shaped; made on a pebble of fine grained quartzite; upper surface shows big as well as shallow flake scars and the under-surface two deep and the rest shallow flake scars; both faces have patches of cortex; chisel like tip; thick pebble butt; sharp, slightly wavy edges; biconvex cross-section and rhomboid cross-section near the tip and the butt, respectively.

Size : 139 x 79 x 51 mm.

NTA-4-(Fig. 1,3) : Spear-shaped; fine grained quartzite; fresh; fully flaked on both faces by detaching shallow flakes by cylinder hammer technique, some stepped flake scars from the edges are also removed, producing a wavy edge running all around including the butt; biconvex cross-section.

Size : 130 x 68 x 35 mm.

Flake

STA-4 : Oval shaped small flake of quartzite; fresh; upper surface boldly flaked from the left side and partly from the right, the rest cortex; primary flake surface makes an angle of 120 degree with the platform.

Size : 82 x 62 x 30 mm.

NOTES

[1] *Indian Archaeology* 1957-58 *A Review*, 25-26; *Indian Archaeology* 1961 *A Review* and R. V. Joshi, 'Stone Age Industries of the Damoh Area, Madhya Pradesh', *Ancient India*, **17** (New Delhi), 1961, 24.

[2] Nisar Ahmad, *Stone Age Cultures of the Upper Son Valley, Madhya Pradesh*, Ph.D. Thesis; Copies in the library of the Deccan College and Poona University.

[3] 64 J/1 1 inch=1 mile map.

[4] Ibid.

[5] NTA=Nawatola.

[6] STA=Salamtola.

A Clay Tablet in Lucknow Museum : An Artistic and Religious Study

by KIRAN KUMAR THAPLYAL

A Lucknow Museum circular (about 2 cm. in diameter) terracotta sealing (S. No. 609) portrays four animals—a bull and a horse facing each other in the upper part and a lion and an elephant similarly disposed in the lower. The bull is shown stepping forward, head sideways, and the horse with its forelegs raised, as prancing. The lion is depicted in a charging attitude. The trunk of the elephant is raised. All the four are evidently full of spirit and movement. The legend in Brāhmī characters of c. 3rd or 2nd century B.C. reads :—

Yakhadāna [1] (Pl. XB).

These animals are ofcourse elsewhere represented individually or variously combined with the others on seals, ringstones, coins and in terracotta, painting and sculpture. But what is unusually striking, they are similarly grouped on the abacus of the Sarnath Lion Capital, in a terracotta plaque in the Central Museum, Lahore [2], on the moonstones from Nagarjunakonda [3] and Anuradhapura (Ceylon) [4] and on a steatite plaque from Akra [5]. Literary evidence, too, refers to these animals together, besides individual inclusions in other groups as well [6].

Different interpretations of the delineation of these animals on the abacus of the Sarnath Lion Capital have been given from time to time. It was held that they were purely ornamental [7]. They were related to certain events of prime importance in the life-story of the Buddha [8]. Contrary to expectations, it was inferred from this creation of the latitudinarian king Aśoka, that they were theriomorphic representations of Brahmanical divinities subordinated to Buddhism [9].

They are also taken to represent the four quarters of the world. The last view is supported by some substantial evidence such as the discovery of metallic images of these animals—a gold lion, silver bull, copper horse and a corroded iron mass seemingly representing an elephant—facing cardinal points, N. W. S and E. in a bronze casket sealed up in a laterite plinth of a small temple at Kedah in Malaya [10], and of bronze figures of these animals in Ceylon facing the same points [11]. They are also attached to a tank as gargoyles in the ancient Khmer capital of Angkor [12] and their images embellished the artificial Meru Parvata in Bangkok [13]. These animals are also associated with the four mouths of the Anavatapta lake [14]. Whatever be the real significance of the representation of these animals on the Sarnath Lion Capital [15], one thing at least is certain : these four were held in very high esteem since remote antiquity. They represented age-old and widespread traditions and like numerous other symbols and motifs were common heritage of various cults interpreted by them in their own way [16].

The legend on our tablet *Yakhadāna* may be translated as 'offering to the Yaksha (or Yakshas)'. The tablet (which has no string marks on the back) was quite likely a votive offering to a Yaksha shrine. The Yaksha-cult is of hoary antiquity [17]. Yaksha and Yakshī figures from the Maurya [18] and Śuṅga [19] period downwards bear ample testimony to the popularity of this cult,

The *Niddesa* mentions three of these with certain other animals and titular deities like Vāsudeva, Baladeva, Indra, Brahmā, Nāgas, Mahārājika gods etc. having their own cults [20]. The *Milindapañho* furnishes a similar list with the addition of a few others and hints at their esoteric nature [21]. The *Nāyadhamakahā* mentions some 40 devatās including the elephant, horse, lion and the cow (instead of bull) [22]. We can postulate that some people would have worshipped more than one animal.

But, as already stated, the tablet, in all probability, was a votive offering to a Yaksha shrine. In fact, this is the earlier of the only two glyptic examples so far known [23], clearly testifying the prevalence of *Yaksha* cult, though the ancient Indian literature so well demonstrated by Coomaraswamy, has copious references suggesting not only the existence of Yaksha shrines but also their commonness [24].

As regards the presence of animals on a tablet used as a votive offering to a *Yaksha* shrine, the association of these with the *Yakshas* in various forms is well known. In Bharhut some of the *Yaksha* figures have been depicted with animal *vāhanas*, Gāṅgeya [25] and Supravāsa [26] each represented with a tusker and Ajakālaka with a composite animal having the tail of the *makara* and the " front part of a quadruped " [27] perhaps of a lion or tiger [28].

The *Yaksha* and *Yakshī* figures have sometimes been conceived in therianthropic form—part human and part animal. A *Jātaka* [29] refers to a horse-faced (*aśvamukhī*) *Yakshī* and such representation in art is known [30]. We may also refer to a terracotta female figure with the face of a cow(or bull) in the Lucknow Museum which probably represents a *Gomukhī Yakshī* and a sculptural piece in the same museum (no. G385) representing a bull-faced *Yaksha* [31]. More significant in the present context is the fact that the *Aupapātra-Sūtra* and *Antagaḍa Dosāo* refer to the practice of decorating the diases of the *Yaksha* shrines with animal figures [32] which include the bull, horse and elephant—three of the four animals that occur on our tablet.

Another evidence suggesting the association of *Yakshas* with animals may also be considered. The possibility of these animals symbolising the four quarters has already been noticed. The *Niddesa* even refers to the cult of quarters [33]. The *Chaturmahārājas* are the guardians of these quarters [34], and interestingly enough, the label inscriptions at Bharhut designate each of them as a *Yaksha* [35].

Our tablet is a rare example among the glyptics of the historical period whereon as many as four animals have been represented together, though such representations are known on hoary Harappan ones [36].

The depiction of four animals in such a limited space, so remarkably life-like and with a strong suggestion of rhythmic movement bears ample testimony to the great skill and high artistic attainments of its maker. The Mauryan sculptures in stone are ofcourse celebrated for their dignity and majesty, but the present tablet is a rare piece of this early period in the medium of clay, remarkable for the realism of its figures with a fine suggestion of animal vigour [37].

NOTES

[1] There is a slanting stroke after *na*. But it does not seem to be part of a letter.

[2] D.R. Sahni, *Guide to the Buddhist Ruins at Sarnath*, 5th ed., 40.

[3] V.S. Agrawala, *Chakradhvaja*, (Varanasi), 1964, figs. 101-104.

[4] D. Gordine, 'Masterpieces of Oriental Art-7' *JRAS*, 1946, 123, Pls. X and XI.

[5] *Op.cit.*, [3] Fig. 93-A.

[6] For various literary and archaeological references see Agrawala, Ibid., 60-63 and 93 and see plates.

[7] *Op.cit.* [2], 40.

[8] B. Majumdar, *Guide to Sarnath*, 2nd ed., 46. The elephant is supposed to symbolise conception, bull Nativity, horse Renunciation and lion the Buddha himself. (Cf "Śākya simha"—a well-known epithet of the Buddha) whose preaching was compared with the roar of a lion.

[9] *Op.cit.* [2], 40.

[10[H.G.O. Wales, 'Recent Malayan Excavations and some wider Implications', *JRAS*, 1946, 142-149 and 145.

[11] V. A. Smith, *History of Fine Arts in India and Ceylon* 1911, 60 fn., *Op.cit.* [10], 145.

[12] B. Rowland, *Art and Architecture of India*, 258, n. 12.

[13] Ibid., 41.

[14] T. Watters, *On Yuan Chwang's Travel in India* I, 32.

[15] For further discussion see author's article 'The symbolism in Sarnath Lion Capital and its Purpose', *JUPHS* (*N.S.*), **VIII**, 1960, 11-19 and Plates; Agarwala, *Op.cit.* [2], 29-40.

[16] Significant human and animal combinations in parts, e.g., Gaṇapati (man elephant), Narasimha (man lion) Nandikeśvara(man bull) Hayaśīrsha (man horse) in the later myths may well be viewed in this light.

[17] Some scholars take certain Harappan figures as proto-type of Yakshas. According to some, Yakshas have been referred to in **RV** 7, 61, 5 and their temples in **RV** 4, 3, 13. (See V.S. Agrawala, *Studies in Indian Art*, 1965, 87). It is however doubtful whether the word 'Yaksha' in **RV** stands for the Yakshas. Sāyaṇa takes it to mean *Yajna.*

[18] The figures from Parkham, Pawaya and Patna are same of the earliest found representations of Yakshas.

[19] Amongst Bharhut sculptures we find inscribed images of the Yakshas (Virūḍhaka, Ajakālaka, Gāngeya Sūchiloma and Supravāsa) and Yakshīs (Sudarśanā and Chandrā).

[20] *Niddesa,* (i), ed. by L. De la Vallee Poussin and E.J. Thomas, (London) 1916, 89, *to hatthivattika ka va honti, assavattika va honti govattika va honti.*

[21] *Op. cit.* [2], 33.

[22] Ibid, 34.

[23] The other one is in the collection of Shri R.C. Tandon of Allahabad. It bears a *makara* figure and the legend which has been read by Professor K.D. Bajpai (kindly conveyed through a letter) as *Mahamdamritaya Yakshasya Dhanyasriyah.* The letters have been partially rubbed off.

[24] A.K. Coomaraswamy, *Yakshas,* I.

[25] B.M. Barua, *Bharhut,* I, 60, and Cunningham, *Stupa of Bharhut,* Pl. XXI, I and p. 134. The inscription reads '*Gamgito*'.

[26] *Op.cit.,* [25], 61.

[27] Ibid, 60.

[28] J.N. Banerjea, *Development of Hindu Iconography*, 2nd ed., 342.

[29] *Padakusalamanava, Jataka,* No. 432.

[30] *Op.cit.* [24] Pl. 12, Fig. 1.

[31] I am indebted to Shri Sankata Prasad Shukla for drawing my attetion to these two pieces in Lucknow Museum.

[32] *Op.cit.* [24], 19-20.

[33] *Niddesa, Op.cit.,* 89, *disvattika-va-honti.*

[34] Vaiśravana—north; Dhṛitarāshṭra—east; Virūḍhaka—south, and Virūpākhsa—west. vide *Dighanikaya,* III, ed. by J.E. Carpenter, (London), 1911, 197-201.

[35] *Op.cit.* [25], 59.

[36] J. Marshall, *Mohenjodaro and the Indus Civilization.* I, Pl. XII, Fig. 17; Ibid., III, Pl. CXVI, no. 14.

[37] We gratefully acknowledge the facilities extended by the Lucknow Museum authorities for study and photograph.

An Episode from Ramayaṇa on a Terracotta Panel

by SURENDRA KUMAR SRIVASTAVA

The Archaeological Survey of India Annual Report for the year 1967-68 brought out a significant statement on the excavated materials of Sahet-Mahet. J. Ph. Vogel published some terracotta panels of the Gupta age which have been drawing attention of scholars for their exquisite beauty, rhythmic effect, technical attainment and successful depiction of mythological stories. The terracotta panel in question displays two figures, a human (male) and (Pl. x, A) a monkey. The latter has been identified by Vogel as *Hanumāna* [1]. The purpose of the present paper is to study this panel once again and to suggest a more appropriate identification.

The human figure in the panel is depicted on the left side holding a sword in his raised right hand and hair being done stylistically in deep incised lines. He also puts on bangles, *kuṇḍalas*, beaded necklace ; an *uttarīya* suspending down from the right shoulder forming a lasso round the waist and an underwear covering the loin. Just to his left stands a monkey figure clothed in an underwear, ornamented with bangles and necklace, kicking the human figure and also lifting a rock in its outstretched hands to throw on him.

Originally the heads of these figures were found detached when excavated and later on were refixed on their proper places [2]. Around the two figures, the three borders of the panel are decorated in criss-cross design executed by incised lines.

Vogel was the first scholar to study this panel in his Sahet-Mahet excavation report. He has identified the monkey with that of *Hanumāna* but says nothing for the other figure [3]. Later, C. C. Dasgupta fully agreed with the views of Vogel, as far as the monkey is concerned, and identified the other figure as *Rākshasa* [4]. M. M. Nagar is also of the same opinion and he describes the figure as Hanumāna and *Rākshasa* at war [5].

The theory of Vogel is to the effect that (i) the depicted scene is from Rāmāyana and (ii) it displays *Hanumāna* and a *Rākshasa* at war. However, certain points do not permit us to accept the later part of this theory.

The first objection is that all other panels related to the *Rāmāyaṇa*, which have been excavated from this temple, illustrate some important incidents from the epic. The panel stating the redemption scene of *Ahalyā* is an example of this fact [6]. Now the question arises as to why the modellers of this particular panel depicted a scene which was not at all connected with some story or incident, while *Rāmāyaṇa* was full of such references. Therefore, it might not be correct to assume that the panel does not represent a particular story and merely refers to an ordinary fight between *Hanumāna* and an unknown ogre.

Another objection is on account of the necklace worn by the monkey figure. There is no reference either in the *Vālmīki Rāmāyaṇa* or in the *Ādhyātma Rāmāyanṇa* to *Hanumāna* putting on a necklace while he was fighting a *Rākshasa*.

Lastly, we also do not find any reference to *Hanumāna* attacking with a rock a goblin who was ready to slaughter him (*Hanumāna*) by his sword.

From the above discussion it becomes almost clear that the depicted scene is neither an ordinary one nor the fight is in between *Hanumāna* and an unknown *Rākshasa*. Now we come to an episode from *Rāmāyaṇa* more akin to the scene depicted in the panel.

In the *Yudha-kāṇḍa* of the *Vālmīki Rāmāyaṇa*, the younger brother of *Bālī* had a combat with *Virūpāksha*, a general of *Rāvaṇa* [7]. When all the famous warriors including *Indrajīt Kumbhakarṇa*, *Dhumrāksha* and *Akampan* etc. of *Rāvaṇa's* army were killed and a great panic was created in the battlefield, *Rāvaṇa* sent *Virūpāksha* to fight against *Sugrīva*. As soon as he came in the battlefield he jumped out of his chariot with his bow, mounted on an elephant and attacked the enemy with a hideous roar [8]. In order to control the worsening situation *Virūpāksha* also aimed at *Sugrīva*, shot arrows and made his army fearless [9]. *Sugrīva*, finding his soldiers in trouble, made a severe attack on the elephant carrying *Varūpāksha* with a tree, resulting in the elephant's retreat to a bow distance. The elephant screamed with pain and sat down [10]. Ultimately *Virūpāksha* had to get down from his wounded elephant's back with a sword and shield. He also chided *Sugrīva*, who was standing steadily [11]. When *Sugrīva* apprehended the seriousness of the situation he lifted a rock in his hands, which was as black as cloud, and tossed over *Virūpāksha* [12]

As regards the necklace of the monkey figure in the *Adhyātma*-*Rāmāyaṇa*, it is mentioned, when *Bālī* was born, *Indra*, his father, gave him a golden necklace and left for his heavenly abode [13]. That golden necklace was amazing and victory adducing. It was so powerful that *Bālī* never failed to put it on whenever he sought war, so much so, when he was fighting *Dundubhi* and his own brother *Sugrīva*, he did not foget to wear it [14]. Later on *Bālī* gave that necklace to *Sugrīva* when he was getting unconscious and was at the verge of collapse. He said, " *Sugrīva*, you put on this celestial necklace of *Lakshmī* before I die, otherwise its *Śri* will disappear "[15]. On these words *Sugrīva* forgot all his previous enmity and adorned himself with that necklace [15]. In *Abhishekanāṭakam* of *Bhāsa* also we have a description that *Bālī*, at the time of his death, gave *Sugrīva* a family *hemamālā* to put on, which the latter accepted with gratitude [17]. Accordingly, the probability is that the necklace, depicted in the panel, is a representation of this necklace, which was given to *Sugrīva* by *Bālī* and which the former did not forget to put on while in combat with *Virūpāksha*.

Thus we conclude that the panel may be better identified as depicting the fight between *Sugrīva* and *Virūpāksha*. This alternative suggestion is nearer to the scene and characteristic features illustrated in the panel. The question as to whether this panel may be associated with some other apt theme also, remains open.

Notes

[1] J. Ph. Vogel, *Archaeological Survey of India Annual Report*, 1907-08, 96. Pl. XXVII.

[2] Ibid.

[3] Ibid.

[4] C. C. Dasgupta, *Origin and Evolution of Indian Clay Sculpture*, 221.

[5] M. M. Nagar, *Sravasti*, 1956.

[6] S. K. Srivastava, *Prajna*, IX (2), 1964.

[7] *Valmiki Ramayana*, Yudha Kanda, Sarg 96.

[8] Ibid.

विरूपाक्षः स्वकं नामधन्वी विश्राव्य राक्षसः ।
रथादाप्लुत्य दुर्धर्षो गजस्कन्धमुपारुहत् ॥१४॥
स तं द्विपमथारुह्य विरूपाक्षो महाबलः ।
ननर्द भीमनिर्ह्रादं वानरानभ्यधावत ॥१५॥

Yudha Kanda, 96—14-15

[9] Ibid.

सुग्रीवे स शरान् घोरान् विससर्ज चमूमुखे ।
स्थापयामास चोद्विग्नान् राक्षसान् सम्प्रहर्षयन् ॥१६॥

Yudha Kanda, 96—16

[10] *Valmiki Ramayana,*

ततः पादपमुद्धृत्य शूरः समप्रधनो हरिः ।
अभिपत्य जघानास्य प्रमुखे तं महागजम् ॥
स तु प्रहाराभिहतः सुग्रीवेण महागजः ।
अपासर्पद् धनुर्मात्रं निषसाद ननाद च ॥

Yudha Kanda, 96, 18-19

[11] Ibid.,

गजात् तु मथितात् तूर्णमपक्रम्य स वीर्यवान् ।
राक्षसोऽभिमुखः शत्रुं प्रत्युद्गम्य ततः कपिम् ॥
आर्षभं चर्म खड्गं च प्रगृह्य लघुविक्रमः ।
भर्त्सयन्निव सुग्रीवमाससाद व्यवस्थितम् ॥

Yudha Kanda, 96-20-21

[12] Ibid.,

स हि तस्याभि संक्रुद्धः प्रगृह्य विपुलां शिलाम् ।
विरूपाक्षस्य चिक्षेप सुग्रीवो जलदोपमाम ॥

Yudha Kanda, 96-22

[13] *Adhyatma Ramayana,*

वाली समभवत्तत्र शक्रतुल्य पराक्रमः ।
तस्या दत्वा सुरेशानः स्वर्णमाला दिवंगतः ॥

Uttara Kanda, ch. 3-92.

[14] *Valmiki Ramayana,*

तमेव मुक्त्वा संक्रुद्धो मालामुत्क्षिप्य काञ्चनीम् ।
पित्रा दत्तां महेन्द्रेण युद्धाय व्यवतिष्ठत ॥

Kishkindha Kanda, 11, 39

[15] *Valmiki Ramayana,*

इमां च मालामधत्स्व दिव्यां सुग्रीव काञ्चनीम् ।
उदारा श्रीः स्थिता ह्यस्यां सम्प्रह्यान्मृते मयि ॥

Kishkindha Kanda, 22, 16

[16] Ibid.,

तद्वालिवचनाच्छान्तः कुर्वन् युक्तमतन्द्रितः ।
जग्राह सोऽभ्यनुज्ञातो मालां तां चैव काञ्चनीम् ॥

Ibid., ch. 22-18.

[17] *Bhasa,*

वाली---सुग्रीव ! प्रतिगृह्यतामस्यत्कुलधनं हेममाला ।
सुग्रीव--- अनुगृहीतोऽस्मि ।

Abhishekanatakam, Bhasa Nataka Chakram, I, Pratham Anka, 21.

A Prehistoric Bronze Anthropomorph in the Patna Museum and Its Identification

by PRITHVI KUMAR AGRAWALA

In my recent visit to the Patna Museum, I got an opportunity of examining a number of the bronze antiquities in the collection of the Museum through the kind courtesy of the Curator Dr. P. L. Gupta to whom I am indebted and thankful for showing me the unique piece described below (Arch. No. 240; ht. 18 cms.; from Manbhum) and allowing the permission for its publication. It is profitable that this piece appears in the accompanying illustrations and apparently adds greatly to our knowledge of the early Gangetic Valley Bronze Hoard [1] material.

Important evidence of early metal industry in Northern India is represented by a series of Copper Hoards discovered from over thirty-six sites in the Gangetic Valley, Orissa and Madhya Pradesh ; and recently added area of Rajasthan by its important site at Khurdi. A comprehensive study of over 600 objects has revealed eight principal types, as constituting these hoards, including a form known as *Anthropomorph*. Artistically, certain barbed harpoons and the ' Anthropomorphs ' from Bisauli, Sirthauli and Sheorajpur are to be regarded ' masterpieces ' of these hoards. Indeed, the anthropomorphic shapes form a unique series themselves from the Gangetic basin. Nowherelse in the world such objects are found. They are named anthropomorphic figures only for convenience's sake as they seem to ' represent a human form with straddled legs and, incurved arms '. But their purpose whether religious or otherwise is highly doubtful. On these few problems the piece described here from the Patna Musuem Collection throws a veritable light.

From it there can be no doubt that it represents a human figure and moreover that of a male since the genital portion is clearly represented. It shows a vertical rendition of a male figure, though crudely made. Yet it is certainly of a high merit as regards ideographic representation. A comparison of this with the Sirthauli or Bisauli ' Anthropomorph ' leaves no doubt that the latter class of representations also intended human figure in a similar attitude and conception of stylisation. How these figures lead to the well known Śrīvatsa symbol of early art is summarily illustrated here. (Fig. 1, 1—4) The first and the second are the renderings of the Anthropomorphs from Bisauli and the third is the piece from Patna Museum. Next is the Śrīvatsa symbol from a Mathurā Āyāga-Paṭṭa of the Kushāṇa period.

Also for a profitable comparison, the human representations from the prehistoric and primitive paintings are shown here (Fig. 2, 1—4) (The " Ape Man ", Singhanpur ; Figure, Adamgarh ; The " Mermaid ", Singhanpur ; Figure, Son Bhadra. After Gordon).

However, the Śrīvatsa symbol known from early Indian artand in a group of Eight Auspicious symbols (*ashṭamaṅgalas*) bears striking resemblance to the anthropomorphic representations mentioned above. This may even go to suggest some cult associations for the anthropomorphic shapes, possibly representing a symbol of the

An anthropomorph from Patna Museum.

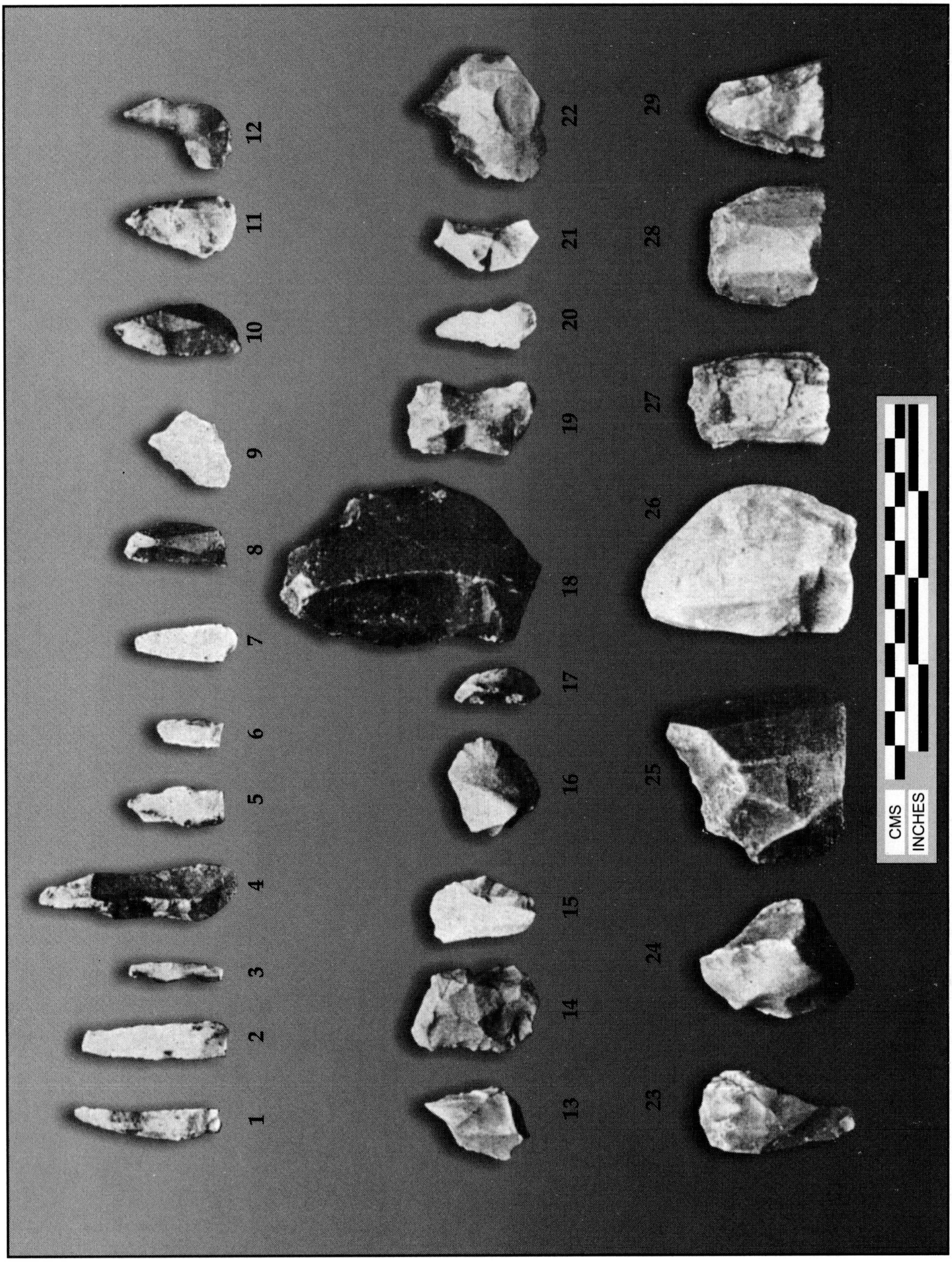

Late Stone Age tools from Shahabad (Bihar).

Fig. 1 (1—4)

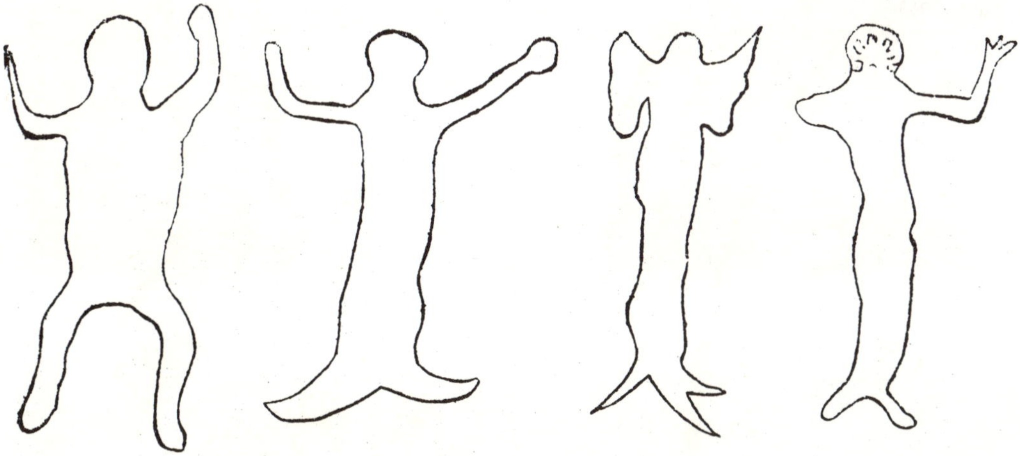

Fig. 2 (1—4)

Fig. 3 (1—2)

Mother Goddess whose cult was widely popular from the earliest ages. She might have been a deity of so much importance in the culture-complexes represented by the Gangetic Copper Hoards that her symbol was in great demand just as the other associated weapons of the hoards appear to be as objects of commodity. A symbol of copper or bronze was obviously an object of value as compared to figurines and emblems of clay, etc.

If so, a comparative class of the above, appears to have been metallic or clay representations, affiliation of which can possibly be with the " Babe of the mother-goddess Śrī " (Śrī-vatsa). For example, one instance in metal comes from the Piprahwa relics (Fig. 3,1) [2]. Another may be cited from Ahichchhatra terracottas (Fig. 3,2) [3].

NOTES

[1] B. B. Lal, ' Further Copper Hoards from the Gangetic Basin, etc.', *Ancient India,* 7 (New Delhi), 1951, 20-39; H. D. Sankalia, *Prehistory and Protohistory in India and Pakistan,* (Bombay), 1963, 223.

[2] V. S. Agrawala, *Indian Art,* (Varanasi), 1964, Pl. XVI.

[3] V. S. Agrawala, ' Terracotta Figurines from Ahichchhatra ', *Ancient India,* (New Delhi) 1948, Pl. XXXVI, 63.

The Tribal Deity of The Vishaṇins

by DEENABANDHU PANDEY

At Mohenjo-daro, Mackay discovered a steatite seal [1] on which a three faced horned god seated in *yogic* pose and surrounded by animals was seen. There were more than one seal with the depiction of horned god out of which two came from lower and two from upper levels [2]. Marshall took the figure as depicting Paśupati and identified it with a prototype of the historic Śiva [3]. Sastri takes the figure to be a representation of a composite god being nearer to a prototype of Vedic Rudra and connects him with the Mahishāsura of the Purāṇic times [4]. According to him the figure is composed of buffalo-head, scorpion arms, tiger waist, and serpent legs. While it may be agreed upon that the figure has only one face, the head being of a buffalo is a far-fetched statement. Neither the form of the head-dress of the figure resembles the buffalo horns nor the stylization proposed by Sastri is convincing. The face is of a human, no doubt a stylised one.

On the pre-Harappan pottery we see the depiction of many animals. In those animals the representation of bovines is of more importance than others. By the time of Kulli culture and in the subsequent Harappa culture the depiction of bull assumes an important place. Whenever a bull is represented, his horns have been depicted in the front view though the bull may be seen in different views. Thus the horns were given importance. It will not be unlikely if we take the head-dress of the figure in discussion to represent an ornamented and stylized form of the horns of the sacred bull. It may also be connected with the *chandralekha* on the forehead of Śiva and his association with the *Nandin.*

Thus we may conclude that the devine figure is a composite form of bull, tiger, scorpion and snake. The form of the god well suits to be a prototype of Vedic Rudra who becomes Siva in later times. The Rudra-Śiva cult seems to be very popular in the Harappa culture [5].

The god under reference may well be identified as a tribal-deity of the Vishāṇins. Vishāṇins mentioned in the Ṛigveda [6] were one of the ten kings in the tribal confederacy against the Bharatas, lead by Viśvāmitra. The Vishāṇin tribe has been grouped by Pusalkar with the five frontier tribes which were of little note [7]. Vishāṇins were located between the rivers Krumu and Gomati. The five frontier tribes seem to be non-Aryans. The word Vishāṇin, is explained by Sāyaṇa as 'holding horns in the hand'. The word has been used in the Epic and Purāṇic literature to mean 'having horns' and 'horned'[8]. Pusalkar suggests that the tribe was called Vishāṇin because their helmets were horn-shaped or ornamented with horns [9]. Thus the proposed identification that the figure in discussion is the representation of the tribal-deity of the Vishāṇins seems very plausible.

NOTES

[1] E. Mackay, *Further Excavations at Mohenjo-daro,* II, pl. XCIV, 420.

[2] Ibid. loc. cit; and pl. LXXXVII, 222 etc.

[3] J. Marshall, *Mohenjo-daro and the Indus Valley Civilization,* I, 53-56.

[4] K. N. Sastri, *New Light on Indus Civilization,* I, 7-13.

[5] V. S. Agrawala, *Indian Art,* 34.

[6] *Rigveda,* 7.18.7.

[7] R. C. Majumdar and A. D. Pusalkar, ed. *The Vedic Age,* 251.

[8] Monic Monier Williams, *Sanskrit-English Dictionary,* 997.

[9] *Op. cit* [7].

A Microlithic Site from Shahabad (Bihar)

by BHUPENDRA PAL SINGH

While the author was engaged in exploration of the famous cave of Gupteshwar Dham in Shahabad District, he collected the following microliths. In general, this area seems to be of an immense archaeological potentiality as evidenced by a chain of sites yielding N.B.P. along the river Durgawati. Again, Jagebaraon, a village situated in the same tehsil in the foothills of Kaimur, yielded a neolithic celt along with N.B.P. and other important materials.

The physiographic features of the area where the present microlithic site is discovered provide an ideal habitational place to the prehistoric man. The place as surrounded by the ring of high hills and the river Durgawati offers seclusion and security of life.

The microlithic artifacts under study, were collected near Karamchat where the Bihar Government is going to construct a dam.

As far our knowledge goes, it is the first microlith-yielding site in Shahabad district. The typological study attempted here may serve as a link between the microlithic complex of Eastern Bihar and that of Eastern U.P. and Madhya Pradesh.

Nature of the Industry

The raw material used in the production of microliths is fine grained silicious element, which includes glassy quartz, flint, jasper, agate, chalcedony, chert, etc.

Most of the tools of the assemblage are surprisingly fresh, only a few having a yellowish tinge of patination. The microliths here constitute a series of flakes, blades and points, often worked, core trimmings and cores. Besides regular artifacts, a large number of cores were also found. Some of the worked cores present in the collection could have been used as scrapers. Some blades are worked out into points. Simple flakes are numerous, fine serrated and ribbed long blades are not many, so is the case with the geometric forms. Some unworked flakes which show sign of use are included in the list [1].

The occurrence of cores of various size, shape and variety and the presence of waste flakes indicates that it was a factory site.

Typological Classification

The artifacts can broadly be classified into two main groups :

(*a*) Finished artifacts

(*b*) By-products

Finished artifacts include the regular microlithic shapes, while the by-products include the core and unutilized flakes. The following table will show the major finished tool types as well as the by-products with their frequency of occurrence.
Finished artifacts include the regular microlithic shapes, while the by-products include the core and unutilized flakes. The following table will show the major finished tool types as well as the by-products with their frequency of occurrence.

	Types		Number
Finished Implements (84)			
(*a*)	Blade	..	52
(*b*)	Point	..	16
(*c*)	Scraper on blade	..	11
(*d*)	Lunate	..	1
(*e*)	Scraper on core	..	4
By-products (56)			
(*a*)	Core	..	45
(*b*)	Flake	..	11
	total	..	140

The table shows that out of a total of 140 microliths, blades (52), points (15) and scrapers (11) constitute the main bulk of the assemblage. Further classification of tool types has been attempted, considering the shapes and their functional aspects.

Blade

The largest number of artifacts belong to this group. These specimens have a great range of size varying from 0.6 cm. to 1.3 cm. According to technique and their forms, they can be divided into following.

(*a*) *Simple Blade* (Pl.XII, 1, 2, 3) These are roughly rectangular with parallel sides with one of the ends pointed. Sometimes, they have in their dorsal surface a pronounced mid-rib, while in others it has been chipped off. Twenty-four specimens are represented in the group.

(*b*) *Backed Blade* (Pl.XII, 4, 5, 6) These specimens also have parallel-sided edges, but one edge is purposely blunted. Mostly, there is single flake scar on the dorsal surface, which intersects the ventral flake surface and the working edge remains sharp. Ten specimens are there in the group.

(*c*) *Blades without parallel sides* (Pl.XII, 7,8) Eighteen specimens are represented in the group. Here the two sides are not parallel to each other, as it is found in other cases. One end is short and blunt, while the working edge remains sharp.

Point

Points are sixteen in number. The specimens have a pointed end which is secured by secondary working. Almost all the specimens are sub-triangular or almond shape. These are simple points, crude and have an unworked main flake surface. In some specimens, retouching has been done along the margins to obtain a pointed shape. Both the sides taper towards the working edge and emerge into a pointed shape. These implements with a thick triangular body may have been used as gravers, drills, etc. Typologically, points may be divided into the following sub-types.

(*a*) *Triangular Point* : (Pl.XII, 9, 10, 11) The specimens of this class are more or less symmetrical and triangular. The pointed end is achieved by the tapering of the margins. Generally, upper flake surface have mid-rib. Eight specimens are grouped in this division.

(*b*) *Asymmetrical Point*: (Pl.XII, 12) The Specimens under this group are asymmetrical in shape. Longitudinal flake scars cover the dorsal surface and the butt-end is blunt. The specimens are five in number.

(*c*) *Tanged Point* : (Pl.XII, 13) The single specimen of this group shows a small tang at the butt-end, while both margins taper to produce a pointed working end.

(*d*) *Tool with curved point* : (Pl.XII, 12) There is a single specimen of this group.

Scraper

This group includes tools, which once served for scraping. This group contributes eleven specimens in the collection. These are mostly thin and flat implements, sometimes with one side more sloping than the rest. Besides the primary longitudinal scars, secondary retouch is also present on the tools. The scraping edge is brought about by the intersection of dorsal flake scars with the main flake surface. According to their technique of preparation they may-be further sub-divided as follows.

(*a*) *Side Scraper* : (Pl.XII, 14, 15) The working edge is confined to the one side only. The flake scars of the dorsal surface are intersected with the main flake surface. Some secondary retouch is present along the working edge. Most of the specimens are prepared out of flake.

(*b*) *End Scraper* : (Pl.XII, 16, 17) The working edge is obtained by the intersection of the dorsal flake scars with the main flake surface. Three specimens are represented in this group.

(*c*) *Side-cum End Scraper* : (Pl.XII, 18) The working edge is not confined to one side. Mostly, specimens of this category are prepared on flakes. This group registers two examples.

(*d*) *End-cum-Concave Scraper* : (Pl.XII, 19, 20) This single specimen is typical in the whole group. The distal end of the dorsal surface shows the flake scars intersecting the main flake surface. The margins are concave due to the retouch.

Lunate (Pl.XII 21)

This group is represented by a single specimen. The arch edge is blunted, while the chord edge is straight and sharp and slightly concave.

Scraper Made on Core

These are some scrapers made on cores which are further classified on the typological grounds.

(*a*) *End scraper* (Pl.XII, 23) The specimen has sharp, often wavy, edge. This is due to either intersection of flake scar on the dorsal side with unworked ventral side or by the interaction of flake scars on both the sides.

(*b*) *Side scraper* (Pl.XII 24) The specimens of this group have the scraping edge parallel to the axis.

(*c*) *Steep scraper* (Pl.XII 25) These specimens are worked on both the sides. Flakes have been detached steeply from base upward while the scraping edge is obtained by the intersection of flake scars , which is often wavy.

By-Products

The by-products of the collection includes the cores, core-trimmings and waste flakes.

Core

About 45 cores are collected from the site. The striking platforms are usually faceted. According to their outward appearance and technique employed, they may further be subdivided as follows.

(*a*) *Having single platform* (Pl.XII, 27, 28) The cores under this category have longitudinal flake scars transited from one platform, in one direction only, running parallel to each other. The technique is fluting. Some of the cores are chipped completely and obtained a conical shape.

(*b*) *Having Double Platform* (Pl.XII, 26) Under this category, the flakes are detached from two platforms which are at right-angle to each other. In other variety, the striking platforms are parallel to each other but flake scars are not parallel.

(*c*) *Irregular Core* (Pl.XII, 29) These cores have an irregular shape, with frequent patches of cortex on the body and have more than one striking platform. Flaking is generally multi-directional and fluted.

Flake

This group includes utilized and unutilized flakes which have no definite shape. The utilized flakes, though cannot be tested as the other regular forms, confirm that they have been used. Generally, these flakes do not exhibit any retouch. They are generally pointed, sub-triangular, trapezoidal, rectangular or irregular in shape. The unutilized flakes include the core-trimmings which owing to their crudity and thickness, rule out the possibility of being taken into use.

Discussion

Typological study of microliths from Gupteshwar Dham reveals that the industry is non-geometric in nature. The foregoing account shows that blades, points and scrapers are the main occupants in the assemblage. The presence of geometric form is represented by a single specimen of lunate which is not very certain. However, from the fact above, we may conclude that the number of geometric form is very insignificant and the industry remains non-geometric. Some of the very common tool types are absent in the collection. This may be due either to inadequate sampling or their complete absence from the site.

With regard to the outward appearance of the artifacts, a few are patinated and the rest are fresh. The specimens are small and crude. Most of these microliths exhibit primary flaking with unprepared striking platform while lesser number of them shows a secondary chipping. Considering the fact that geometric elements come in the later stages of development[1], this industry with its crude non-geometric tools attests to a comparatively older antiquity. It is, however, difficult to assign some definite date to the industry, unless the finds are scienti fically processed in the stratigraphical context.

When the typological comparisons are drawn, it appears to be in full agreement with microliths especially of Mirzapur region[2]. Considering its crudeness, non-geometric nature and use of raw material, it may safely be linked up with the microliths of Singrauli Basin[3]. The present industry is not associated with any kind of pottery and bones.

NOTES

[1] D. H. Gordon, 'Stone Industries in the Holocene in India and Pakistan', *Ancient India*, 6, 1950.

[2] V. D. Krishnaswamy, and K. V. Soundara Rajan, 'The Lithic Tool Industries of the Singrauli Basin, District Mirzapur', *Ancient India* 7.

[3] B. P. Singh, 1962 Stone Age Industries on Balia Nadi in Mirzapur District (unpublished M. A. Thesis).

Reviews

Khajuraho—A Study in the Cultural Conditions of Chandella Society, by Vidya Prakash, M.A., Ph.D., Department of Ancient Indian History, Culture and Archaeology, Banaras Hindu University; Publisher : M./S. D. B. Taraporevala Sons. & Co., Bombay, 1967, pp. xxviii+217 with 110 photographs and 350 line-drawings, Rs. 65/-.

Khajuraho is an important centre of the art and architecture of early medieval India. Inspite of the ravages of time there still exist nearly thirty temples at the site to tell the glory that was Khajuraho. These temples are flooded with innumerable sculptures on the facades and in the niches and cellas inside the temples. The sculptures cover a large range of subjects. Besides the religious images there are countless scenes portraying various aspects of life of the people.

Vidya Prakash has given a new turn to the study of Khajuraho sculptures by treating them as records of social and cultural history of central India between A.D. 800 and 1200, the period when these temples were erected. The author has drawn upon these carvings to throw useful informations on the cultural conditions of central India in general and Chandella Society in particular. How did the people of these times live, love and fight ? What and how did they wear ? What were their ornaments and hairstyles ? Did they use cosmetics ? What were their games, amusements and pastimes ? What arts did they cultivate and what professions did they follow ? What were the main triats of their religious life and mode of education ? What sort of everyday life did they live ? What kind of furniture and household articles did they possess ? What were their moral and social values ? These are some of the questions that the author has very ably answered by critically analysing and interpreting the carvings of Khajuraho. He has corroborated his observations from contemporary literature and inscriptions and has refrained from being imaginative. The photographs have been well chosen and several of them are published for the first time. The line drawings and maps, which alone are a testimony to several year's hard labour, provide an added merit to the work.

The book consists of sixteen chapters, one appendix, a comprehensive glossary of technical terms and a select bibliography. First two chapters are introductory and give general informations about the political and cultural background of Khajuraho temples and the salient features of their art and architecture. In the section on sculpture the author has analysed the stylistic features of Khajuraho art. 'The figure sculptures of Khajuraho', he observes, 'display a distinctive physiognomy. Generally the face is oval and the chin round. The nose and the lips are prominent and the eyes and the eyebrows are sharply carved. The figure is tall and slender but the legs are sometimes unusually long and the poses difficult and tortuous' (p. 18). Next two chapters deal with dress, ornaments and hairstyles. The author has discovered a number of varieties of interresting garments in the sculptures. For example, 'a very close-fitting pair of trousers with folds formed above the ankles' (p. 27). People had a strong passion for ornaments but it is significant to note that Khajuraho sculptures 'do not provide any example of nose ornaments of any type' (p. 32). In the next three chapters cosmetics, music and dance, and amusements have been dealt with. The section on dance is very well written but it could have been further improved by identifying the dance sculptures with known poses of dance in technical literature of the subject. Eighth and ninth chapters deal with the military life and weapons. The chapter on the latter gives an exhaustive account of all the varieties and sub-varieties of swords, daggers and spears etc. delineated in the Khajuraho carvings, but one would have expected the technical Sanskrit names of all the varieties of weapons which the author has not given. Chapters ten and eleven discuss industrial arts, professions of the people and the household furniture and articles of daily use. The author has drawn attention to several types of bags and baskets which appear quite modern in their look (plate XXII). Chapter twelve deals with education and learning. Some of the observations made in this chapter are based on flimsy grounds and need corroboration. In chapter thirteen the religion and religious life of the people have been discussed and the author observes that a very important feature of the religious life of Khajuraho was the mutual tolerance amongst the followers of different sects (p. 144). He does not regard the religious life painted by Krishna Mishra in the *Prabodhachandrodaya* which is full of hatred and contempt for the Buddhist and Jainas to be reliable, since he was a staunch Vaishnavite and his vision was coloured by his fanatic zeal.

In the last two fairly long chapters has been discussed the controversial problem of the erotic sculptures of Khajuraho, one giving a background of *mithuna* theme in Indian art, literature and religion, and the other providing an interpretation of the erotic figures of Khajuraho. The treatment of the subject is most exhaustive, critical and throughly documented. The author is of the opinion that 'the erotic sculpures of Khajuraho were a logical outcome of a number of factors already present in the religious life and usages of the times'. One will be certainly fascinated and swayed by the arguments and interpretations of Vidya Prakash even though he may not agree with him on all points.

The book on the whole is a very valuable contribution to art and archaeology, and it will equally interest the social historians of India. The book, I am sure, will serve as a model for similar intensive studies on the other monuments of India. The publishers also deserve praise for the quality printing and fine get-up, which are unfortunately rare in Indian publications on Art.

A. K. Narain

Khajuraho ki Deva Pratimayen (Hindi), By Ramashrya Avasthi, M.A., Ph.D., Lecturer, Department of Ancient Indian History & Archaeology, Lucknow University; Publisher: Oriental Publishing House, Civil Lines, Agra; 1967, pp. 22+285, Plates 72; Rs. 70/-.

Khajuraho group of temples in the Central India is world famous for its architectural grandeur and wealth of sculptures. These temples were constructed during the reign of the Chandellas, a medieval dynasty of Rajputs between 9th and 12th Centuries. Khajuraho has been attracting the archaeologists and art historians since the time of Cunningham. During recent years also several outstanding works on the subject have appeared from Indian and foreign scholars discussing one or the other aspect of the art and architecture of Khajuraho. But in no work any serious attempt was made to discuss the iconography of innumerable gods and goddesses depicted on the temple walls. Ramashrya Avasthi has very ably undertaken this task and deserves the credit of being the first scholar not only to describe and discuss the deities of Khajuraho with great detail but also to corrorborate them from the available iconographic texts. It is also the first authoritative work in Hindi on Khajuraho.

The work under review is a revised version of the thesis submitted for the degree of Ph.D. of Lucknow University in 1966. It has been divided into seven chapters. First chapter is introductory one and gives a brief account of the political history of the Chandellas and the existing temples. For the latter the author has largely depended on Krishnadeva's writings. In chapter 2 to 6, Ganapati, Vishnu, Sūrya, Navagraha and Ashṭadikpālas have been discussed. In the last chapter some general observations have been made. There is a good bibliography and a useful index. Thus it will be seen that Avasthi selects only a few deities of Khajuraho for exhaustive discussion and analysis. We expect that he takes up soon the remaining deities also to form the subject matter of his other volumes. In the present one the selection of deities has been rather arbitrary. It would have been better if a certain well defined basis was adopted to select the deities for discussion in a particular volume.

The gods selected for the present volume (Ganapati, Vishnu, Sūrya, Navagrahas, Aṣṭadikpālas) have been critically analysed. The author has done well to give a brief history of the origin and evolution of each god which serves as a good background for the study of Khajuraho specimens. He has scientifically analysed the prescriptions of available iconographic texts and has made an extensive use of *Aparājitprichchhā* which appears to have derived much from the images of Khajuraho. The discussion is most exhaustive and even the minutest detail of icons has not escaped the notice of the author. Several unknown or hitherto unnoticed images of iconographic importance have been brought to light and identified. The arguments for the identification of deities have been critically and clearly set forth, though it is hard to agree on all points.

The work of Avasthi will undoubtedly serve as a valuable reference book on the iconography of early medieval India. It is a useful work for the students and scholars alike. So far this is the only work of its kind in Hindi and let us hope that this will inspire younger scholars to write original works on art and archaeology in Hindi and other Indian languages. Though the plates need improvement, the printing and get-up of the book are fine for which the publishers deserve congratulation but they are not justified to price the book so exorbitantly.

Vidya Prakash

The Arts of India and Nepal : 'The Nasli and Alice Heeramaneek Collection (An illustrated catalogue) by Rosenfield *et. al.*, Publisher : Museum of Fine Arts Boston, U.S.A., 1966, pp. 185, Eighty seven illustrations including twelve colour plates, Price not given.

Nasli Heeramaneek, the son of a Parsee dealer in art and antiquities, was born in Bombay. He inherited from his father the love and devotion for art which only grew with years and he became one of the better known connoisseurs of Asiatic art. He came into contact with Ananda Coomaraswamy and became a great admirer of the Museum of Fine Arts. Nasli had a vast collection of sculptures, bronzes, miniature paintings, bronze vessels, jewellery, ceramics and other art antiquities belonging to India, Nepal and other places. His valuable collection which is named after him and his wife Alice now forms a part of the Museum of Fine Arts, Boston. The work under review is a finely printed and sumptuously illustrated catalogue of this very collection of Indian and Nepalese works of Art.

There is a total number of 283 entries in the catalogue of which 1—109 are stone sculptures and bronzes and the rest are palm leaf manuscripts, painted book covers, manuscript paintings, Tankas, textiles, ceramics and minor works of art. These objects represent almost all the phases of art from the Indus Valley terracottas to 19th century brocades. The objects have been arranged chronologically and region wise. The entires are provided with all possible useful informations such as date, provenance, size and material of particular object. Whenever possible they have been compared with similar pieces known at other places. The description of objects is very minute and exhaustive. It bears testimony to the painstaking labour and wider perspective of Asian art on the part of those responsible for catalogue (entries).

Time and circumstances have deprived us of our own past heritage. It is a matter of satisfaction and pleasure that this catalogue will give an opportunity to the world of scholars to know closely the art subjects which have gone out of the homeland. Students of Asian Art are sure to benefit from this very valuable publication.

Vidya Prakash

The Iconography of the Buddhist Sculptures (Caves) of Ellora by Ramesh Chandra Gupta M.A., Ph.D., Head of the Department of History and Ancient Indian Culture, Marathawada University, Aurangabad : Publisher: Marathawada University, 1964, Rs. 45/-.

The Buddhist caves of Ellora have widely attracted the attention of scholars for their Sculptural wealth. But unfortunately the hundreds of Buddhist icons have never been thoroughly studied and analysed. The work of Dr. R.S. Gupta attempts at an exhaustive and intensive treatment of the subject. It is a good addition to the literature on Buddhist iconography.

The book consists of ten chapters. First two chapters are introductory, giving the significance of Ellora and the economic and historical background of the cave temples. In chapters three, four and five the author discusses the sculptures of the Buddha, Bodhisattvas and Buddhasaktis, There are five appendices dealing with the symbols, flying figures, dress and ornaments of the icones. There is a short glossary of technical terms and a biblography. The work is enriched by 80 half-tone, 300 line-drawings and two maps. The author apparently has put hard labour in preparing the work but the treatment is clumsy and lacks brevity. His chapters are disjointed and he fails to have grip over his material. It is more of the nature of a catalogue of the sculptures of Ellora and there is little of critical approach.

Vidya Prakash

Indian Palaeography by Ahmad Hasan Dani, Oxford : At Clarendon Press, 1963, pp. XVIII. 297, with 23 plates.

For long, Bühler and Ojha were considered as the most important books on Indian palaeography. The discovery of the Harappa culture, which could have brought revolution in the field of Indian palaeography failed to give any definite direction to scholars and the Indus script, inspite of several attempts, still remains a frozen mystery. However, discovery of large number of inscriptions, introduction of scientific methods in the field archaeology and increasing interest in the concepts of cultural anthropology gave new filip to the study of antiquities and paleography. During the last twenty years several books have come out on Indian paleography, but I have no hesitation in saying without in any way minimising the importance of other contributions, that A.H. Dani's is the most thorough treatment of the subject.

Dani has rightly divided the history of the study of Indian palaeography into three definite stages. The first, which covers the late eighteenth and early nineteenth centuries, was the period of the discovery of the inscriptions and the decipherment of the scripts used in them. The second stage starts with James Prinsep completing the process of decipherment in the thirties of nineteenth century. Cunningham, Burgess, Burnell, Ojha, Fleet, Bühler and many others collected, compiled and studied the inscriptions and prepared faithful charts of the letters. The main idea behind it was to use palaeography as chronometre by producing as accurately as possible the charts of the various writings from the original records so as to collect at one place all the scripts for the guidance of those who wished to read and interpret them. This was natural under the circumstances in which the decipherment of the inscriptions started. Bühler's Indian Palaeography marks the climax of this stage and his techniques were regarded, until recently, as standard. The third stage of compilation and publication of the inscriptions along with their facsimiles started with the issue of regular volumes of *Epigraphia Indica* from the close of the nineteenth century. This step brought epigraphy and palaeography to larger readers and, more and more persons found themselves interested in its study and interpretation and new contributions were made. But it is Dani who gave Indian Palaeography the status of an independent subject to be studied for its own sake. Thus he has ushered in the fourth stage, if I may say so.

The real contribution of Dani in the field of Indian Palaeography is his attempt to interpret and explain the evolution of writing in cultural context. Now several scholars consider writing as an item of culture and interpret it as such and Dani seems to be in line with them. His study of Indian script in cultural context and in the light of technique employed and the tools used gives it a new dimension. He does not lay much emphasis on the exact reproduction of the letters; rather, he emphasises the movement of the hand which is more important in the formation of the letters. With a deep insight he classifies and traces the evolution of script and solves many problems satisfactorily. To him script is no longer a time-scale but is an item of culture.

Dani analyses and classifies all the five hundred and thirty seven symbols of Indus Valley script into eight categories of living beings, nineteen categories of stylized objects and many other categories such as Ovals and their parts; Triangles, Angles & Crosses; Quadrangles and their parts; Numerals, Brackets and others. As a result of this classification and analysis he observes that 'the actual number of signs in the Indus script is twenty seven objects and twenty seven geometrical forms, besides numerals, brackets, and two magic emblems.' (p. 19). He further opines that the number "is increased to four hundred and seventy four (the remainder sixty three being numerals, etc.) by following two principles, namely :

(i) by combination with other signs;

(ii) by addition of strokes (a) internal, (b) external, from 1 to 6, besides the arch-like signs.

The combinations are always with some recognizable objects, and strokes are found added to all but the homo-, snake-, wheel-, vehicle-, and bow-and-arrow- signs." (p. 19). Whereas it is difficult, in the present state of the materials, to asses correctly Dani's contribution to the study of Indus script, his reviewer has no reason to doubt that it will be of help to all those who are actively and optimistically engaged in the task of deciphering the Indus script.

While dealing with the origin of Brāhmī script, Dani analyses and classifies Brāhmī characters into two categories: original forms and those made by additional strokes, C.S. Upasak also classifies these characters into original and derived forms. Dani regards three vowels—*a*, *i* and *u*, and nineteen consonants—*ka*, *kha*, *ga*, *cha*, *ja*, *ta*, *tha*, *da*, *na*, *pa*, *ba*, *ma*, *ya*, *ra*, *la*, *va*, *sa*, *sa* and *ha*—a total of twenty two letters as original forms, a number which coincides with the number of signs found in North Semitic or Aramaic. Out of these twenty two forms he could find only eleven signs from the North Semitic and Early Phoenician combined, which are somehow similar to corresponding Brahmi signs. He also correlates all these twenty two sounds of Brahmi with the twenty two letters of North Semitic except *u* and *o* in Brahmi and *Kheth* in North Semitic. On this ground he considers that 'Indus Brahmi was created on the basis of North Semitic letters (p. 28).

But a careful examination of Dani's classification, Fig. 2, p. 27, shows that the number twenty two, arrived at by him, is an arbitrary one. For example, among the vowels he considers the triangle only three formations of *a*, *i* and *u* and ignores the triangle form of *e* which on the same grounds should be included in the original forms. Among the consonants also, he has selected letters to suit his purpose. For example he considers *ga* and *sa* as original form but actually *sa* is made by adding a stroke to the left leg of *ga*. Similarly *sa, sha, ha, la ya, pa*, and *pha* can be regarded as derivatives of only one sign which can be formed with the help of adding strokes of various points. Some more instances of this type can be pointed out.

As regards the similarity of the letters of Brahmi on one hand and North Semitic and Early Phoenician on the other, he has repeated the technique of Buhler, which has already been controverted by Ojha, Pandey, Upasak and others.

While dealing with the origin of the script such as Brahmi, one must consider that there are two elements in any script, ,viz. form and the sound. Actually no correlation between the form and the phonetic value can be expected in any system of writing of the world and Brāhmī is no exception. Simple geometrical forms such as the Brāhmī letters need not be the monopoly of anyone among the ancient peoples. On the other hand the scientific classification of the *aksharaṣ* of the Sanskrit *varnamala* on phonetic basis was already known before Asoka. We do not understand why so much exercise is made to correlate the origin of Brahmi with any of the known systems of writing ? Why so much emphasis on the monogenesis of writing ?

Dani rightly includes Ceylon and South-East Asia in his study for Indian culture along with the Indian script reached these places. However, he does not include the Brāhmī script prevalent in the Central Asia and Tibet. While dealing with Kharoshṭhī script he explains its origin and development in India and Central Asia in the same cultural context.

No review of the book can be complete without expressing on admiration for the hard labour the author has put in collecting the data for illustrations, and which are so well produced.

A. K. Narain

Shaikhan Dheri Excavation (1963-64 Seaosns) Published in Ancient Pakistan, Bulletin of the Department of Archaeology, University of Peshawar, Vol. II—1965-66 by Ahmad Hasan Dani, pp. 16-214, plates 51, line, drawing, figures 58, site plan, several charts etc.

The excavations at Shaikhan Dheri, which were undertaken in search of the second city of Pushkalavati, in two seasons 1963 and 1964, have revealed undoubtedly a city founded by the Indo-Greeks who came from Bactria. Sir Mortimers' excavations at the Bala Hisar mound provided a definite sequence of cultures in Ghandhara from circa 6th to 1st centuries B.C. Dani's excavations at Shaikhan Dheri, which is opposite Bala Hissar, about twenty two miles north of Peshawar, continues the story upto the end of the Kushana power. Needless to say the results of Dani's work at the site are of great value.

According to Dani, the city was most probably founded by Menander, in about the middle of the second century B.C. The chronology suggested by Dani is strengthened by radio-carbon dates he has obtained for the samples from his excavations of the site. On the topmost layers a number of coins of Vasudeva I (Siva-Bull type) were recovered and these were the last coins on Shaikhan Dheri. It is clear that the site was given up during his reign, perhaps on account of flood. It has been claimed by the excavator that the materials, unearthed so far, which include as many as 475 coins, have to say something definite on the various knotty problems related to the chronology of the Indo-Greeks, Sakas, as well as those of the Gandhara art.

Apart from the coins the site has yielded a lot of antiquities of almost every kind. Special mention, however, must be made of the statue of Hariti (pl. XVI) and that of the Buddha (pl. XVII) from the House of Naradakha (pl. VIII No. 1), a Buddhist *acharya* whose name was recorded at the base of a pedestal (pl. XXII) belonging to a relic casket, and who flourished during the hey day of the Kushanas.

Dani also arrives at certain conclusions regarding the chronology of the Yavana-Saka kings on the basis of the stratigraphy and material remains he has obtained at the site. He agrees with the reviewer's date of Menander, and the chornological proximity of Agathocles with Menander. But he also considers Apollodotus as chronologically close to Menader and therefore disagrees with the reviewer's theory of two Apollodotuses. In view of the limitation of space we propose to discuss this matter as well as Dani's opinion about the place of Soter Megas elsewhere, for we still feel the necessity to agree to differ with the author.

We are glad that the Shaikhan Dheri excavations have provided the material and the insight for what Dani remarks on pp. 39—40, "Any school of art has to be studied in its total circumstance within the area and society where it develops. Its chronology has to be built on its own right".

A. K. Narain

Religion in Art and Archaeology, (Vaishnavism and Saivism) by J. N. Banerjea, M.A., Ph.D., F.A.S., F.N.S.I., Formerly Carmichael Professsor & Head of the Department of Ancient Indian History and Culture, University of Calcutta; Publishers: University of Lucknow, 1968; pp. 134, Plates XIX, Rs. 30.

The workers in the field of Art, Iconography and Religion are already indebted to the late Prof. J.N. Banerjea for his monumental book on Iconography and many illuminating papers on one or the other aspect of art and religion. The publication under review is another significant work from the pen of the learned author. It is a collection of a series of five lectures delivered by Prof. Banerjea under the auspices of the Radhakumud Mookerji Endowment lectures at the University of Lucknow in 1961-62. It is a matter of profound regret that Prof. Banerjea did not live to see the publication of his highly learned and informative discourses. It is also unfortunate that Lucknow University took nearly five years to publish these lectures.

Five lectures of the learned author form five chapters in the book, first two chapters are devoted to Vaishṇavism in archaeology and art. The first clear mention of the word *bhakti* in theistic context, observes Prof. Banerjea, appears in the *Śvetāśvatara Upanishad* and the later Vaishṇavism owed its origin to the deification and worship of the human hero Vāsudeva Kṛishṇa. The cult, of which Vāsudeva Kṛishṇa was the central deity, gradually incorporated Vedic Solar deity Āditya, Vishṇu and the cosmic deity Nārāyaṇa described in the later Vedic, Epic and Smriti texts. Banerjea has analysed the archaeological and sculptural data to throw useful light on the origin, and subsequent evolution and growth of Vaishṇavism and its prevalence in different parts of India during pre-Gupta, Gupta and post-Gupta periods, until the end of the early medieval period in the 13th century A.D.

Chapters three and four deal respectively with Śaivism in archaeology and *linga* worship and Śaivism in art. The literary data about the prevalence of the worship of Śiva in the north during the centuries immediately preceding the Christian era have been supported by the archaeological evidence mainly numismatic and glyptic. The author, however, admits the absence of any epigraphic evidence belonging to pre-Christian era to throw any light on the nature of Śaivism in early days. Banerjea has discussed the Mathura stone inscription in relation to the Lakulīśa sect. He regards the earlier hypothesis of R.G. Bhandarkar about the approximate period of Lakulīśa, being first quarter of the second century B.C., to be untenable. He reiterates his earlier opinion that 'Lakulīśa might not have been the actual founder or the Pāśupata order, but his contributions to it as its first systematiser and organiser were so great that in later tradition he was given this role' (p. 52). Prof. Banerjea discusses the role of Mattamayūra form of Śaivism referred to in the central Indian inscriptions of 10th-11th centuries A.D. He has thoroughly analysed the views of other competent authorities on the subject and has differed from them at several points. For example, he would not agree with V.S. Pathak who suggested the region of Panjab for the location of the place with which the name Mattamayūra was associated (p. 59). Similarly he regards the suggestion of Goetz 'peculiar and unwarranted' that the Mattamayūra Śaivas were associated with the unsocial Kaula-Kāpālikas and that they were indirectly responsible for some of the grossly erotic reliefs on the medieval temples of Khajuraho (p. 63). The author of this review, who had occasion to discuss this problem with the late Prof. Banerjea, agrees with him that there is no clear literary or archaeological evidence to justify association of this moderate Śaiva order with the erotic theme of Khajuraho temples. The association of even the Kaula-Kāpālikas with these carvings is doubtful. The chapter on Śaivism in art attempts to discuss critically the phallic representations of Śiva and its different phases. Śiva has been depicted anthropomorphically in thousands of sculptures in various forms. These have been scientifically classified and analysed with the help of select examples. The treatment of the images illustrating Śaiva tenets, like Lakulīśa, Nṛityamūrtis and syncretic icons is particularly interesting.

Fifth and the last chapter deals with the relationship of architectural art with Vaishṇavism and Śaivism in ancient and medieval India. Important existing Vaishṇava and Śaiva temples have been studied from the cult point of view. Prof. Banerjea observes that the ritual needs of the sectarian worshippers were responsible to a great extent for the architectural types of temples. The position of certain images were rigidly fixed in the architectural complex. Thus 'in many of the Vaishṇava temples of the early medieval period, both in northern and southern India, the three incarnations of Vishṇu, Vāräha, Narasiṃha and Vāmana-Trivikrama were shown as the Pārśvadevatās on the southern, western and the northern faces respectively'. (p. 91).

The book is an outstanding work, full of informations which the learned author has presented in his characteristic critical style. Though many of the views contained in this work were already expressed by him in his earlier writings, the value of the work is unaffected. The greatest merit of this book is its quality of precision and intelligible treatment of a highly complex subject. It will be immensely useful to the students and researchers of Indian religion and iconography.

Though the get up and type face is generally satisfactory, there are a number of printing mistakes. On page 92 alone four printing mistakes can be detected (Trivikrama is written as 'Trivikarama', Narasiṃha as 'Narashimha', Krishṇāyana as 'Krishnaana' and Devala Mitra as 'Devata Mitra'). Such errors in standard publications are unfortunate. The plates also do not come upto standard. Considering the amount of printed matter, the price of the publication is too high. At least University publications, the primary aim of which is not profit, should be priced moderately.

A. K. Narain

The Dynastic Arts of the Kushans by John M. Rosenfield, University of California Press, Berkeley and Los Angeles 1967, pp. xliv+377, 16 plates of coins and seals+50 plates illustrating 167 text figures, 3 maps and several line drawings.

It is an irony that despite most abundant source material the history of the Kushanas should be replete with unresolved problems of every kind. John Rosenfield's book which primarily deals with the 'place and importance of the royal portraits of the Kushan emperors in their relationship to India and the Near East' is a major contribution and deserves high praise for tackling a little trodden aspect of Kushana art and civilisation. Although the work essentially intends to be a history of art, it is a mine of information on Kushan history which the author has presented with clarity of vision and critical scholarship. He has a perfect grip over the sources. His mastery over the intricacies of Kushana art and numismatics in particular and Indian Art and iconography in general are reflected in every page of his writing. The amount of painstaking labour the author has put in collecting his illustrative material is most impressive.

The book consists of nine chapters and three appendices. There is an exhaustive bibliography at the end which hardly excludes any work even with slightest relevance to Kushana history. Starting from an account of the beginnings and creation of Kushana empire in chapter I, the subsequent chapters upto V deal with Kushana kings, and the Saka and Parthian rulers. The author has given first, a detailed account of the biography of these rulers and the history of their times, and then analysed the portrait delineations from their known coinage. The minute and objective study of these portraits by the author reveals many new facets about the changing patterns of Kushana royalty, and stylistic evolution of the art of portraiture. The author rightly observes that the standing figure of Vima Kadphises on copper coins is 'the most direct prototype' for the stone statue of Kanishka at Mathura and that it 'helps demonstrate a close correspondence between the art of the dynastic shrines of Mathura or Surkh Kotal and the symbolic spirit of the Kushana coins' (p. 26). The author does not favour the theory of any interregnum between Vima Kadphises and Kanishka and points out the close agreement between Vima's and Kanishka's imperial symbols on their coins on the one hand and between monumental sculpture on the other as an additional support (p. 40). The account of the history of Kanishka, his conquests, empire and the various legends connected with him are lucid and readable. With the help of Kanishka's portraiture on coins and the Mathura portrait, the author observes that from the time of this ruler spear became a prominent part of royal regalia which was probably intended more as an emblem than as a weapon in a practical sense. Similarly he regards the goad held in the hand of Kanishka on his coins as an attribute of a master of ancient India's greatest instrument of warfare. Rosenfield makes a closer observation of the types of headgear carved on the Huvishka coins and suggests that this evokes the memory of the opulence of Assyrian kingship. One may not disagree with this suggestion particularly when the parallel examples are noticed in the Hatra and Kommagene royal images.

Chapters VI and VII are intended to study in detail the Mathura portraits from the Gokarnesvara mound and the Mat shrine and the Kanishka and Iranian portraits. According to the author the royal portraits of Mathura or Surkh kotal were not an isolated phenomena. They reflect a strong awareness of activities within the Iranian culture sphere. Chapter VIII, dealing with the stylistic and iconographic aspects of the Mathura imperial portraits, attempts at a minute and critical study of clothing and the attrients in the hands. The author advances sound arguments in favour of the view that the squatting Surya image were derived from Kushan royal portraits. The last chapter is a thorough analysis of the Kushan figures as donors and devotees in Buddhist sculpture. Rosenfield has rightly noted that "these images help to place the Kushans in a cultural milieu of considerable detail, showing factors of patronage and spiritual conviction which underlay the vigorous activity of the Buddhist sculpture workshops" (p. 215).

The three appendices at the end on (i) the date of Kaniskha (ii) the Kanishka reliquary and (iii) the inscriptions pertaining to the Indo-Scythian dynasties at Mathura are very useful. It is indeed most gratifying for the present reviewer to note that his view on the date of Kanishka, as discussed by him in the Kanishka seminar held in London in 1960, finds acceptance by the author of this book. The table of dated inscriptions given in Appendix III will be found by the readers as of great help. The illustrations are very well chosen and the reproductions are of the highest quality.

Needless to say, this contribution of Rosenfield is not only very substantial but one whose great impact will be felt by all future students of Kushan art and history.

A. K. Narain
